Salvation and Sin

SALVATION

AND

SIN

Augustine, Langland,
and Fourteenth-Century Theology

DAVID AERS

University of Notre Dame Press
Notre Dame, Indiana

BT
751.3
.A38
2009

Library of Congress Cataloging-in-Publication Data

Aers, David.
    Salvation and sin : Augustine, Langland, and fourteenth-century
theology / David Aers.
        p.   cm.
    Includes bibliographical references (p.   ) and index.
    ISBN-13: 978-0-268-02033-0 (pbk. : alk. paper)
    ISBN-10: 0-268-02033-7 (pbk. : alk. paper)
        1. Salvation—Christianity—History of doctrines.   2. Sin—
Christianity—History of doctrines.   3. Augustine, Saint, Bishop
of Hippo.   4. Langland, William, 1330?–1400? Piers Plowman.
5. Theology—England—History—Middle Ages, 600–1500.
I. Title.
    BT751.3.A38   2009
    230'.24209023—dc22

                                                        2009008134

To my parents, Pam and Ian, with love.

V. Panem de caelo praestitisti eis.

R. Omne delectamentum in se habentem.

—Thomas Aquinas, "O Sacrum Convivium"

CONTENTS

"That is soth," y saide, "and so y beknowe
That y haue ytynt tyme and tyme myspened;
Ac ȝut y hope, as he þat ofte hath ychaffared
And ay loste and loste and at þe laste hym happed
A boute such a bargayn he was þe bet euere
And sette his los as a leef at the laste ende,
Such a wynnyng hym warth thorw wyrdes of grace:
Simile est regnum celorum thesauro abscondito in agro;
Mulier que inuenit dragmam.
So hope y to haue of hym þat is almyghty
A gobet of his grace and bigynne a tyme
That alle tymes of my tyme to profit shal turne."
"Y rede the," quod resoun tho, "rape the to bigynne
The lyf þat is louable and leele to thy soule."
"Ȝe! and continue," quod Conscience, "and to þe kyrke ywende."
                    William Langland, *Piers Plowman,* V.92–104

THE EPIGRAPH TO THIS PREFACE IS A GRIPPING MOMENT IN A WORK
that is central to this book, a moment of conversion and summons
into the Church. But *Piers Plowman* unfolds a more complicated account of
the processes of conversion than the penitent Wille anticipates. He prays
for the divine grace that alone can redeem time laid waste and lost. Conscience tells him that the place of beginnings to which his reason urges
him is the Church in which he had already been born in baptism. In the

lines following the epigraph Wille obeys. But gradually Langland discloses the opacity of the converted will to the introspective powers of the soul and its unacknowledged resistance to the gifts of redemption. He also discloses how the gift of God in which Wille is called to redeem the time, "þe kyrke" founded by the sublime acts of Christ and the Holy Spirit, is also historically constituted by the acts and habits of sinners (chapter 4). So here the interactions of agency become extremely complex and desperately opaque to Wille as he searches for what he finds and loses, what is present and absent, revealed and hidden. Perhaps drawn on by Langland, *Salvation and Sin* explores different models of the mysterious relations between divine and human agency together with models of sin and its consequences. Theologies of grace, versions of Christian identity, and versions of community, especially the Church, are its pervasive concerns. I am especially interested in figurations of how God found out a remedy that would bring the long-wandering prodigal from a distant, insatiably hungry and warring land "to the city of the living God, the heavenly Jerusalem" (Heb. 12.22).[1] As Shakespeare's Isabella (in *Measure for Measure*) tries to remind the godly and revolutionary judge of Vienna who has just insisted that her brother "is a forfeit of the law":

> Alas, alas!
> Why, all the souls that were were forfeit once,
> And He that might the vantage best have took
> Found out the remedy.[2]

About to enter the cloister, Isabella evokes an extraordinarily powerful image of salvation and the consequences of sin. In a poetry of radiant beauty she grasps how human salvation is inextricably bound up with divine patience. The divine judge, he who "is the top of judgement" (2.2.76), the lord of time, patiently took time to find a way that would be "the remedy" to sin and its catastrophic consequences. The remedy she invokes is the incarnation, crucifixion, and resurrection of Christ (Phil. 2.6–11). In the face of the magistrate's reintroduction of the death penalty for sexual unions outside marriage, she recalls the transformation of the relations between law, justice, justification, and mercy in Christ: "all have sinned and fall short of the glory of God; they are now justified by his grace as a gift through the redemption that is in Christ Jesus"

(Rom. 3.23–24). Her recollection invites the human judge, Angelo, to consider the entailments of worshiping the God who enacts this humility, patience, and self-abandoning service. Angelo rejects her invitation to take the time he has been given to find out these entailments for himself and the polity he governs. In doing so he rejects an invitation to conversion. This charged scene identifies some central preoccupations in *Salvation and Sin*. How do the writers it studies envisage the consequences of sin, the conversion of sinners, and the resistances to conversion?

Four chapters of *Salvation and Sin* are on fourteenth-century writers, two of whom wrote in Latin, two in English (although one of these, as the epigraph illustrates, makes use of Latin). But the book sets out with Augustine, who died on August 28, 430. His presence, however, is not confined to the first chapter, for he becomes a major interlocutor throughout *Salvation and Sin*. The first chapter shows the reading of Augustine relevant to this book while it introduces a vocabulary and grammar that will help me to explore representations of divine and human agency, grace, and sin in all the other writers explored here. Augustine's role in shaping my inquiries should not set up expectations that I have any interest in contributing to a history of putative "Augustinianism."[3] Augustine was certainly a major authority in medieval Christianity, but investigating the extremely complex mediations of his work, and others' work thought to be by him, is not my task. I do hope, however, that the first chapter, together with the later readings of Augustine (especially in chapters 4 and 5), may recollect fascinating strands of Augustine's work that have largely been occluded from literary studies.[4] Indeed, I hope that literary scholars, both medievalists and early modernists, may be encouraged to expand their engagement with Augustine's perpetually searching, monumentally intelligent, and endlessly generative range of writings (including his abundant homilies) and to do so before deciding what is or isn't "Augustinian" (chapter 4).

The second chapter begins the book's engagement with fourteenth-century theological writing. This chapter was the outcome of research provoked by the current scholarly consensus that Langland's theology is "semi-Pelagian" or "Pelagian" and that his most important affiliations are with "modern" theologians ("moderni") and especially with William of Ockham. My own previous engagements with Ockham, Langland, and Augustine had not given me confidence in this thesis, but it clearly dealt with matters central to the present project. So I decided to explore an especially relevant cluster of issues in Ockham's theology. These are his understanding of grace (including sacramental grace), human agency, sin, divine forgiveness, and salvation together with his versions of freedom. Both Augustine and Aquinas help me to bring out the consequences of Ockham's model of grace, in which salvation is cut off from both the network of mediations displayed by Augustine (chapter 1) and any substantive Christology. This, it will emerge in chapter 4, is a very different theology from Langland's.

From Ockham I turn in chapter 3 to a theologian generally considered to be "Augustinian" and engaged in a battle with fourteenth-century "modern" theology and what he took to be its incorrigible Pelagianism. Recent scholarship on Thomas Bradwardine has been particularly concerned with scientific interests (physics, natural philosophy, astrology, astronomy), together with his work in mathematics, logic, and metaphysics. But my own engagement is restricted to aspects of his treatment of sin and salvation, conversion, and the Church's sacraments. Once more my questions are facilitated by my reading of Langland, Augustine, and St. Thomas. Given the customary classification of Bradwardine as "Augustinian," a judgment doubtless encouraged by his copious quotations from Augustine, I was particularly surprised to find a thoroughly un-Augustinian sidelining of Christology in the massive work undertaken on behalf of the God worshiped by Christians, *De Causa Dei*. This, so it seems to me, is accompanied by an equally un-Augustinian approach to the mysterious relations between divine and human agency in the processes of conversion and lives of Christian discipleship.

Having considered a "modern" theologian and a renowned anti-"modern" one, I move to Langland's theology of sin, grace, and reconciliation in *Piers Plowman,* a long multigeneric poem written and rewritten in the later fourteenth century. I concentrate both on the distinctive dialectical strategies of Langland's poem and on some minute particulars that illuminate his understanding of sin's consequences, individual sin, and collective sin. Such attention is essential because the poem's modes of writing are intrinsic to its theology. Christian doctrine is never simply independent of the forms of writing and practice in which it is manifested, but Langland's work compels theologians to remember a fact that their habitual procedures have often occluded, a fact to which

Aquinas drew attention in his exposition of the Lord's Prayer:[5] Langland is profoundly and pervasively attentive to the person and work of Christ in whom God is revealed. Here I show some of the ways in which his theological understanding, to which his ethics belongs, is shaped by his Christology. In doing so, I hope to suggest how arguments about "Pelagianism" are inextricably bound up with Christology, although this seems to have been largely forgotten. But it is not forgotten by Langland or Augustine.

Anyone trying to write a historical survey of Langland's relations with fourteenth-century theology would doubtless follow up these considerations with accounts of other theologians.[6] But I have no such ambitions, a fact further manifested by the subject and modes of discussion in the book's final chapter. This brings Julian of Norwich's profound, compassionate, and much-admired theology into conversation with Langland and Augustine. I confess that I found the processes and outcome of this really gripping. The conversation unfolds important difficulties in Julian's account of agency and sin as these relate to salvation and Christology in the *Showings*. I hope this critical engagement with Julian's great work encourages further exploration of her thinking about human agency together with her theology of sin and the reconciliation between God and humanity effected in Christ (2 Cor. 5.16–21).

Salvation and Sin has been written from both an English department and a divinity school. It is indebted to discussions in courses taught across a customarily sharp divide, courses that included both students in theology and ones in English medieval studies, courses such as one exploring theologies of grace from Augustine to Luther through Langland. The book's choices of texts, preoccupations, and modes of inquiry reflect this site of production. So it is unsurprising that *Salvation and Sin* is more theological in its arguments than work habitually done in English departments, even when this work addresses Christian writing in the Middle Ages or the Reformation.[7] But *Piers Plowman* is not known in divinity schools, yet it plays a central role in *Salvation and Sin*. Moreover, the book often attends to the minute particulars of the text in a manner that suggests an apprenticeship in literary studies. I appreciate that this may cause problems for some theologians who have never encountered *Piers Plowman*. Such problems are an inevitable part of any attempt to work across disciplinary divides that are alien to the medieval and early modern writings and practices we study. My hope is that what is shown of *Piers Plowman* in chapter 4 will encourage those who have not read the poem to do so and to ruminate on it. But perhaps some who come from a divinity school or department of theology without having met *Piers Plowman* may find it helpful to go from the chapter on Augustine (chapter 1) to the chapter on Langland (chapter 4). This will at least give some substance to the passing allusions to Langland in the chapters on Ockham and Bradwardine.

I have written and ordered *Salvation and Sin* as an inquiry into different models of salvation and sin, setting out from Augustine, whose presence pervades the book. But it is neither a historical narrative nor, as I have already indicated, a historical survey. Because the book is an exploration of different writers, of peculiar force, addressing common and central topics in Christian teaching and forms of life, it is possible to read its interlocking chapters, after the Augustinian prelude, in an order other than the one I prefer. It does seem to me, however, that were *Piers Plowman* to be studied in divinity schools or theology departments it might elicit a fruitful exploration of the fate of Christian teaching and practice in the modes of theological reasoning propagated by Ockham, Bradwardine, and their successors. Be that as it may, I hope that my attempts to engage with the works I explore will convey something of the joy I have received from them and will encourage others to develop congruent critical practices.[8]

IN THE NOTES TO THIS BOOK I HAVE TRIED TO ACKNOWLEDGE THOSE to whom I know I am indebted, past and present. I want to thank with especial gratitude the two people who have been most closely involved and most sustaining in the making of this book, Stanley Hauerwas and Sarah Beckwith. Stanley Hauerwas commented on everything here. He brought his capacious learning and intense theological concentration to the task of helping me understand what I want to do. My debts to him, his friendship, and his generosity are immense. Sarah Beckwith also read everything. I have benefited hugely from her creative and critical intelligence at all stages of composing this book. I am fortunate indeed that she remains at Duke University. I thank Derek Pearsall and Denise Baker for reading early versions of material on Langland, Kate Crassons for conversations about *Piers Plowman,* and Brian Cummings for commenting on the Bradwardine chapter. I am grateful to Lynn Staley for reading the work on Langland and for a particularly detailed and helpfully resistant engagement with the chapter on Julian of Norwich. I thank James Simpson for inviting me to lecture on Augustine at the Harvard Conference on Conversion in 2005 and for his comments on a lecture that grew into the book's first chapter. Many aspects of this study benefited from discussions in graduate courses involving students from the Divinity School and the English Department at Duke University; thanks go to those students for the pleasure and privilege of working with them. Among these, I thank Cara Hersh and Rachael Deagman, who were my research assistants during the making of this book, and especially Rachael Deagman, who provided me with inestimable help and support during the major part of its completion. I thank Greg Jones, dean of the Divinity School, and the provost and deans at Duke University, who have given the leaves to help me complete this book. I also give warm thanks to Catherine Beaver for making the English Department at Duke such a benevolent environment. I am grateful to Barbara Hanrahan at the University of Notre Dame Press for her invaluable support of this project and her generous, patient advice. I have been greatly helped by Elisabeth Magnus, who skillfully edited the manuscript for the University of Notre Dame Press, and by Michael Cornett of Duke University Press, who, with equal skill and care, worked on the edited text. Finally I thank Christine Derham, who continues to be my closest friend and my wife. For her, still criss-crossing the Atlantic, some words from Bob Dylan's recent song, "Beyond the Horizon": "Beyond the horizon / Across the divide / Round about midnight / We'll be on the same side."[9]

CHAPTER I

Augustinian Prelude

Conversion and Agency

That bread which you can see on the altar, sanctified by
the word of God, is the body of Christ. That cup, or
rather what the cup contains, sanctified by the word of
God, is the blood of Christ. It was by means of these
things that the Lord Christ wished to present us with
his body and blood, which he shed for our sake for the
forgiveness of sins. If you receive them well, you are
yourselves what you receive. You see, the apostle says,
We, being many are one loaf, one body (1 Corinthians 10.17).

—Augustine, Sermon 227

IN THIS CHAPTER I WILL CONSIDER SOME ASPECTS OF AUGUSTINE'S
writing about conversion as a way of approaching his theology of agency,
grace, sin, and salvation. This account will be developed in some later
chapters (chapters 4 and 5), but it offers a framework for my explorations
of fourteenth-century writing on forms of agency, sin, and salvation.[1]
Here I set out from *The City of God* (413–26/27), where Augustine envisages history through the figure of two cities, the earthly city and the city

of God.[2] Augustine's understanding of conversion and the agency involved in conversion has to meditate on these differences: From what forms of life are Christians converted? And to what forms of life, to what practices will they be drawn?[3]

In the earthly city people live according to "the rule of self" [secundum se ipsum]: that is, by a rule that imagines humans as autonomous subjects independent of God (*CG* XIV.3). Its peace is correspondingly defined in terms of the distribution and possession of material goods mediated by contingent cultural values, such as a cult of honor or a cult of glory derived from military triumphs or civic works (XIV.1). In the earthly city, exemplified at its providentially shaped best by Rome, people's wills, their loves, are fixed on glorification of the self ("amor sui," XIV.28). In seeking to secure themselves they seek dominion over others, and their lust for dominion comes to dominate their lives ("dominandi libido dominatur," XIV.28).[4] The rulers of the earthly city are "interested not in the morality but the docility of their subjects," and laws are organized around the protection of property and its accumulation. This is called freedom (II.20). Those who challenge this version of the virtues will be attacked as a public enemy ("publicus inimicus"), and the licentious multitude ("libera multitudo") will exile or kill them (II.20).[5] In fact the earthly city normalizes and institutionalizes the roots of sin.[6] Adam's will to autonomy from God and Cain's city founded on fratricide are its origins (XIII.13–15; XV.1, 5–8).

Not that the earthly city necessarily rejects religion. On the contrary, it fosters the worship of gods and the generation of many kinds of mediator. Augustine exhibits this in a sustained account of religion and ritual in Rome. The city's gods and their cult are shown to function as ideological and social cement in the compromise of conflicting wills and competing lust for dominion. Even Platonic philosophers participate in their polity's religion.[7] For through the shared worship of demonic mediators and pagan gods competing citizens are bound together. It thus becomes virtually impossible for "a weak and ignorant individual" nurtured in such a culture to escape from its social and demonic ties (IV.32). The cultural norms are internalized and secured in collective worship (VI.4). Furthermore, worship itself is directed to sustain "the enjoyments of vices and an earthly peace," to prolong the dominion over others (XV.7). All this description and critical analysis is elaborated with a theological hermeneutic centered on the one true mediator between the triune God and humanity.[8]

What then is the city to which Christians are converted, those forms of life that Augustine calls the city of God? Whereas the earthly city embodies love of self becoming contempt of God, the city of God is made by the love of God becoming the contempt of self, a love whose fulfillment and glory are not in a putatively autonomous self but in God (XIV.28). This city fashions well-directed wills that make emotions ("motus"), the acts of will, praiseworthy (XIV.6).[9] Such duly directed wills love God, their truly felicitous end, and they love their neighbors not according to human determinations ("non secundum hominem") but according to God ("secundum Deum"). In Scripture this is usually called charity ("caritas"), though it is also known as love ("amor," XIV.7). But the power and detail of Augustine's vision of the earthly city, instantiated by Rome, pose the question of how anybody formed in this city could find, let alone pursue, those very different and strange forms of life called the city of God, the kingdom of God, or the kingdom of Christ.[10] To put the question in terms shared by Langland and Augustine (as we shall see in chapter 4), how can the half-alive/half-dead man of Jesus's parable, the man attacked by thieves, stripped naked, bound up, and left lying in a wilderness, how can such a person become a free member of the city of God (Luke 10.29–37)? Is the requisite conversion perhaps totally inward? Could it be a totally inward act taking the Christian into an invisible city, a Wycliffite version of the true Church?[11]

There are certainly powerful accounts of Augustine that go along such lines. Adapting his Neoplatonic heritage, Augustine calls people to a turn away from the temporal and material world in which they have been fragmented and entrapped, a turn inward on a contemplative journey that will return them to God. Perhaps, like Milton's Archangel Michael, Augustine calls Adam to find "A paradise within thee, happier far" (*Paradise Lost,* XII.587).[12] One of the most widely diffused readings of Augustine in this direction appears in Charles Taylor's monumental *Sources of the Self: The Making of the Modern Identity.*[13] According to Taylor, Augustine invents a core component of "modern identity," the one Taylor calls "inwardness." Indeed, Augustine's invention of "inwardness" anticipates Descartes.[14] He quotes from Augustine's early work *On True Religion* (*De Vera Religione*): "Do not go outward; return within yourself. In the inward man dwells the truth." Not without reason, Taylor comments: "Augustine is always calling us within. What we need lies '*intus*,' he tells us again and again."[15] For Augustine, "inward lies the road to God" (129). In fact, Augustine's turn to the self was a turn to "radical reflexivity" (131).[16]

In an important review of *Sources of the Self,* Stanley Hauerwas and David Matzko offer criticisms of Taylor's version of Augustine. They argue that this version entirely displaces the story of the city of God as "a counter-commonwealth of forgiveness and peace." Taylor, they maintain, fails to grasp the role of the city of God in Augustine's understanding of the "inward" route to God.[17] If this criticism is warranted, as I believe it to be, it still leaves us with the question I put two paragraphs above: How can those of us who are habituated dwellers in the earthly city even perceive the city of God, let alone become its citizens? Augustine has shown that we are preoccupied by temporal goods, power, and honor, that we generate multiple strategies for shoring up our anxious selves against others, against death, and against God. In these preoccupations are we not likely to support our city's means of self-defense, its military power on which our own security against assorted barbarians depends? Do not ties of patriotic solidarity, sacrifice, and collective glory bind us together into our earthly city? Yes, of course they do. So could not "radical reflexivity," that famous inward turn, merely contribute to these given desires, anxieties, and bonds? Could it not actually shore up the very self produced by, in, and for the earthly city? And when I make the inward turn is there any good reason to think I will not find a god made in the image of the earthly city that has taught me how to honor the gods together with myself? Might not the earthly city even have taught me how to meditate? Taylor's inquiry does not ask these questions. Yet they are among the very questions Augustine's *City of God* has taught us to ask and has actually taught us to make central in any study of the self and its loves. In book VII of the *Confessions,* considering the converted Christian, Augustine says that while such a person may delight in God's law according to the inward person ("secundum interiorem hominem"), and so show himself to be a rebel within the earthly city, "what will he do with 'the other law in his members fighting against the law of his mind and bringing him into captivity under the law of sin, which is in his members?'" (*Confessions,* VII.21.27, quoting from Rom. 7.22–23).[18] Unlike some of his readers,

Augustine does not give us good reason to trust that the "radical reflexivity" of the "inward" turn will take us to God. It is salutary to remember that one of the features of the kingdom of God, the heavenly city, is the supersession of privatized, deep, secret interiorities: "The thoughts of our minds will lie open to each other" (*CG* XXII.29). In fact the fall of humanity is inextricably bound up with forms of privatization, with a rejection of common goods, the bonds of community, and transparency.[19] So we may suspect that far from being "the principal route to God," "radical reflexivity" could become bound up with the forms of privatization and inwardness cultivated in the earthly city as a means of accommodation with its life.[20] Far from inciting conversion, such inwardness could integrate us more comfortably and resourcefully in the earthly city.

Conversion from this city, the "kingdom of death" (*CG* XVI.1), to the city of God will involve not so much a privatized inward journey as the conversion of the whole person from one home ("domus") to another.[21] It will mean converting from a city seeking an earthly peace structured on the will for dominion and dismissal of the triune God to a city whose members understand themselves as pilgrims in a foreign land worshiping this God. And the triune God has given the promise of redemption in the divine judge who was crucified by the judges of the earthly city ("under Pontius Pilate," as the Nicene Creed states), the risen Son of God reconciling God and humanity in the Church, itself a divine gift. This city, Augustine says, calls out citizens from all nations to join a society of aliens ("peregrinam colligit societatem") that has its own religious laws ("religionis leges") and remains indifferent to the customs, laws, and institutions of the earthly city with which it lives. This indifference, however, will necessarily involve not inward emigration but dissent. And dissent will encounter anger, hatred, assaults, and persecution (XIX.17). So conversion is not to a city that is only invisible, a home in a privatized interiority.

Conversion is to the city of charity (*CG* XIV.7). This is the Christian religion itself ("ipsam religionem Christianam, ipsam civitatem Dei"), whose king and founder is Christ ("cuius rex est et conditor Christus," XVII.4).[22] Here all sacrifice is directed to the triune God revealed in Christ. It is offered "in every act which is designed to unite us to God in a holy fellowship," present and future. These sacrificial acts are acts of "compassion" involving neighbors and self, inseparably collective and in-dividual, offered to Christ, the community's "great Priest" (X.6). They constitute and build up the city that is the Church, the body of Christ. Au-gustine quotes Paul: "We are many, but we make up one body in Christ" (X.6; Rom. 12.3–6). And here, characteristically, he turns to the Eucha-rist: "This is the sacrifice which the Church continually celebrates in the sacrament of the altar, a sacrament well-known to the faithful where it is shown to the Church that she herself is offered in the offering which she presents to God" (X.6).[23] This brings us toward the heart of con-version in Augustine's theology. Conversion is into the embodied life and story of the Catholic Church in which Augustine held the office of bishop. As he says, pagan philosophers were right in thinking that the wise man's life is social. But Augustine insists on affirming this "much more strongly than they do."[24] As Oliver O'Donovan notes, Augustine wishes to stress the "distinctive" capacity of Christian thought "to break free of an individualist vision of the good" and develop "a social one."[25] For the city of God from "its first start" through its pilgrimage in this his-torical world could not "attain its appointed end [debitos fines] if the life of the saints were not social [socialis]" (XIX.5). And so, living a life in his-tory, "as a *civitas,* the Church is for Augustine itself a 'political' reality."[26]

Here it is necessary to acknowledge a contested area in readings of the *City of God*: the relations between the Catholic Church and the city of God. My own view will already have emerged implicitly, but I think it should be articulated, however briefly. The Church is both visible and in-visible, a city and a mystical body, the body and bride of Christ. Augustine explains his understanding of the relation between the Catholic Church and the kingdom of heaven, the New Jerusalem, in a sermon preached around 414.[27] He tells his congregation that "the Church which now is," "this Church, which gathers in good and bad together," is also "called the kingdom of heaven." It is the net of Christ's parable, given to collect all kinds of fish into a truly mixed body until the Last Judgment (Matt. 13.47–50). Augustine stresses that Christians teaching good things but "doing bad things" are certainly, for now, "in the kingdom of heaven, that is, in the Church as it is in this time."[28] Similarly in book VIII of the *City of God* he writes that the city of God, which is the holy Church, "is now being built in the whole world," built of those who once converted be-come like living stones (VIII.24; 1 Pet. 2.5). The Church includes both "tares" and "wheat," which the Lord allows to grow together until the final harvest. God's "kingdom" thus includes "stumbling-blocks," yet it is "the Church in this world" (XX.9; Matt. 13.39–43). Such locutions resist any dichotomization of visible and invisible Church. Augustine observes that his book is a defense of "the City of God, that is to say, God's Church" [defendimus civitatem Dei, hoc est eius ecclesiam] (XIII.16). So Catholic Christians are "the citizens of the Holy City of God" who are "in the pilgrimage of this present life" (XIV.9). Our allegorical reading of the Old Testament must always be practiced "with reference to Christ and the Church, which is the City of God," both within and beyond history (XVI.2).[29] The Church is certainly the heavenly city on pilgrimage, a determinate community of historical beings. But as we have noted, it is equally certainly a mixed body. Against the Donatists' fantasies of a pure Church, Augustine insisted that the Church in its pilgrimage has wrinkles and spots, unlike the bride of Christ in her final form (Eph. 5.25–27).[30] Just as Augustine's language resists dichotomization of visible and invisible Church, so it resists any simple, unqualified identification of the city of God and the Catholic Church. The Church both already is the city of God and is not yet the city of God. This is a structure of theological reflection pervading Christian understanding of the relations between the kingdom of God already revealed in Christ and the kingdom of God prayed for and awaited, an eschatological event.[31] In history, with its wrinkles, spots, tares, and wickedness, "the Church even now is the kingdom of Christ and the kingdom of heaven," albeit a kingdom "at war" (XX.9).[32]

With this reading of Augustine's language concerning the Church and the city of God in mind, I return to the issue of conversion from the earthly city, that kingdom of death (*CG* XIV.1), to the city of God. This undoubtedly includes some kind of return to oneself from being assimilated to "externals" [foris].[33] But this moment must not be isolated from the movement into the community that constitutes the city of God in its historical pilgrimage. It must involve the whole, embodied person in a process that is never completed in this life.[34] Conversion is from a home in a city organized around fragile compromises over wills competing for dominion and wealth to one centered on the promises of redemption, the precepts and gift of God, namely the Church (XIX.17). And it entails the public act of baptism. In a sermon preached around 419–20

Augustine tells his congregation that in the Church sins are forgiven that "are not forgiven apart from the Church."[35] Indeed, sins "must be forgiven in that Spirit by which the Church is gathered together in a unit" (71.28). Why? "Because the Church has received this gift, of sins being forgiven in her in the Holy Spirit." Indeed, "You can tell you have received the Holy Spirit if you are held in the bond of peace of the Church, which is spread out among all nations. That's why the apostle says, *Eager to preserve the unity of the Spirit in this bond of peace* (Ephesians 4.3)" (71.28). As for training in what Taylor called "radical reflexivity,"[36] Augustine emphasizes that baptism into the Church, with the gift of divine forgiveness constituting this act, is conversion even if the Christians do not yet perceive that they have actually received the Holy Spirit (71.30–31). He reflects, characteristically, on the limits of our self-awareness: "Nor should it strike you as odd that someone should have something and be ignorant of what it is they have. To say nothing of the power of the Almighty and the unity of the unchangeable Trinity, who can easily grasp by knowledge what the soul is?" (71.31).

Time and again, in different genres of writing, Augustine affirms that "the words of God," represented in Scripture, "make it perfectly clear that, apart from community with Christ, no one can attain eternal life and salvation." And that, he writes in *The Punishment and Forgiveness of Sins and the Baptism of Little Ones* (411–12), is why we baptize people, however young.[37] Through this sacrament "they are joined to the body and members of Christ" (III.4.7). Christ himself "willed that this rebirth be brought about by baptism" and instituted this sacrament of conversion (I.18.23). So while God "is the light of the interior human being," he "helps us to turn to him" (II.5.5) in the ways he has given people in the Church, which is his body. Conversion "begins with the forgiveness of sins," but this "interior" renewal continues from day to day (2 Cor. 4.16) in the Catholic Church, where the fruits of the Holy Spirit are bestowed (II.7.9). Preaching to his congregations in the Church at once very visible and invisible, he often stresses that if the forgiveness of sins in Christ "were not to be had in the Church, there would be no hope of a future life and eternal liberation. We thank God, who gave his Church such a gift," the gift of the baptismal sacrament.[38] And, of course, thanks are given for the sacrament of unity where Christians are daily incorporated in the body of Christ.[39]

In just this thoroughly social way the city of God on pilgrimage seeks to remedy the privatizing individualism of the Fall. Conversion cannot be an inward emigration. Nor can it be like the salvific journey of the awakening Plotinian soul returning alone to its always unfallen self in union with the One it has never truly left, an inward journey of the alone to the alone. On the contrary, as John Kenney has recently shown, Augustinian contemplation is Christocentric, scriptural, and thoroughly ecclesial. The Church, he argues, offers "an ecclesial locus for contemplation, nesting it within an institutional structure."[40] Christian conversion is to a city that calls ("evocat") and collects ("colligit") a community (*CG* XIX.17). It makes a determinate society developing a form of life faithful to God revealed in his Word. Augustine's arguments and iconography here are congruent with Karl Barth's insistence that the disciple of Christ cannot attempt "'inner emigration' in which he will not be offensive, or at least suspicious, or at the very least conspicuous, to those who still worship their gods. It is not merely a matter of saving his own soul in the attainment of a private beatitude. He loses his soul, and hazards his eternal salvation, if he will not accept the public responsibility which he assumes when he becomes a disciple of Jesus."[41] But conversion is not only from one city and its present form of life to another. It is also from a history, from a past that has constituted a person's identity: one's senses, emotions, thoughts, fears, loves, dreams—indeed, memory upon memory.[42] This past truly binds us. In the seventh book of the *Confessions,* Augustine addresses the *how* of conversion: "What will wretched man do?" With St. Paul's help he reformulates the question and gives an answer that is strikingly different from Taylor's account of the "principal route" to God through an "inward road": "'Who will deliver him from the body of death' except your grace through Jesus Christ our Lord," the "coeternal Son," the innocent Lord who was killed by the prince of the earthly city and freed humankind from the decree that was against us (VII.21.21; Rom. 7.24; Col. 2.14; see too VII.9.113–14).

Turning back to the *City of God* we receive the same answer: "The hostile power . . . is conquered in the name of him who assumed human nature and whose life was without sin, so that in him, who was both priest and sacrifice, remission of sins might be effected, that is through the mediator between God and mankind, the man Christ Jesus, through whom we are . . . reconciled to God" (X.22). Christ is the "one road," Augustine writes, the goal and "the way" (XI.2). Here is the source of the grace that awakens and calls the Babylonian subject to begin the movement into that other city. But this answer still leaves open questions about agency, about the weight of the past, the temporalities of human identity. A person drawn by grace into the community that Bishop Augustine now inhabited would, however uncertainly and diffidently, become estranged from her past. Yet the memory of that past, its presence, is not expunged.[43] Nor must it be, despite its formation in the earthly city. For in our memory, that abyss with its fields, vast palaces, and treasures, is a massive power ("vis"), a sublime ("horrendum") mystery where we find God. For if I find you outside my memory ("praeter memoriam meam"), Augustine confesses to God, I forget you; and how shall I find you if I am not remembering you (*Confessions*, X.17.26)? But this encounter with one's memory bears little, if any, relation to Taylorian accounts of the Augustinian "inward" journey and the "road" to God. For the tenth book of *Confessions* displays how the converted and baptized person, living in the new household, has become extremely opaque to herself. Augustine observes how he has become a "quaestio" to himself (X.33.50), has been made to himself a difficult land, hard to labor (X.16.25). Indeed, joyful conversion shows how his self-reflexivity yields neither clarity nor certainty but lamentable darkness in which his obscure potentials are hidden (X.32.48). The different and abandoned past still returns and, at least in dreams, can elicit consent to old, rejected habits and pleasures (X.30.41). So the converting agency of divine grace does not repress the past. Rather, it enables that past, its power and consequences, to be grasped, at last, with clarity but, crucially, without panic. In his homily on Psalm 136, Augustine notes that if we truly become citizens of Jerusalem, the memory of Jerusalem will gradually supersede our memories of Babylon, our former home and, as we can only now see, our prison. But the danger remains that as we are still pilgrims, encompassed by the earthly city, we can aestheticize this city of confusion, turning it into songs, and gradually forget Jerusalem in the reinvigorated memories of Babylon.[44] Once again we are led to see how conversion is an exhilarating, restless, and dangerous process. Nothing could be more misleading than to assimilate such descriptions of the grace of conversion to some irresistible force that concludes the struggles of conflicting memories, ends the need for searching, and provides transparent self-knowledge in the light of divine clarity.[45]

Some words from Barth's treatment of the doctrine of reconciliation are congruent here:

> There can be no question of an act of compulsion on the part of the Lord. . . . He certainly exercises power, putting down the mighty from their seat and exalting them of low degree (Luke 1.52). Nor is there any power in heaven or earth compatible with or superior to His. But it is not a blind, brute power. . . . His is not a rampaging numinous which strikes man unconditionally so that he can only be petrified and silent before it, yielding without really wanting to do so. He does not humiliate or insult man. He does not make him a mere spectator, let alone a puppet.[46]

Views that take the account of Paul's conversion in Acts 9 as paradigmatic of Christian conversion will be addressed as I now pursue the issue of conversion and agency.

In his preface to *On Christian Teaching* Augustine insists that Christians, however replete with divine gifts, must accept that the Holy Spirit teaches through human mediations. Learning from others within the community is not only a learning about Christian practice and doctrine but also a training in humility. It is the demonic pride learned in the earthly city that seeks to persuade people that as vessels of the Holy Spirit Christians do not need human mediations of the Word. The outcome of such perversity is likely to be refusal "to go to church in order to hear and learn from the gospel, or to read the Bible, or to listen to anybody reading it out and preaching it; and into expecting to be snatched up to the third heaven, *whether in the body or out of the body,* as the apostle says, *and there hear unutterable words which it is not lawful for man to speak* (2 Cor. 12: 2–4), or there see the Lord Jesus Christ and listen to the gospel directly from his mouth rather than just from other people."[47] Once again, we learn that ideologies and spiritualities that isolate us from the community of believers, the actually existing Catholic Church, are the product of pride, the will to autonomy and privatization enacted in the Fall. Augustine would doubtless have encountered Christians whose model of conversion was taken from Luke's story of Paul's conversion (Acts 9 and 22). Perhaps he would also encounter some who interpreted his own conversion as an echo of this story. So he warns his readers: "Let us be on our guard against all such dangerous temptations to pride, and let us rather reflect on how the same apostle Paul, although he had been struck down and instructed by the divine voice from heaven, was still sent to a man to receive the sacraments and be joined to the Church [ad hominem tamen missum esse ut sacramenta perciperet atque copularetur ecclesiae]" (Preface, 6).[48] Similar arguments are relevant to Cornelius in Acts 10. An angel tells him that his worship is accepted by God and then hands him over to Peter both to receive the sacraments and to learn what should be believed, hoped, and loved (Preface, 6). The human condition would be truly abject ("abiecta") if God seemed unwilling to minister his word to human beings through humans ("per homines hominibus," Preface, 6). God, however, certainly wills such ministry. For without human mediations in the Church "there would be no way for love, which ties people together in the bonds of unity, to make souls overflow and as it were intermingle with each other" (Preface, 6.13).[49]

In a work written against the Donatists, *On Baptism,* Augustine also reflects on Cornelius's conversion. There too the emphasis is on the need for Cornelius to be "incorporated in the Church by the bond of Christian brotherhood and peace." He learns about Christ through Peter. Baptized by Peter, "he was joined by the tie of communion to the fellowship of Christians, to which he was bound by the likeness of good works." Augustine observes that it would have been disastrous for Cornelius had he despised what he had not yet received, communion with the Church, "vaunting himself in what he had."[50] Augustine's teaching is as incompatible with Wycliffite ideology, identifying the only true Church as an invisible one of currently unknown, unknowable predestinates, as it is with Plotinian understanding of the "inward" way to salvation. For Augustine, in Christian conversion the divine will is that such conversions be made and sustained by human mediations that constitute the body of Christ, the kingdom of Christ in its earthly pilgrimage, the city of God in its historical form.[51]

This systematic emphasis on human mediation and the actual Catholic Church in conversion does not sideline divine agency, grace.[52] Characteristically, Augustine confesses to God, "You converted me to you" [convertisti enim me ad te] (*Confessions,* VIII.12.30). Indeed, a common perception I have already alluded to has been that Augustine's theology of grace overwhelms and dissolves human agency.[53] Yet in the *Confessions* God is shown patiently drawing people to active acknowledgment of conversion in the Church. Victorinus exemplifies this (VIII.2.3–4.9). A famous, erudite pagan, he has been a worshipper of idols, a proponent of "sacrilegious rites," and a defender of these cults for many years. But reading holy Scripture and Christian writings he is drawn to Christianity. He comes to see himself as a Christian and informs his Christian friend and priest Simplicianus. The latter, however, replies, "'I shall not believe that or count you among the Christians unless I see you in the Church of Christ.'" Victorinus rejects what he takes to be a superfluous externalism of belief and laughingly asks, "Do walls make Christians?" This "joke" is used to avoid any public identification of a move between communities, one that would certainly be offensive to his pagan friends. He wishes to keep conversion an inward and private matter. But as he continues to ruminate on the demands of discipleship outlined in Scripture (such as Luke 12.9) he comes to see that conversion entails catechism and baptism in the Church. So he decides to make "profession of his salvation before the holy congregation" (VIII.2.5). For Augustine this is a model of God's grace creating both joy for the converted person and communal joy in the Christian community where the conversion incorporates the convert (VIII.2.5–3.6). And it prefigures Augustine's own conversion, to which the story of Victorinus belongs. For in Augustine's conversion God acts through a dense network of mediations, a veritable cornucopia of interlocutors. We encounter the roles, sometimes direct, sometimes oblique, of many: Faustus the Manichee, Neoplatonists' writings, Monica, Ambrose, Anthony, Ponticianus, Victorinus, a child's voice, Paul, divine admonitions. Describing this network, Ann Matter concludes that "the example [of Augustine's conversion] given is not Paul, either as described in Luke or in his own writings, but a Chinese box of stories of conversion."[54] In converting Augustine through such interlocutors, God was converting Augustine into the Church, that network of mediations where he would be a bishop. The words he quotes from Simplicianus to Victorinus speak to his own deferral of baptism: "I shall not count you among the Christians unless I see you in the Church of Christ" (VIII.2.4).

Attention to the complex relations between divine and human agency pervades Augustine's work from his response to seven questions put to him by Simplicianus in around 395.[55] Here I wish to illustrate the form of this attention by considering the opening of the thirteenth book of the *Confessions*. This book discloses the divine covenant embodied in the Church while reading the covenant in the creation saga of Genesis. It begins by invoking God:

> I call you [invoco te] my God, my mercy, you who made me, and, when I forgot you, you did not forget me. I call you into my soul [invoco te in animam meam], which you prepare to seize to yourself through the desire which you have inspired in this soul. Do not desert me now as I am calling you [invocantem te], you who before I called you [invocarem] preceded me and with increasing urgency pressed upon me with callings [vocibus] in many ways so that I would hear you from far away and be converted [converterer] and call you calling me [vocantem me invocarem te].[56]

The first word of the final book makes a clear claim to human agency: "Invoco," I, Augustine, call God. The same word opens the second sentence, now stressing what was implied before: I call you into my soul. But the word is broken into a play of voices other than that of the confessing subject, voices that seem to flow from the one whom Augustine invokes. Indeed, the one to whom Augustine calls turns out to be calling Augustine ("vocantem me") even as he himself invokes God. Not only is the one whom Augustine addresses actually calling Augustine, he is pressing upon Augustine with many kinds of mediations, with many callings ("vocibus"). As Augustine remembers having forgotten God, he recalls how God has never forgotten him but always preceded him ("praevenisti"), ensuring that he would hear God from far away and so be turned back to God, converted.

    This image carefully evokes one of the recurring models for conversion in the *Confessions*, the story of the prodigal son in Luke 15.[57] God's agency reaches the one who wanders obliviously into a far country; "de longinquo" here echoes Luke's "in regionem longinquam" [into a far country] (Luke 15.13). In these words Augustine also recalls a moment from book VII. There Platonic books admonished him to return to himself (VII.10.16).[58] Led by God through these books into his "innermost citadel" [intima mea], raised up by God, he glimpses "the immutable light," the light that made him and that love knows. Yet Augustine's contemplative vision discloses that in fact he is "far from you [God] in the region of dissimilarity" [longe me a te in regione dissimilitudinis] (VII.10.16).[59] There, in the recognition of alienation from God who is both revealed and hidden, he hears, as the voice of God, one calling him ("tamquam audirem vocem tuam"). The voice calls him to the eucharistic banquet where he, the agent who eats the bread of life, will be changed, one could say converted, "into me" [in me] (VII.10.16). Later in this book of the *Confessions* he has still not been able to receive this food, being not yet reconciled to the fact that the enjoyment of God he so desires is inseparable from "the humble Jesus" (VII.18.24). The latter has provided the food humanity needs by mingling the divine word with flesh so that divine wisdom might produce milk for "our infant condition" (VII.18.24). Conversion in Augustine is inseparable from Christology.

Tracing these examples of Augustine's attention to divine and human agency helps us see its suppleness and subtlety. Who is doing what to whom? Whose voice is speaking? Who is listening? These are shown to be complex questions. Syntax, wordplay, echo, and allusion in the extraordinary prose of the *Confessions* compose a distinctive grammar of grace. The initiative of divine agency, often hidden or obscurely mediated, is prevenient and pervasive but addresses human desire and elicits human agency. The delicate account of invocation, exemplified in the passage considered above from book XIII, gradually answers a question asked near the opening of the *Confessions*: "How shall I call upon my God?" [Et quomodo invocabo deum meum?] (I.2.2). He comes to see that what he took to be God's absence was actually Augustine's absence and that God "called and cried out loud" (X.27.38). The act of human invocation (XIII.1.1) is inextricably bound up with divine acts of invocation.[60] We encounter a version of "double agency."[61] And this is a sacrament, a mystery.

In the *Confessions* Augustine not only displays a dense texture of mediations eliciting his conversion but also shows how puzzlement and unpromising delights draw him toward the city he had held in contempt. For example, in book V he relates how his love of eloquence drew him to Ambrose although he had absolutely no hope in God's Church but rather contempt for Christian teaching and sacraments (V.12.23). But without his knowing this ("nesciens") it was to emerge that his free agency was being led through his rhetorical pleasures by God so that, through Ambrose, he would be drawn, now knowing ("sciens"), to God. Still far off ("longe") he notes that little by little he was drawing near (he uses the active verb *propinquabam*) although he did not know this ("nesciens" [V.12.23]). Little by little ("sensim"), he was drawing near. This is very different from the Paul of Acts 9.1–7 (also Acts 22.3–11). Even late in book VI Augustine emphasizes that he was still wanting and able to delay being converted ("converti"), that he postponed ("differebam") finding life in God although "I did not postpone the fact that every day I was dying within myself" (VI.11.20).[62] But intrinsic to his own will and long-ings, divine grace lures him toward the community into which he will be converted to live a life of continuing conversion.[63]

Augustine's explicitly anti-Pelagian writings are not famous for their subtlety and nuance. But I will now consider two moments from these that suggest that a certain rereading of these might be fruitful. The first comes from *The Grace of Christ and Original Sin* (418).[64] During his discus-sions of inadequacies in Pelagius's teachings on human and divine agency, Augustine addresses one of the questions from which this chapter set out with *The City of God*. How do humans change from being bad trees pro-ducing bad fruit to being good trees producing good fruit? In *The Grace of Christ,* Augustine quotes Christ's observation that an evil tree cannot bring forth good fruit.[65] On the contrary, from the root of a bad will grows evil fruit in thoughts, words, and deeds. Only when a human being receives ("accipit") God's grace is such a strange conversion possible (I.19.20). And then it is grace that cooperates ("cooperatur") with the good trees in producing good fruit, a cooperation that is both through the means of grace in the community and through the agency of grace within ("intrin-secus," I.19.20). Here we see how the crucial inward turn is a gift formed by Christ. As for evil, this is not a new nature but rather the activity of the will seeking autonomy from the source of its life (I.19.20). Once again there is no question of rival agents or of an irresistible power, extrinsic to the human will, overwhelming it. The processes of conversion are both "intrinsic" and bound in with the means given the Christian community (I.19.20–22). The *City of God* likewise describes the citizens of the city of God being restored to health by the Holy Spirit, who works internally ("intrinsecus") to make effective the necessary medicine, which is applied externally ("extrinsecus") in the Church of pilgrims (XV.6).[66]

One of Augustine's models for displaying his argument about human and divine agencies in the gift of conversion comes from a reading of St. Peter's denials of Christ in Luke 22.[67] These denials occur as Jesus is being interrogated, mocked, and assaulted by his captors (Luke 22.52–71). Peter has just witnessed the will of the earthly city to destroy the founder and king of the city of God. Confronted with this unimaginable determination, Peter has fled. But he has returned to follow Jesus, albeit from afar ("a longe," Luke 22.54). This following has brought him into exchanges with those hostile to Jesus. He is challenged to disclose his identity (Luke 22.55–60). Peter's response is understandable terror at being identified as an alien within the earthly city. He insists that he really does belong to this city, that he is no alien. Accordingly he denies all knowledge of the captured stranger whom he has so recently acknowledged as Messiah, beheld in the divine vision of the Transfiguration, and promised to accompany to prison and death (Matt. 16.16; Luke 9.28–36; Luke 22.33). In panic Peter forgets more than his promises to Jesus. He forgets why he ever made such promises, why he continued to accept Jesus's initial call, "Follow me" (Matt. 4.19). He has forgotten to what community he has been called.[68]

Augustine approaches Peter's denial of Christ and his ensuing tears of penance through Ambrose's commentary on Luke. Once more he uses the language of cooperation to describe the relations between divine and human agency while insisting, with Ambrose, that "no one even begins anything without God" (*Grace of Christ,* I.44.48). Even the love by which one loves God "is due to the gift of grace," a gift from the Lord who "cooperates" [cooperatur] with our will and commitments. He turns his attention to penance. This, he observes, is certainly something the will does. But like the love to which it belongs, it is something done with the Lord's mercy and help (I.45.49). Augustine's reading is a nice example of the complex way in which he envisages the relations of divine and human agency in his later work.

He follows Ambrose in noting that in his first denial of Jesus Peter "did not weep, because the Lord had not looked upon him. He denied him a second time and did not weep because the Lord had not yet looked upon him. He denied him a third time. Jesus looked upon him and he wept most bitterly" (*Grace of Christ,* I.45.49, quoting Ambrose on Luke). Luke's gospel shows, Augustine writes, that at this point Jesus was being

interrogated by the chief priests within the building while Peter was outside in the courtyard with the servants at the fire. So, he comments, one
cannot say that the Lord looked upon him with bodily eyes, admonishing him in a way that Peter could see. For this reason the language of interiority becomes essential as we grasp the narrative's implications: "The
action which scripture reports, *The Lord looked upon him* (Luke 22:61) took
place interiorly [intus actum est]; it took place in the mind; it took place in
the will. By his mercy the Lord in a hidden manner helped him, touched
his heart, recalled his memory [memoriam revocavit], visited Peter with
his interior grace [interiore gratia sua] and produced passion of the inner
man which moved him to tears."[69] Christ's hidden agency is prevenient
and intrinsic. It touches Peter and calls to his own memory, his own inner
and outer acts. So the language of interiority ("intus . . . in mente . . . in-
terioris hominis") belongs to conversations that have been brutally interrupted, and it draws Peter back to these. The summons of grace to the
inner person is simultaneously a summons to a shared history. This is
nothing like Plotinian self-reflexivity and contemplation.

In fact Peter experiences just what Augustine recollected in the
passage from the opening of the thirteenth book of the *Confessions* discussed earlier in this chapter. "When I forgot you," Augustine invokes
God, "you did not forget me" (XIII.1.1). And how delicate is the work of
divine memory, memory that is that divine patience also known as grace.
Augustine sees the absent Christ working with mercy in Peter's mind,
will, and heart. He sees Christ calling back Peter's own memory, and there
is absolutely no trace of an irresistible, "rampaging numinous" that would
make the human a puppet or, at best, a spectator at her or his own conversion.[70] Divine grace enables an art of remembrance that truly remembers Peter, recalling him to his identity as a member of the community that is the body of Christ. Remembered, he remembers his betrayals:
"And Peter remembered [recordatus est] the word of the Lord . . . [and]
wept bitterly" (Luke 22.61–62). These are the tears of penance that belong to Peter's conversion. Christ had prayed for this event when he had
anticipated Peter's denials: "I have prayed for thee, that thy faith fail thee
not: and thou, being once converted [conversus], confirm thy brethren"
(Luke 22.32). Tears of penance, tears of conversion: Peter moves and is
moved toward the broken community to be remade at Easter. As in the
City of God, conversion is about the formation of that strange commu-

nity, mingled with the earthly city, a thoroughly mixed community but nevertheless Christ's kingdom on earth, the Church (*CG* XX.9; XIII.6; XVII.1).

In one of his final works, *The Predestination of the Saints* (between 427 and 429), Augustine gives us yet another model of conversion.[71] This is taken from Acts 16, the conversion of Lydia. Acts 16 summarizes Paul's formation of Christian communities guided by the "spirit of Jesus" (16.7). At Philippi Paul addresses a group of women including Lydia, a seller of purple. While Lydia listens to Paul, the Lord opens her heart to what Paul says. The act of attention is hers and leads to her decision to be baptized with her whole household, her "domus" (16.1–15). Although Augustine does not explore the forms of agency in the detail of his reflection on Peter in *The Grace of Christ,* he observes that Luke's narrative shows how the gift of divine grace is given: "When God wills the accomplishment of something which only willing human beings can do, their hearts are inclined to will this, that is, he inclines their hearts who produces in us in a marvelous and ineffable way [in nobis mirabilis modo et ineffabili operator] the willing as well" (20.42). Once again we have a model of divine and human agency in which there can be no question of competition or rivalry. And once again there is no doctrine about the pursuit of a desocialized, autonomous interiority through which God will be found. Furthermore, the processes of conversion belong, yet once more, to the formation of the community that is the city of God on earth: inward "emigration" is simply not an option. Augustine would agree with Karl Barth that "to be awakened and to be added to the community are one and the same thing."[72] As for agency, some words from a sermon of 416 preached against the Pelagians sum up major components of his views as he discusses "justification":

> But the whole thing is from God; not however as though we were asleep, as though we didn't have to make an effort, as though we didn't have to be willing. Without your will, there will be no justice of God in you. The will, indeed, is only yours, the justice is only God's. There can be such a thing as God's justice without your will, but it cannot be in you apart from your will. . . . While he made you without you, he doesn't justify you without you. So he made you without your knowing it, he justifies you with your willing consent to it.[73]

Once again, Augustine displays his version of double agency in conversion. The model is not of an irresistible power overwhelming a passive creature, or of a grace whose action is extrinsic, but of a transforming gift whose work is intrinsic to the will.[74] And the gift is through the humility of Jesus Christ, who "emptied himself taking the form of a servant" that "we might do the justice of God in him" (169.2; Phil. 2.6–7; 2 Cor. 5.21). In the power of Christ's resurrection, Augustine tells his congregation, "recognize here your own justification" (169.12). The sermon thus typically opposes Pelagianism on Christological grounds, an issue I will return to at greater length in chapter 4.

THIS CONCLUDES MY AUGUSTINIAN PRELUDE TO THE READINGS OF fourteenth-century theology that follow. But although I have mentioned Augustine's emphasis on the ecclesial mediations involved in Paul's conversion, I wish to address some other potentials in Luke's narrative.[75] Luke relates that Paul (then known as Saul) had been "breathing out threatenings and slaughter against the disciples of the Lord," determined to capture Christians for trial in Jerusalem. As he went to Damascus, "suddenly a light from heaven shined round about him. And falling on the ground, he heard a voice saying to him: Saul, Saul, why persecutest thou me?" Asked who speaks, Paul is told, "I am Jesus whom thou persecutest. It is hard for thee to kick against the goad." Paul asks what the Lord would have him do and is told to go to Damascus, where he will learn. Paul rises from the ground, now unable to see anything (Acts 9.1–8). In *The Predestination of the Saints,* Augustine observes that "the beginnings" of Paul's faith "are very well known because they are frequently read in the Church." He describes these "beginnings" in this way:

> When he was turned away from the faith which he was persecuting and was strongly opposed to it, he was suddenly converted to it by a more powerful grace. He was converted by him to whom the prophet said, as he was about to do this, *You will convert us and give us life* (Ps 85:7). He not only became someone willing to believe from someone who was unwilling, but from a persecutor he became someone who suffered persecution in the defense of that faith which he

was persecuting. It was given to him by Christ not only that he believe in him but also that he suffer for him. (2.4)[76]

Although the emphasis here is on the statement that Paul was "suddenly converted," Augustine also emphasizes Paul's transformed will and its faithful perseverance. The persecutor becomes someone who willingly endures persecution for what he experiences as the joy of communicating the gospel (Phil. 4.4–13). Yet Luke's narrative can be read to emphasize the overwhelming force involved in conversion.[77] In an anti-Pelagian sermon preached on the feast of the apostles Peter and Paul, Augustine himself comments on the narrative as one that illustrates a coercive form of divine grace: "He's coerced into sparing, so that he may be spared himself. The wolf is changed into a sheep; that's nothing, into a sheep; in fact, into a shepherd. By the voice from on high he's slain and brought to life, struck down and healed" (299.6).[78] This language generates the possibility of a reading that concentrates on violent coercion rather than the processes of mediation, resistance, and gradually transformed attention that Augustine traces elsewhere. And it is just this narrative of Paul's conversion that has been seen in Augustine's change of mind concerning the use of imperial laws to compel Donatist Christians to become Catholic Christians.[79] The scholars making this argument seem to draw not on sermons but on Augustine's letters, especially the famous one to the soldier Boniface in 417 that Augustine himself described as a book called *The Correction of the Donatists*.[80]

In this letter (185), Augustine justifies the application of imperial laws compelling Donatist Christians to become Catholic Christians. Having recounted the murderous violence of Donatist militants against Catholics (shades of unconverted Paul), Augustine argues that it is licit and best for the Donatists' own eternal well-being that they should be compelled to join the Catholic Church. He turns to the conversion of Paul:

> For who can love us more than Christ, who laid down his life for his sheep? And yet though he called Peter and the other apostles by words alone, in dealing with Paul, who was first Saul and later a great builder of his Church, but before that its fierce persecutor, he did not restrain him by words alone but laid him low by his power.

And to press the man who was raging in the darkness of unbelief to desire the light of his heart, he first afflicted him with blindness of the body. If that were not a punishment, he would not have been healed of it later, and if his eyes were healthy when he saw nothing, though his eyes were open, scripture would not report that at the imposition of Ananias' hands some sort of scales that prevented his seeing fell from his eyes so that his sight might be restored. What happens to their usual cry, "One is free to believe or not to believe. With whom did Christ use force? Whom does he compel?" See, they have Paul the apostle; let them acknowledge in him Christ first using force and afterward teaching, first striking and afterward consoling. It is amazing, however, how that man who came to the gospel forced by bodily punishment, labored more for the gospel than all those who were called by words [1 Cor. 15.10]. And though greater fear drove him to love, his *perfect love cast out fear* (1 Jn. 4:18).[81]

It seems clear that Paul's conversion is seen as an unusual form because it involves peremptory compulsion. Yet it too displays Christ's saving love for Paul and the body of Christ that Paul had been persecuting. This divine act delivers the Church from a zealous destroyer and gives her "a wise architect," gifted by grace to lay "the foundation" of the mission to the Gentiles (1 Cor. 3.10). Augustine goes on to explain how his earlier rejection of coercion against Donatists has changed in response both to their violence against Catholics and to the way coercive imperial legislation has actually driven them to the Church, where the gifts of the Holy Spirit have led to their conversion (185.23–51). Despite these reflections Augustine retains the acknowledgment of nonviolent human mediation of divine grace through Ananias's healing hands.[82] But his emphasis here is certainly on a decisive act of overwhelming divine power as a model to legitimize the empire's coercion of Christians who oppose the Catholic Church. Why, he asks, should not the Church, a loving mother, "force her lost children to return if these lost children were forcing others to perish," and why should she not then embrace those whom she has compelled to return home? Does not, he asks, a shepherd use coercion as well as persuasion in preserving his sheep? Because Paul was "forced by Christ" to his salvation, "the Church, then, imitates its Lord in forcing the Donatists" to return to their true home (185.6.23). And, of course,

Augustine is not applying these analogies to the treatment of unbaptized people.

Paula Fredriksen notes that Augustine had used the image of Paul's conversion in his reply to Simplicianus twenty years earlier.[83] Yet on that occasion, as in the anti-Pelagian Sermon 169 discussed above, Augustine was trying to illustrate how conversion is not something one can simply effect autonomously. As he said in Sermon 169, the attempt to build oneself in such autonomy leads to the building of a ruin (169.11). Yet even in his reply to Simplicianus Augustine wrote about the impossibility of conversion without sources of delight to move the will (I.22), thus briefly anticipating the modes and motions of conversion in the *Confessions* and so many sermons. Here, as we have seen, he composed an extraordinarily complex, nuanced grammar of grace that is antithetical to any model of instantaneous, coerced, and utterly decisive conversion. As Rowan Williams writes, "Augustine, more than almost any other Christian thinker, gives full value to the centrality of change and growth in human selfhood."[84] Given this, it would be mistaken to impose the anti-Donatist model of coercion, drawn from Luke's Paul, onto the accounts of conversion in the *Confessions,* the *City of God,* or sermons such as those considered above and in chapter 4.

That distinction does not mean one should ignore the use of Paul's conversion in Augustine's legitimization of coercing violent and schismatic Christians. Indeed, we should set this usage alongside his influential application of Jesus's parable of the great supper (Luke 14.15–24) in the same letter (185.6.24). In this parable people invited to the feast make excuses not to come. The angry Lord orders his servants to bring in the poor, the weak, the blind, and the lame. When this is done, there is still room. So the Lord tells the servant: "Go out into the highways and hedges and compel them to come in, that my house may be filled" (Luke 14.23).[85] Augustine finds that the Lord's move from gentle invitation to coercion has implications for the present situation of the Church. It figures forth the way God has led rulers to become Christians who have now decided to compel into the Church those Christians "found on the roads and pathways, that is, those in heresies and schisms." Such compulsion brings these Christians to the Lord's banquet, which is "the unity of the body of Christ not only in the sacrament of the altar but also *in the bond of peace*" (185.6.24; see Eph. 4.3). It is important to remember that

Augustine opposed the death penalty for Donatists who had committed murder and insisted that Catholics should not cooperate with imperial prosecution of Donatists for murder even if this made them feel free to kill Catholics.[86] So Henry Chadwick is undoubtedly right to insist on the chasm between Augustine's writings against the Donatists and the late medieval Church's practice of burning heretics to death.[87] Yet in terms of my own reading of Augustine's theology and politics of grace in conversion, his use of Acts 9 and Luke 14 to justify the use of imperial law to force Donatists into the body of Christ, the Church, goes against the grain of his own models of grace in the *Confessions,* the *City of God,* and elsewhere.[88] For there he developed a supremely delicate grammar of grace and human agency showing how conversion from the earthly city is a daily and continuing process within the Church under the guidance of divine patience that eschews compulsion. This process, he emphasizes, was enabled by a God who "emptied himself, taking the form of a servant." So Christ "humbled himself, becoming obedient unto death, even to the death of the cross," the mediator between God and humanity, the goal and the way for human beings.[89]

CHAPTER 2

Illustrating "Modern Theology"

Sin and Salvation in Ockham

Garriebam plane quasi peritus et, nisi in Christo, Salvatore
nostro, viam tuam quaerrerem, non peritus sed periturus
essem. [I chattered on loquaciously as though I were an
expert and yet unless I searched for your way in Christ our
savior I would have been no expert but perished.]

Augustine, *Confessions,* VII.20.26

I

I will begin this brief account of Ockham on sin and salvation with his
commentary on the first book of the *Sentences.*[1] Ockham sets himself
the following question: "Utrum praeter Spiritum Sanctum necesse sit
ponere caritatem absolutam creatam, animam formaliter informanten"
(III.440). He characteristically argues that "de potentia Dei absoluta"
God can accept the soul to final salvation without any divinely given form
inhering in the soul: that is, without any habit (III.445−46). The key to
Ockham's approach is that whoever is accepted by God is for that reason
worthy of eternal life (III.446; see similarly 455−56). The focus is on divine acceptance. It is neither on the consequences of sin for the powers

of the human soul and her separation from God nor on the transforming, healing powers of divine grace. Ockham's habitual use of *de potentia
absoluta* facilitates this focus. So, for example, God "in potentia Dei absoluta," could accept or not accept one informed with a supernatural form,
or somebody who had received the divine gift of charity could be un-
lovely and unacceptable to God: "tales non esset carus et acceptus Deo"
(III.453; see too 449). Indeed, God could give such a gift and then annihilate it before he gave eternal life to its subject (III.453–54). Of course,
Ockham's deployment of the dialectic of *potentia absoluta* and *potentia ordinata* never collapses the former into the latter.[2]

Ockham affirms traditional teaching on divine agency in the redemption of humanity and is certain that his theology is free from any traces
of Pelagianism. There has been a long debate, in both medieval and modern times, about Ockham's relations to semi-Pelagianism or Pelagianism.
Rega Wood, among the most learned of Ockham scholars, has fully supported Ockham's claims, whereas Marilyn McCord Adams, an equally
learned author of a massive, indispensable two-volume work on Ockham, has determined that his theology of salvation is "semi-Pelagian."[3]
Ockham's defense of his position is that Pelagianism is constituted by
the claim that a "good act" obliges God to confer eternal life on its subject and that such obligatory acceptance is not solely a matter of God's
free grace (III.455–56). That is, Pelagianism puts God under necessity to
accept someone, whereas Ockham's pervasive dialectic of *potentia absoluta*
and *potentia ordinata* maintains God's freedom and so, according to Ockham, keeps the theologian far removed from Pelagianism. Rega Wood's
recent defense of Ockham's self-defense concedes that Ockham maintains that grace is not required for virtue, that pagans can love God above
all else, that sinners can do good works disposing them to grace, and that
foreseen merits precede predestination.[4] But she asserts that only an
"ultra-Augustinian" would accuse Ockham of "semi-Pelagianism" because Ockham is actually "like Augustine" in maintaining "the thesis that
God completely controls the economy of salvation."[5] This is a fascinating judgment made in very revealing language. For Wood has allowed
Ockham's version of divine power and divine freedom in "the economy
of salvation" to determine her own view of Christian tradition and Augustinian orthodoxy. As we will see, the key issue is in the term *controls*.
Pelagians allegedly deprive God of "control," whereas the orthodox, "like

Augustine," do not. The risk of such language is that the theology of the reconciliation between God and humanity in Christ gets swallowed up in a language of power and control, albeit in Ockham's case a "control" deferred until the display of the final divine decision to accept or not to accept. Furthermore, such language and the debate to which it belongs can occlude many of the issues that concern this book and its readings of Augustine, Ockham, Bradwardine, and Langland. So, in the present case, both Ockham and the modern commentator sideline issues concerning the consequences of habitual sin for the powers of the sinner's intellect and will, the consequences for her love of God and love of neighbor. Issues concerning the perfectionist expectations of Pelagianism also disappear. Instead of addressing such questions, we are drawn into a discourse in which the decisive matter is acknowledging divine freedom and power.

But rather than addressing what is sidelined, I will briefly consider how Ockham does deal with sins, repentance, and forgiveness. He maintains that God could decree (in his absolute power) that anyone who, after mortal sin, grieved for his sin out his natural powers ("ex puris naturalibus"), without any divine grace, should have his sins forgiven and be received into eternal life after death, as long as he did not sin mortally in the intervening time (III.460). This argument illustrates a characteristic and frivolous failure to reflect on the consequences of sin for the will and its habits, a failure that involves a refusal to learn from the minute display of the formation and bonds of habit in Augustine's *Confessions,* from his *City of God,* and from medieval explorations of sin and confession around the sacrament of penance. Just how does one who has become a mortal sinner never sin again mortally *ex puris naturalibus*? In Langland's terms, how does Semyuief become alive, how do the utterly slothful sinners and the lost Wille "do well," encounter Christ, and find the elusive way (chapter 4)? Ockham's talk of the divine forgiveness of mortal sins leaves divine forgiveness and the human transformations that such divine agency elicits utterly *extrinsic* to the sinning agent. There is no attempt to display how divine forgiveness engages and transforms the sinner's will, intelligence, and choice. But given the focus on divine acceptance, after this life, such reticence is not at all surprising.

Ockham moves on to consider another question, closely related: "Utrum actus voluntatis posset esse meritorius sine caritate formaliter animam informante" [Whether an act of the will can be meritorious without charity formally informing the soul] (III.467–75). Not at all unusually, Ockham disputes with St. Thomas, here choosing *Quaestio disputata de caritate.*[6] St. Thomas had argued that "merit" depends on charity informing the subject since this theological virtue (a divine gift) exceeds the power of our nature. Ockham rejects Thomas's traditional arguments.[7] He does so because, he asserts, God can accept, from his grace, a good movement of the will elicited from purely natural powers. Such an act will be meritorious (that is, salvific) through God's graciousness ("quia bonum motum voluntatis ex puris naturalibus elicitum potest Deus acceptare de gratia sua, et per consequens talis actus ex gratuita Dei acceptatione erit meritorius"). Thus no gift is needed from the Holy Spirit for the development of transformed habits (III.469). Indeed, Ockham claims that a virtuous habit would destroy our freedom (III.470). In 1326, the Avignon masters who examined Ockham's teaching saw this response to Thomas as smacking of Pelagian heresy. Against Ockham's claims that charity is not required, they quoted St. Paul on charity and salvation (1 Cor. 13.1–3). They also criticized his use of *de potentia absoluta* as a habitual device to protect him from the charge of heresy, observing that his argument actually goes ahead without the condition *de potentia absoluta.* The masters argued that Ockham's denial that charity was in itself praiseworthy ("de se laudabilis") was against Scripture, and they again invoked 1 Corinthians 13. This denial, they asserted, was heretical.[8] As Rega Wood observes in her edition and translation of Ockham's *On the Virtues,* Ockham "minimizes the role of the kind of habit described by Aquinas and maximizes the direct role of divine acceptance."[9] In this systematic minimizing of habits, Ockham refuses to pay attention to the processes, the forms in which divine grace and human agency work to transform the human subject toward a life lived in reconciliation, obedience, and love to God. In doing so, he cultivates a universe of discourse that is different not only from St. Thomas but also from Augustine and Langland.

Continuing his objections to Aquinas, Ockham asserts that a meritorious act and a charitable act do not surpass the power of unaided human nature. Every act of charity in the common course of life is possible by one's unaided natural powers ("ex puris naturalibus"). It certainly does not exceed our natural powers (III.472). For Ockham, the point is that what lies beyond our powers is not charity but simply what

God will freely accept as meritorious. Merit, he emphasizes, is entirely a matter of divine acceptation: "in libera Dei acceptatione" (III.472). To make sure we get the point, he insists that God could reject the act of charity: "The very same act which was just now elicited from one having charity [i.e., the habit of charity] and is meritorious, God can, through his absolute power [de potentia absoluta] not accept and then it will not be meritorious. And yet it remains the very same act and the very same charity" [Unde idem actus qui modo elicitur ab habente caritatem et est meritorius, posset Deus de potentia Dei absoluta non acceptare eum, et tunc non esset meritorius, et tamen esset idem actus et caritas eadem] (III.472–73). Once more he says that when an act emerges from the habit of charity (a divine gift, we recall) it is not an act from our will and therefore not a voluntary act ("Ita si Spiritus Sanctus causaret actum caritatis et non voluntas, non esset actus voluntarius, hoc est, illa voluntas non libere vellet," III.473). Ockham seems to envisage divine gift and human agency in some kind of either/or terms, a model of rivalry, as though God and humanity were two people competing for power.

Ockham's theology of grace, his theology of the reconciliation between God and humankind in Christ and the conversion of humans to God, is remarkably different from both Augustine's and Langland's. Indeed, I am doubtful that he develops anything that is congruent with a language of conversion, although he does sometimes use such language. It is therefore worth turning to a text in which we can watch Ockham using such language. In *De Connexione Virtutum* (On the Connection of the Virtues) he addresses "aversion from God and conversion to God."[10] Ockham considers a question concerning conversion to God by an act of charity and aversion from God by an act of loving what God does not want us to love, as in the case of fornication. His response to the question is very striking. Conversion to God and aversion from God are not formally or naturally irreconcilable. On the contrary, the theologian asserts, "they are compatible in the same subject as far as the nature of the acts is concerned. They are incompatible only by virtue of an extrinsic cause—namely God, who ordains that the created will should in no way love a certain creature [sed solum repugnant per causam extrinsecam, puta per Deum ordinantem talem creaturam nullo modo a voluntate creata diligi]" (162–63). So the difference between conversion to God and aversion from God is "solely on account of the ordination of such

an extrinsic cause" [et ideo propter ordinationem talis causae extrin-
secae videtur solum repugnantia] (164–65). And here Ockham comes up
with his model for thinking about God's relations with his human creatures living in the new covenant: "This is evident, since if the statutory
law [lex statuta] were revoked, these acts of love [i.e., conversion to God
and rejection of God] would thenceforth be compatible in the same subject. Moreover, if the law were to command that the creature be loved,
then not only could the acts coexist, but the will would then love the
creature meritoriously" (164–65). Ockham can imagine God only as an
"extrinsic cause" whose statutes are both thoroughly orderly and thoroughly arbitrary. This is a somewhat strange way of thinking about the
gospel and its form as the law of Christ.[11] But this is characteristic of
Ockham's theological writing and symptomatic of its approach to sin,
grace, and salvation. Divine commands, like divine grace, remain utterly
extrinsic to their subjects. Statutes, Ockham's model, are not the ran-
dom acts of a crazed voluntarist, since they have intelligibility and order.
But they are simultaneously rational *and* quite arbitrary in relation to the
good intrinsic to their subjects. Hence Ockham's choice of analogy and
the emphasis that the statute or divine command is an utterly "extrinsic cause" unrelated to any intrinsic flourishing or any destructiveness of
the acts the decree addresses. In her commentary on this passage, Rega
Wood writes:

> What is interesting here is Ockham's emphasis on the statutory
> nature of divine precept—its potentially arbitrary nature. . . . What
> is important is Ockham's claim that God could have ordained a sys-
> tem in which acts that are correctly considered sinful in the estab-
> lished order of salvation would lead to beatific vision [Ockham's
> example is "fornication"]. . . . Beatific vision and damnation do not
> depend on the intrinsic nature of things but solely on the will of God.
> Hence the rules of salvation are an external order not unlike the legal
> systems of human rulers, who regulate rewards and punishments by
> statute.[12]

This is an accurate gloss on the passage I quoted. But Wood does not notice any of the theological problems it generates, problems I have begun
to outline. One of the most important issues that emerges in passages

such as this is how detached the theologian's thinking is from Christology, how extrinsic to it is the form of reconciliation given in the incarnation, crucifixion, resurrection, and ascension of Christ.[13] Here a brief comparison with St. Thomas Aquinas can clarify the theological problems with the approach we have found in Ockham. It can also remind us that his successors would have to evaluate the differences between Ockham's approach and the tradition represented by Aquinas, choosing to reject or develop one or the other.

Reflecting on the relations between the Old and the New Law, St. Thomas considers their common end: to bring humans obediently to God.[14] He also considers a difference relevant to the present division. The Old Law is as a schoolmaster ("paedagogus puerorum," Gal. 3.24), whereas the New Law is a law of perfection because it is the law of charity (Col. 3.14). The mode of education appropriate to the subjects of the former entails persuasion to virtuous acts by an extrinsic cause ("ex aliqua causa extrinseca"). Aquinas illustrates such extrinsicism by someone who undertakes actions motivated by the fear of punishment or the promise of payment (such as honors or riches). The latter, the law of perfection, is very different. Here the subjects are drawn to virtuous action by love of virtue. They are not motivated by fear of punishment or desire for extrinsic reward ("non propter aliquam poenam aut remunerationem extrinsecam"). So "the New Law, consisting primarily in spiritual grace itself implanted in men's hearts, is called the *law of love* [lex amoris]." Divine agency draws people to charity "not as to what is external to them but as to what is their very own" [non quasi in extranea, sed quasi in propria] (*ST* I-II.107.1, resp. and ad 2). As St. Thomas explains later, grace implants in the human soul a divine gift that draws humans beyond their natural limitations to participate in divine life (I-II.110.1). And as Fergus Kerr observes, the fact that God is beyond the capacity of creatures does not mean that God is utterly extraneous. He quotes from the *Summa contra Gentiles*: "The divine substance is not beyond the capacity of the created intellect in such a way that it is altogether foreign to it, as sound is from the object of vision, or an immaterial substance is from sense power."[15] The divine agency of grace is envisaged as the light of the soul and in this way is imagined as bestowing illumination in the soul (*ST* I-II.110.1, sed contra). It gives humans an intrinsic inclination to fulfill their supernatural end. This rejection of an extrinsicist account of saving grace also involves a rejection of simply forensic accounts of sin and salvation.[16] Ockham's decision to offer an extremely thin account of divine acceptation, modeled on statutory law, the cornerstone of his theology of grace, seems closely bound up with his extrinsicist theory of grace. While he may have been encouraged on this path by Duns Scotus, it constituted a major break with Augustinian and Thomist theology and psychology. It was a crucial break that was not followed by all late medieval theological writers.[17]

II

I now want to consider Ockham's treatment of some related issues in his discussion of predestination during his commentary on the first book of the *Sentences* (d. 41, IV.595–610).[18] In her invaluable commentary on Ockham's *De Connexione Virtutum*, Rega Wood states that the treatment of predestination in his work on the *Sentences* offers "the strongest evidence that his detractors can present" to show his "alleged Pelagianism." Here she is referring to his view not only that good acts are "possible in the state of mortal sin" but that "in some sense they can be a reason why God confers grace." Wood determines that even here "it is incorrect to call Ockham a Pelagian or a semi-Pelagian," because he "accepts predestination" and sees such "good works" as producing "a disposition for grace in the sinners" without rendering sinners "acceptable to God."[19] Fascinating as are the conflicting interpretations of Ockham's positions, I have no ambitions to adjudicate these, since I think that these classifications can impede the discussion of the issues that most concern me, particularly the representation of sin and redemption. Ockham organizes his study in the first book of his commentary on the *Sentences* by putting the following question: "Utrum in praedestinato sit aliqua causa suae praedestinationis et in reprobato aliqua causa suae reprobationis" (IV.597).[20] In this sequence, Ockham's arguments include the assertion that the saints and doctors teach us that although works done in mortal sin do not bring eternal life they are rewarded temporally and should be performed by the sinner so that God gives the grace that deserves eternal life (i.e., so that God accepts the sinner doing well) (IV.600).[21] Therefore, he argues, such good works done in mortal sin, though not meriting divine acceptance,

dispose the human agent to grace and consequently to the effect of predestination (IV.600). Despite undoubtedly tricky aspects of Ockham's
claims here (not least being the semantics of *cause*), it seems that, in Ockham's view, the mortally sinful person does initiate good works that do
"prepare us for grace."[22] Once more, the arguments about classification
among the terms *Pelagian, semi-Pelagian,* and *neo-Pelagian* can distract readers from attending to Ockham's assumptions about the powers of the
fallen soul and the effects of sinful acts on the agent. We are, yet again,
witnessing a trivialization of sin; yet again we encounter a discourse on
sin without any recognition of the ways in which sinful acts become compulsive chains, habits shaping the will, guiding our uses of intellect and
conscience, separating us from God and neighbor. To these processes
both Augustine and Langland pay profound attention, attention that is intrinsic to repentance and confession. By contrast, Ockham's text displays
an extraordinary blandness about sin.[23]

Here it will be helpful to consider the discussion by Aquinas that
Ockham attacks (*ST* I.23.5).[24] St. Thomas observes that nobody would
be crazy enough to say that human merits are the cause of divine predestination. The question is whether divinely foreseen human merit has a
causal role in predestination. Exploring this, he notes that Pelagians maintain that the beginning of Dowell ("initium benefaciendi") is from us ("ex
nobis") while the consummation is by God. In this way, predestination is
the consequence of our own agency, our own preparation. Against this,
however, he quotes Paul: "We are not sufficient to think anything of ourselves, as of ourselves [quasi ex nobis]" (2 Cor. 3.5). And no beginning
preceding thought can be found. As he works his way through the standard conflicts (I.23.5, resp.), Aquinas observes that we simply cannot distinguish what is "ex libero arbitrio" and what is "ex predestinatione" any
more than we can distinguish exactly what is caused by a secondary cause
and what is caused by a primary cause. God's providence, as he has already shown (I.22.3), works through secondary causes. So what is enacted
"ex libero arbitrio" is enacted "ex predestinatione." Agency is thoroughly
complex, doubled. God, we can say, preordains ("praeordinavit") himself to give glory to someone on account of her merits and also preordains himself to give grace to that person so that she can merit glory.
But we must acknowledge that in totality the effects of predestination
have a cause other than ourselves. Indeed, we must confess that whatever

prepares us for our salvation is entirely understood as the effect of predestination; and this includes the very preparation for grace ("ipsa praepa-
ratio ad gratiam"). Here Aquinas quotes Lamentations 5.21: "Convert us
[converte nos] to you, O God, that we may be converted [convertemur]."
Aquinas goes on to emphasize that predestination is entirely about God's
goodness (I.23.5, ad 2). In fact, both in I.23 and in III.24, following Augustine closely, he presents predestination as the eternal preordination of
the divine goodness enacted in time by the grace of God (III.24.1, resp.;
I.23.1–2). Aquinas emphasizes that eternal life with God exceeds our created nature and power: it is "supra naturam cujuslibet creaturae" (I.23.1,
resp.). And the consequences of sin massively exacerbate this gulf, de-
priving our nature of the grace in which it was created before the Fall
(I.23.7, ad 3). Brian Davies encapsulates Thomas's view: "Beatitude, or
life with God, is a gift. . . . It has to be brought about by God and may,
therefore be spoken of as a matter of predestination."[25] St. Thomas approaches predestination as the eternal preparation of divine grace, the
eternal decision not only to bring humanity into the divine life beyond
the powers of created nature but also to overcome the consequences of
sin through the grace embodied and poured forth in Jesus Christ (III.7.9,
resp.; III.24.1).[26] So the theology of grace at some point will enter into
conversation with the language of predestination. This Langland also acknowledged, as we shall see later (chapter 4). But for the moment, I hope
that this brief discussion of St. Thomas's treatment of predestination, attacked by Ockham, can illuminate the choices Ockham made in his theological modes and their outcomes. The latter includes a trivialization of
sin and an approach that makes grace extrinsic to the Christian in this
life. It also involves a failure to follow St. Thomas in thinking about predestination in terms of divine gift and, most crucially of all, Christology.
The sidelining of Christology is extremely important and makes especially baffling Wood's statement that Ockham's treatment of predestination shows "essential similarity" to Aquinas's.[27]

III

One of the best-known characteristics of the "modern" theology with
which so many literary scholars wish to align *Piers Plowman* (see chapter 4)

is the emphasis that God will freely but unfailingly give grace and final salvation to all who do that which is in them ("facientibus quod in se est, Deus non denegat gratiam"). The presence of this view in late medieval theology has been amply documented, and here I will consider it briefly.[28] I do so especially to help our evaluations of claims about the relations between Langland and the *moderni*. W. J. Courtenay, in *Schools and Scholars in Fourteenth-Century England,* describes how Ockham maintained Scotus's belief "that God had of his own free will committed himself to reward with the gift of grace those who, on the basis of what remained of their natural powers after the Fall (*ex puris naturalibus*), did their best to fulfill the commands of God (*facientibus quod in se est Deus non denegat gratiam*)."[29] With all due caution Courtenay finds that this theology suggests "man can initiate the return to God, and that God will reward with grace and final acceptation those who do their best (*facientibus quod in se est, Deus non denegat gratiam*)."[30] This confirmed Heiko Oberman's important study on Holcot and Luther entitled *"Facientibus quod in se est Deus non denegat gratiam."*[31] Concentrating on Holcot's widely read lectures on the Book of Wisdom, Oberman displayed this concept at work and its relation to Ockham: "God is committed to give his grace to all who do what is in them."[32] He provides one characteristic example: a wicked old man becomes penitent at the point of death and intends to make satisfaction for his sins if he can ("si posset"). This suffices to elicit divine mercy because if a person wills to do that which is in him toward penitence God accepts this in his mercy.[33] Those theologians who propagated such teaching were sure that they eschewed Pelagianism because they taught within a model that emphasized that God had freely established the *pactum* and freely accepted those who did what was in them toward fulfilling it. But Oberman concludes this essay by showing how that late medieval Catholic theologian Martin Luther raised substantial questions about this defense by 1517. In his *Disputatio contra Scholasticam* of that year, he explicitly rejected "the doctrine of the *facere quod in se est.*" He argued that this teaching mistakenly assumed that we have that within us which can remove obstacles to grace. It completely occluded the consequences of sin on our will and intellect, consequences of rebelliousness and ignorance toward God.[34] And Luther had late medieval forerunners in the attack on the *facere quod in se est* such as Bradwardine and Gregory of Rimini.[35] However, here I will conclude my brief recollection of this strand of late medieval theology by returning to St. Thomas's anticipatory objections to it. They are ones that are thoroughly Augustinian. They also help us focus on the issues raised by the apparently benevolent "facere quod in se est" with the kind of clarity we need in exploring the relations between Langland and "modern" theology (chapter 4).

In his treatise on grace in the *Summa Theologiae,* St. Thomas considers the necessity for grace. He asks whether someone can will and do good without grace.[36] The objector argues that we can will and do good ("velle et facere bonum") without grace (I-II.109.2, obj. 1–3). Against that, Aquinas sets quotations from Paul and from one of Augustine's anti-Pelagian works: "Paul says, *it is not of him who wills,* namely to will, *nor of him who runs,* namely to run, *but of God who shows mercy* [Rom. 9.16]. And Augustine says, *without grace, men do no good whatsoever, either by thinking, or by willing and loving, or by acting* [*De Correptione et Gratia,* 2]." In his response, St. Thomas argues that in the state of fallen nature ("in statu naturae corruptae") humans cannot even do what is proportionate to their given nature, let alone the good exceeding that and relevant to eternal life. Of course, the sinner can perform such good acts as building houses or planting vines, but he cannot "perform the whole good which is connatural to him." Sinful humanity is like a sick man who cannot move properly without healing medicine. Later he asks whether someone can fulfill the precepts of the law by natural powers unaided by grace (I-II.109.4). Against the claims that one can, Aquinas comments: "Augustine says that it belongs to the heresy of the Pelagians *to believe that man can perform all the divine commandments without grace*" (I-II.109.4, sed contra). In his reply, Thomas insists that fallen humanity certainly cannot fulfill the divine commands "without healing grace." Article 6 of question 109 rejects the view that we can prepare ourselves for grace without the assistance of grace. In doing so, Aquinas draws on a text used frequently by Augustine in his anti-Pelagian teaching, Christ's words in John 6.44: "*No one can come to me unless the Father who sent me draws [traxerit] him*" (sed contra). God so draws us "by the gratuitous assistance of God moving him within" [per auxilium gratuitum Dei interius moventis] (resp.).

This model of divine help working powerfully, noncoercively, and "within" the human agent is congruent with the model of conversion discussed in chapter 1. It is a model that is characteristically set aside in the Ockhamist focus on divine acceptation with its extrinsicizing of grace and its emphasis on God's help of those who help themselves. Aquinas defends the role of *liberum arbitrium* in human decision and action, including the "conversio" to God, but insists that *liberum arbitrium* can only be turned to God ("ad Deum converti") when God turns it to himself (*ST* I-II.109.6, ad 1). Recalling Christ's statement "Without me you can do nothing" (John 15.5), Thomas argues that "when man is said to do what is within him, this is said to be in his power in so far as he is moved by God" [cum dicitur *homo facere quod in se est,* dicitur hoc esse in potestate hominis, secundum quod est motus a deo] (ad 2).

So here is the explicit attack on the *facere quod in se est,* an attack implicit in the whole treatment of grace, salvation, and sin in the *Summa Theologiae.* It is pursued in article 7 of question 109: Can someone rise up again from sin without the help of grace? Against the claims that one can (obj. 1–3), Aquinas again quotes Paul in the sed contra: "*If a law had been given which could justify, then Christ died in vain*" (Gal. 2.21). In his response, Aquinas argues that "man can in no way rise up again from sin by himself without the assistance of grace." Such rising up entails restoration of what has been lost by sin, a healing of the consequences of sin. Sin includes "a stain, a spoiling of his natural goodness, and a debt of punishment" (as he has shown in I-II.85.1, 86.1, and 87.1). Sin is a terrible deformity that disorders our whole being and makes our will disobedient to God. This subjects us to that final separation from God, damnation. Here is a grasp of the consequences of sin that offers a sharp contrast to Ockhamite theology. In Thomas's account, the consequences of sin shape our forms of life, our very desires, turning them against the love of God and the law of Christ. He maintains that only God can restore what has been lost and form again what has been habitually deformed, habitually turned away from the fulfillment of our being in the divine life. There can be no do-it-yourself remedy, a self-disposition or self-preparation that is accepted as doing the best we can (I-II.109.7, ad 2 and ad 3). In article 8 of question 109 he continues this strand of argument: fallen, sinful humankind "needs habitual grace to heal nature" (resp.). As usual, grace is not split off from divine acceptance but heals and transforms during this life.

This is emphasized in question 113 of *ST* I-II, the question on justification ("De justificatione"). Justification involves the right ordering of our own powers, our own dispositions, a change from a state of injustice (to God, to others, to ourselves) *through the forgiveness of sins* (113.1). So much more is involved here than in the *facere quod in se est* model of divine acceptation, a model nicely illustrated in Holcot's example of the wicked old man noted above. Aquinas's approach develops a theology of the Triune God's reconciliation with sinners; this involves, through Christ's work, the transforming love of divine forgiveness in the present, with the peace this offers (113.2, resp., ad 1 and ad 2). But in Ockhamist or "modern" theology the fallen, sinful person is perfectly capable of loving God above all else and for Godself without the transforming grace and love of God, capable, in fact, *ex puris naturalibus*.[37] If Langland is to be aligned with "modern" theology this would certainly be one of the markers of his alleged affinity and his departure from Augustine and St. Thomas.

IV

I will now consider another characteristic of "modern" theology, namely its wide deployment of the distinction between God's ordained or ordered power and God's absolute power, the distinction between what God does *de potentia ordinata* and *de potentia absoluta*. It was known and used at least from the twelfth century, but it gained new inflections and a new centrality in Ockhamist theology. Part of the novelty seems to have been the introduction of analogies from the treatment of papal sovereignty in canon law, but the history of the distinction is very complex and still unfolding. The consequences of the distinction in late medieval theology are also still contested. The mid-twentieth-century view that the distinction was used to generate a version of God incompatible with tradition, a capricious figure sponsoring skepticism, has been largely abandoned by historians of late medieval theology. W. J. Courtenay's careful arguments to show that most theologians were sure that God had bound himself to his revelations and promises have transformed research in this field. It would be possible, from Courtenay's scholarship, to think that the use of the distinction in Ockhamist theology largely left traditional doctrines concerning God and revelation unchallenged. But not all recent scholars have been persuaded that the treatment of divine freedom makes as little theological difference as one might gather from Courtenay or from Oberman's later work, although this does not necessarily entail returning to the older view expressed so influentially (among literary critics) in the early work of Gordon Leff.[38] Despite the complexity of the materials and debates in this area, I am persuaded that the distinction at issue was intrinsic to a "modern" version of divine freedom and played a shaping force in Ockham's way of doing theology, envisaging divine power, and portraying the relations between God and humanity. It is certainly a characteristic mark of Ockhamist theology, and one would expect to find determinate signs of it in *Piers Plowman* if that poem is to be licitly aligned with such theology. This is one of the main reasons for offering an outline of the topic here.

Perhaps the most obvious place from which to begin such an outline is Ockham's *Quodlibetal Questions*. Here he offers an apparently lucid and full account of the distinction in question, entailing a somewhat lengthy quotation:

> I claim that God is able to do certain things by his ordained power and certain things by his absolute power. This distinction should not be understood to mean that in God there are really two powers, one of which is ordained and the other of which is absolute. For with respect to things outside himself there is in God a single power, which in every way is God himself. Nor should the distinction be understood to mean that God is able to do certain things absolutely and not ordinately. For God cannot do anything inordinately.
>
> Instead, the distinction should be understood to mean that "power to do something" is sometimes taken as "power to do something in accordance with the laws that have been ordained and instituted by God," and God is said to be able to do these things by his ordained power. In an alternative sense, "power" is taken as "power to do anything such that its being done does not involve a contradiction," regardless of whether or not God has ordained that he will do it. For there are many things God is able to do that he does not will to do. . . . And these things God is said to be able to do by his absolute power. In the same way, there are some things that the Pope is unable to do in accordance with the laws established by him, and yet he is able to do these things absolutely. (VI.1.1)[39]

Ockham makes this distinction in answering the question "Can a human being be saved without created charity [i.e., the gift of divine grace]?" The Franciscan theologian is perfectly aware of the traditional answer given this question in the Catholic Church. In his own words: "No human being will ever be saved or be able to be saved without created grace, and no human being will ever elicit or be able to elicit a meritorious act without such grace." As usual, at least at this stage of his life, Ockham gives unqualified obedience to the Church's teachings that are also Scripture's: "I hold this because of Sacred Scripture and the teaching of the Saints" (VI.1.1). But, also as usual, he seems more interested in exploring what God's freedom allegedly could have performed than in exploring what God has actually revealed and done in Christ with humanity. The purpose in this is to defend God's omnipotent freedom, composing a version of freedom at the heart of "modern" theology in the fourteenth century. So even as he declares his obedience to Scripture and the tradition of the Church, he says, "I claim . . . that a human being is able by the absolute power of God to be saved without created charity" and asserts that "by God's absolute power a will placed in a purely natural state is able to elicit a meritorious act." This claim, he says, is not Pelagian because it makes salvation entirely dependent on "God's absolute power" (VI.1.2). He had made similar moves in *Quodlibetal Questions* III.10.2. There he acknowledges that the writings of the saints teach us that original sin is removed "only through created grace." Ockham assents to this. But he continues: "Yet through God's absolute power, original sin could be removed in some other way"—such as, he suggests, God simply not having obligated us to have justice and simply not imputing lack of justice to the man lacking justice (III.10.2). In *Quodlibetal Questions* VI.4, Ockham uses the distinction between God's absolute and ordained power to argue that "by his absolute power God can, if it so pleases him, remit all guilt, both original and actual, without any infusion of created grace. . . . By his absolute power God could, if it so pleased him, accept a sinner for eternal life without grace" (VI.4.1). Once again we encounter a version of divine freedom being composed in abstraction from the God revealed in Jesus Christ.[40] This is the aspect of the dialectic and its version of divine freedom that most interests me. It could never be described as Christocentric, and that should be recalled when we think of Langland's relations with "modern" theologians.

Before elaborating these comments on "modern" versions of divine freedom and the marginalization of Christology, I will exemplify this freedom a little further. In his commentary on the fourth book of the *Sentences,* Ockham discusses a cluster of questions around the sacrament of baptism. The fifth question asks whether all punishment is remitted in baptism.[41] This leads to a consideration of sin as nothing other than an act through which one is owed punishment (VII.44). Later Ockham elaborates this view in his treatment of the sacrament of penance (VII.195–98). He denies that sin causes substantial change in the sinner: it neither corrupts nor removes anything in the soul (VII.197–98). Whatever counts as sin depends entirely on God's free determinations. And just as God's freedom has no obligations, so, it seems, our freedom cannot be bound by our acts. The arguments deployed here are related to Ockham's model of saving grace as a free act of divine acceptation that remains entirely extrinsic to the graced human subject. Marilyn Adams rightly observes that Ockham's denial that mortal sin is anything real, or positive, rests "on the twin theological assumptions of divine omnipotence and divine freedom!" (*William Ockham,* 2:1276). These "twin theological assumptions" shape other aspects of Ockham's commentary on baptism.

Ruminating on why unbaptized infants are owed eternal punishment when such infants have never acted sinfully, Ockham does not pause to subject such doctrine to the pressure of God's reconciliation to the world in Christ. Instead he merely affirms that punishment is due because God so ordained. Ockham's affirmation is strikingly disengaged from Scripture and from the range of teachings on this topic within the Church. Because God creates creatures out of his untrammeled will, he can do whatever he pleases with them ("quia sicut Deus creat creaturam quamlibet ex mera voluntate sua potest facere de creatura sua quidquid sibi placet," VII.55). This conception of freedom is characteristically freewheeling, unformed by the Christological and Trinitarian theology of revelation. On similar grounds he argues that if someone always loves God and does all the works acceptable to God, God can annihilate such a loving, obedient person without any injury. Or, he surmises, God can with equal justice give that person eternal punishment. Such is Ockham's model of divine freedom, of God being free from all obligation. Of course, if God were indeed to act in the way Ockham hypothesizes, a way so unlike the chosen dispensation, then it would still be classified as acting "ordinately" because, as we observed (*Quodlibetal Questions*, VI.1.1), whatever God does is, by definition, done ordinately and hence done justly (VII.55). Here Ockham actually brings Jesus Christ into his discussion. Does this initiate a Christological revision of his theology of freedom? Not at all. Christ is invoked because Ockham assumes Christ illustrates the validity of Ockham's thesis concerning the damnation of infants and divine freedom. How can this be? Because the sinless Christ was grievously punished even to death ("Patet enim quod Christus nunquam peccavit, et tamen fuit punitus gravissime usque ad mortem," VII.55).[42] Once again, what seems remarkable in such theology is the isolation of its speculation from any Christological discipline. Even when Jesus Christ is mentioned he remains extrinsic to the argument and to the theological paradigm in which Ockham constitutes divine freedom. We thus encounter a theologian habituated to exploring divine sovereignty quite independently of the redemption of humanity in a distinctively Christian tradition. It is not entirely surprising that in this paradigm Ockham should have entertained the possibility that God's freedom means that we must affirm that God can command us to hate God ("Deus potest praecipere quod voluntas creata odiat eum," VII.352 and IV, q. 16). Rega Wood has recently stressed that Ockham later rejected this bizarre claim. While this is clearly important, it is more important that such rejection did not come from a rejection of the model that generated the rejected proposition. Ockham rejects his statement because he thinks he has identified a lack of good logic in its composition. He does not call into question anything about the paradigm and the version of God to which both original assertion and later rejection belong.[43]

I will conclude this excursus into "modern" theology's approach to divine power and freedom with some reflections that I hope may also contribute to discussions about Langland's relations to fourteenth-century theology. Once again I emphasize that such discussions should foreground the ways in which this distinctly "modern" construal of divine freedom is abstracted from the Word made flesh and from the Word revealed in Scripture. It proceeds as though these events were not actually revelations of God but rather costumes chosen by divine power in a freedom that could as well, and as ordinately, have chosen utterly contradictory costumes. It is helpful to recollect one of Ockham's own definitions of freedom: "It should be noted that what I am calling freedom is the power by which I can indifferently and contingently posit diverse things, in such a way that I am able both to cause and able not to cause the same effect when there is no difference anywhere else outside that power" [Quod voco libertatem potestatem qua possum indifferenter et contingenter diversa ponere, ita quod possum eumdem effectum causare et non causare, nulla diversitate existente alibi extra illam potentiam] (*Quodlibetal Questions,* I.16.1, IX.87). This is a lucid statement of Ockham's understanding of freedom as it pertains to his thinking about both divine and human agency. It illustrates very clearly what Adams and others have observed: for Ockham freedom is understood simply as *liberty of indifference.* Adams, in an essay on Ockham's "moral theory," addresses this issue in relation to Ockham's commentary on the second book of the *Sentences.*[44] There Ockham acknowledges that "given existing divine precepts" the human is obliged to love God (V.352). Nevertheless, as Adams notes, "In His liberty of indifference, God could command the acts now labeled 'hatred,' 'theft,' 'adultery,' etc.; He could dictate that creatures hate Him; and He could find such hatred so pleasing as to reward it with eternal life, and be so revolted by whole-hearted love of Himself as to meet it with eternal punishment. In doing so, He would revoke present legislation, because—according to Ockham—divine commands cannot lead in contradictory directions."[45] God could thus readily change the constitution, like the pope, who is able to do things "absolutely" that he is "unable to do in accordance with the laws established by him" (*Quodlibetal Questions,* VI.1.1). Having acted thus, "absolutely," and so exemplified divine freedom, God could produce a new constitution that would obligate the created will to acts "now labeled 'hatred,' 'theft,' 'adultery,' etc." Such acts, under the new constitution, would "be done meritoriously by a pilgrim" [meritorie possunt fieri a viatore].[46] Adams puts the major issue very well: "Behind this reasoning lies Ockham's doctrine that both divine and created wills have the liberty of indifference, by which each can will, not merely good under the aspect of good, but also evil under the aspect of evil."[47] This version of freedom abstracts freedom from the intrinsic bonds connecting reason, will, and *liberum arbitrium* with their divinely given teleology (the true, the good, beatitude participating in the divine life), intrinsic bonds characteristic of Augustinian and Thomistic Christianity.[48] With this version of freedom Christian ethics was encouraged to abstract itself from the theology of the virtues and habits envisaged as gifts poured into human hearts by the Holy Spirit (Rom. 5.5), since these now seemed a threat to human freedom and so could not make humans worthy to participate in eternal life.[49] But most decisively of all, such theology sidelines Christology. I have kept returning to this not only because it is an important and often overlooked aspect of Ockhamist theologizing but also because it should be one of the most crucial areas of comparison between fourteenth-century "modern" theology and the profoundly Christocentric theology of Langland's *Piers Plowman*.

I will now pull together these strands in my discussion by recalling Hans Urs von Balthasar's ascription to Karl Barth of "a noticeably *Augustinian concept of freedom*."[50] In this conception, "freedom is primarily a life lived in the intimacy of God's freedom. This freedom, in other words, cannot be defined negatively, as merely a neutral stance toward God, as if freedom were merely presented with [a] 'menu' of options from which the *liberum arbitrium* would make its selection." In fact, "God has prepared the human race for communion with him," and we can only "know what *true* freedom really is when it encounters the event of revelation" in Christ.[51] This, I will show in chapter 4, is thoroughly congruent with Langland's vision, but I wish to stay with von Balthasar's statement and its linking of Augustine and Barth. For the latter offers some illuminating remarks on the version of freedom that is fascinated by generating a discourse on what God might do *de potentia absoluta* (acknowledging that thereby, as I have said, whatever was done would be done ordinately, opening out, doubtless, more talk about the *de potentia absoluta* in this new situation). In *The Doctrine of God,* Barth has a section entitled "The Being of God as the One Who Loves Freedom."[52] Here he writes, again in a thoroughly Augustinian mode, that "God is sufficiently free to indwell the creature in the most varied ways according to its varying characteristics" (314). This freedom "to be wholly inward to the creature and at the same time as Himself wholly outward: *totus intra et totus extra*" is "how He meets us in Jesus Christ" (315). This model of agency is congenial to the ones displayed by Augustine and discussed in chapter 1. In it there is "no caprice about the freedom of God" (318). For it is a freedom revealed in Jesus Christ, for Christian tradition the only way

God is known and so the only determinant of how theologians envisage divine power and freedom (see 318–20). As Barth observes, "Christology, therefore, must always constitute the basis and criterion for the apprehension and interpretation of the freedom of God in His immanence" (320). In the same volume, Barth writes a treatise on "the constancy and omnipotence of God" (490–607). During this he explicitly addresses the distinction between divine power considered *de potentia absoluta* and considered *de potentia ordinata*. He sets out from St. Thomas's use of this distinction in his *Summa Theologiae* (I.25.5, ad 1). Barth shows how the use of the distinction is carefully limited to recollecting the divine sovereignty without which "the grace of creation, reconciliation and redemption would not then be grace"—that is, gift (539). But he then distinguishes later developments of this distinction from St. Thomas's, as in fact Marilyn Adams does in her work on Ockham.[53] Barth describes the development in question as one in which the Thomistic *potentia absoluta* becomes *potentia extraordinaria*. He finds that this affected discourses about "the essence of God," leaving marks on Luther's theology of the *Deus absconditus,* that being who is "wholly Other" to his revelation (541). Barth finds such development theologically "intolerable": "It is both true and important to maintain with Thomas that this capacity [i.e., divine power] is most certainly to be understood as free, but it is completely invalid to ascribe to Him a capacity different from that which He has in fact revealed in His work, and one which contradicts it" (541).

Of course Ockham denies that his use of the terms in question ascribes to God two powers: "With respect to things outside himself there is in God a single power, which in every way is God himself" (*Quodlibetal Questions,* VI.1; affirmed in *Opus Nonaginta Dierum,* ch. 95). But his remorseless deployment of the "absolute" power of God, freed from the "ordained" power, together with his examples of such "absolute" power, composes a discourse that proceeds as if there were indeed a "capacity different from that which He has in fact revealed in His work." Such discourse certainly conveys the impression of a very different god from the God revealed to humanity in Jesus Christ reconciling all to himself. It encourages, instead, the kind of freewheeling speculations about God that Langland associated with the dinner parties of the rich.[54]

V

In the final part of this chapter I will address aspects of sacramental theology in Ockham. The links with the issues we have just been considering are made clear by Marilyn Adams in her chapter "Grace, Merit, and
the Freedom of God" in the second volume of her book on Ockham:

> Since for Ockham, God is utterly free in the redemptive process,
> God is not bound by sacraments any more than He is bound by any-
> thing else. Not only are sacraments not logically necessary or suffi-
> cient for the infusion of charity or grace. Ockham denies that they
> are its efficient causes either. . . . Rather they are causes *sine quibus*
> *non*. By divine ordinance, there is a constant conjunction between
> someone's receiving the sacrament of baptism under certain circum-
> stances and his being infused with grace. But this constant conjunc-
> tion holds, not because of any power (*virtus*)—whether natural or
> supernatural—inhering in the sacrament, but because God wills to
> produce grace in the soul whenever the sacrament is thus received.[55]

But, as we have seen, Ockham also argued that salvation depends entirely
on the free decision of divine acceptance and that God's freedom (envisaged in Ockhamist modes) logically entails that God does not now need
to accept anyone who has been gifted with such grace.[56] We recall that in
this version of *acceptatio divina* salvation and the particular qualities of actions are split apart. Habitual virtues cultivated by the gifts of grace have
no other necessity or meaning than that the divine lawgiver happens
to have mandated them and could as ordinately change the current constitution. He could do so, Ockham imagines, without transforming humankind into a different kind of species. Freedom envisaged as the liberty
of indifference fits well with his denial of traditional forms of teleology,
Augustinian and Thomistic. As Marilyn Adams shows, Ockham does not
define "transcendental goodness" as the proper object of appetite, and
because of "the liberty of indifference" he perceives goodness as "inci-
dental" to an object filling the role of end.[57] Indeed, Ockham "denies the
will any *natural* inclination to act for the sake of the good, of right reason,
or for God's sake!"[58]

I now wish to remember the forms of sacramental theology repudiated by Scotus and Ockham. This helps one recollect what was at stake both in the earlier fourteenth century and later, when Langland was presented with a range of possibilities in his own theology of grace, sin, and redemption. What was being rejected in the areas that concern me can be represented by considering St. Thomas Aquinas on the sacraments. I have observed the strong ties that bind his theology of grace with Augustine's, and his sacramental theology builds on Augustine's bequests to Christian tradition. In the *Summa Theologiae,* Aquinas's treatise on the sacraments comes immediately after his extremely substantial treatise on Jesus Christ. The latter addresses the Incarnation, Christ's grace, Christ's mystical body (the Church), Christ's humanity (a dazzling display of Chalcedonian Christology in his own idiom), Christ's predestination, the life and work of Christ (including his account of justification), the Resurrection, the Ascension, and Christ's life at the right hand of God the Father (as judge and priestly intercessor) (*ST* III.1–59). Only after this are we led to consider the sacraments of the Church. The form of presentation enforces Aquinas's repeated emphasis on Christ's life as the source of the sacraments and the sacraments as divine gifts through which we are led to fellowship with Christ. David Bourke's introduction to volume 56 of the Blackfriars *Summa Theologiae* (containing III.60–65) identifies "one key idea" of the treatise on the sacrament: "the idea that the new life of the redemption wrought by God in the incarnate Word is communicated to man through created media, physical things, or arts combined with words."[59]

I intend to focus my discussion of this great, unfinished treatise on the small portion where Aquinas addresses and rejects the line that was to be pursued by Scotus and Ockham, one illustrated above in the words of Marilyn Adams. This discussion comes in the third question of the treatise on the sacraments, and I will summarize the path by which it is reached. The first question asks "what a sacrament is," responding with articles on signs, their purposes, and the forms they take in the Old Law and in the New Law (III.60). The second question explores the necessity of the sacraments for the specific kind of creatures human beings are and have become through sin (III.61).[60] The third question concerns "the chief effect of the sacraments, which is grace" (III.62). The first article asks whether the sacraments are a cause of grace (III.62.1). Setting out from Augustine, Aquinas argues that the sacraments of the New Law do cause grace, since through them mankind is incorporated into Christ (III.61.1, resp.). But how do sacraments cause grace? Aquinas now takes note of those whose approach anticipates the line to be taken by Scotus and Ockham. Some ("Quidam") say that the sacraments are "not the cause of grace in the sense of actually producing any effect, but rather that when the sacraments are applied God produces grace in the soul."[61] And here we come to an extremely illuminating narrative image that was to be discussed both by Ockham and by his Thomistic adversary, the former chancellor of Oxford University, John Lutterell. St. Thomas relates it as follows. They put "forward the example of one who on offering a leaden denarius receives a hundred pounds by the order of the king. This is done not because the denarius he offers is in any way the cause of him receiving so great a sum of money. Rather this effect is produced solely by the king's will" (III.62.1, resp.).[62]

What is wrong with this model? Aquinas objects because it makes sacraments merely signs, to speak anachronistically, merely Zwinglian signs ("iste modus non transcendit rationem signi," III.62.1, resp.). "For a leaden denarius is no more than a certain kind of sign of the royal prescription directing that the man presenting it is to receive a sum of money." In this case the sign in itself contributes nothing other than being a sign of royal power and will. It is intended to be as transparent as any sign can be. This model makes the sacraments of the New Law "nothing more than signs of grace" [nihil plus essent quam signa gratiae]. This is what Aquinas rejects as a rupture with Catholic tradition: "We have it on authority of many of the saints that the sacraments of the New Law not merely signify but actually cause grace [quod sacramenta novae legis non solum significant, sed causant gratiam]" (III.62.1, resp.). Given this reality, Aquinas says we must take a different approach to sacramental grace. We need one that will distinguish two kinds of efficient causes, "principal and instrumental." First, the principal cause of grace in the sacraments is God alone. For grace is "a certain shared similitude to the divine nature," quoting 2 Peter 1.4 to illustrate this view. But there is a second cause too. This is the "instrumental cause." Although it acts only through the initiating agency of God, it too is a causative agent. In this second way, as an instrumental cause, the sacraments of the New Law cause grace. Indeed, it is precisely for this reason that God gave us the sacraments. So once again in Aquinas, as in Augustine, we meet the commitment to complex versions of doubled agency in thinking about the ways in which God draws human beings to God. Aquinas emphasizes this aspect in his second answer to the objections he had composed to his argument. An instrument, he says, acts in two ways: first by producing effects entirely in the power of the principal agent and second by producing effects that belong particularly to itself (III.62.1, ad 2). The distinction allows St. Thomas to make a crucial move, one that is at the heart of his understanding of sacramental grace. In the sacraments God gives us gifts that "touch the body and so produce upon it the sort of effects which are connatural to them as physical entities." It is imperative that, in producing such effects, they act as instrumental agents producing effects on the soul through God's power (ad 2). He gives the example of water in baptism and turns again for confirmation to Augustine. So the sacraments are gifts appropriately chosen for embodied spirits and must be talked about as such. In this perspective a theology that is content to illustrate sacramental grace with the example of the lead denarius will be guilty of at least two things: (1) disastrous misunderstanding of our existence and needs as embodied spirits and (2) wretched ingratitude toward the wonderful appropriateness of the divine gifts designed so carefully for our particular form of life.

Later in *ST* III.62 Aquinas returns to these issues. The fourth article asks whether there is any power ("virtus") in the sacrament to cause grace. Through the objections he will oppose, Aquinas lays out arguments that assume a sharp disjunction between spirit and body, familiar kinds of dualism. In their view, sacramental grace must be aligned purely with spiritual power ("virtus spiritualis") and a distaste at the thought of divine power committed to the contingencies of matter (see especially III.62.4, obj. 1 and 3). St. Thomas's answer again sets out with Augustine. His response returns to those for whom sacramental grace is best envisaged through the example of the king, the leaden denarius, and the royal will that the one who offers the lead should be paid gold in abundance. "Those who assert that the sacraments do not cause grace except through a certain concomitance deny that there is any power [virtus] in the sacrament to produce the effect of that sacrament" (III.62.4, resp.). That is, they insist that the divine power acts without carnal mediations. The whole celebration of the Eucharist is merely, as it were, a performance that happens to be the occasion for the utterly alien divine power to act on the individual soul. Aquinas once again rejects the line that would be pursued by Scotus and Ockham. Now he does so by elaborating his understanding of the sacraments through the language of instrumental causality. The sacraments are given a certain kind of instrumental power that is "made proportionate to the instrument." Invoking his comments in III.62.1, which I have just rehearsed, he reiterates that while the role of the principal agent is certainly principal, the principal's instrument is also an agent with a power proportionate to its own mode of being, a power that is intrinsic to the effects of the particular sacrament. We must, that is, recognize a certain instrumental power ("virtus instrumentalis") in the divine gifts.

In his *ad primum*, St. Thomas offers an analogy that helps our reflections on different models of grace and what is at stake in the differences between them. He is addressing the objection that spiritual power ("virtus spiritualis") simply cannot be in a body (obj. 1). Aquinas agrees that spiritual power cannot dwell permanently and completely in a body. But this does not mean that spiritual powers cannot be in a body instrumentally. A body can be moved by a spiritual substance inducing a spiritual effect. And here he gives the analogy I have just mentioned:

> There is nothing to prevent a spiritual power being in a body provided it is instrumental—in other words in virtue of the fact that a body can be impelled by some spiritual substance to produce some spiritual effect. Thus too in the human voice itself as perceptible to the senses a certain spiritual power resides to arouse the mind of the hearer in virtue of the fact that it proceeds from a mental concept, and in this way there is a spiritual power in the sacraments in as much as they are ordained by God to produce a spiritual effect. (*ST* III.62.4, ad 1)

In this beautiful counterimage to that of the leaden denarius and the royal will, Aquinas identifies the inextricable bond between body and spirit, showing that it is through this very bond that the God who chose incarnation has graced humanity. The voice itself has a certain spiritual and intellectual power to arouse, to awaken the human intellect. The carnal voice proceeds from the mind's conception and, through material mediations, arouses the intellectual powers of other human beings who are joined in the conversation in which any hope of a just community is rooted. The sacraments are constitutive of that human community we call the Church and thus inseparable from ecclesiology (see, for example, III.73.2; III.73.4; III.79.1). Using the human voice, human understanding, and conversation, St. Thomas creates a picture of the sacraments very different from one based on the arbitrary imposition of value on a leaden denarius. His picture discloses how appropriately the sacraments are ordained by God to elicit spiritual effects for embodied spiritual creatures. How well he would have appreciated the profane "Ecstasie" of a renegade Roman Catholic who was to become a great preacher in the Church of England: "Loves mysteries in soules doe grow, / But yet the body is his booke" (John Donne, "The Ecstasie"). From here St. Thomas focuses on the way the sacraments derive their power from Christ's passion (III.62.5). His concern is to show us how Christ is "the primary sign and cause of God's life in us. . . . By means of Christ's life and death," says Aquinas, "people are actually brought to share in God's life."[63]

So this is the model of sacramental grace that Scotus and Ockham rejected. It pictures the divine mode of working intrinsically to carnal and social mediations, work that composes complex forms of multiple agencies that are simultaneously extrinsic and intrinsic, individual and communitarian, divine and human. Let us now return to Ockham, from whom this discussion began, by recalling his assertion that sacraments are no more than "causae sine quibus non." In his commentary on the fourth book of the *Sentences* he necessarily considers the sacraments. He puts the familiar question: "Utrum sacramenta novae legis sint causae effectivae gratiae?" [Are the sacraments on the New Law effective causes of grace?][64] Ockham attacks St. Thomas's account of sacramental grace in his early commentary on the *Sentences*.[65] He argues that Aquinas is wrong to think sacraments cause grace as instrumental causes (VII.12–13). They are certainly instituted by God, but a sacrament is no more than a "causa sine qua non" (VII.14; see, too, VII.17–18). He chooses the image of the leaden denarius to express his own model of the sacraments. Imagine that a king ordains that whoever receives a leaden denarius should receive a certain gift. The leaden denarius becomes a "causa sine qua non respectu illius doni." That is how sacramental grace works (VII.6). As for the passion of Christ, that is the "causa sine qua non respectu gratiae"

(VII.8). He denies Aquinas's view that sacraments have causal effects in the souls of those participating, and he insists that as spiritual power cannot be embodied it is not in the sacraments ("virtus spiritualis non potest esse subiective in re corporali, igitur non est in sacramentis," VII.11; see VII.9–11). He reiterates that sacraments are not causes of grace: "dico quod sacramenta non sunt causa gratiae" (VII.12). Again and again we are told that sacraments can be said to cause grace only in the sense of a divinely instituted cause "sine qua non," a sense exemplified so well in the image of the king and the leaden denarius (VII.18–19).

Writing in the second half of the fourteenth century, Langland had options that included both "modern," Ockhamizing theology and a theology of grace and the sacraments that was Augustinian and Thomistic (chapter 4). Because some recent commentators on Langland exclude both Augustine and St. Thomas from his contexts, it is worth pausing over an attack on Ockham's investment in the image of the leaden denarius, an attack contemporary with Ockham. In 1323 a provincial chapter of Ockham's own order required him to answer questions about his teaching, and by 1324 he was in Avignon facing charges concerning its orthodoxy.[66] The commission examining his work was composed of doctors of theology from the religious orders together with John Lutterell, who had been chancellor of Oxford University from 1317 to 1322.[67] Lutterell, "a committed Thomist," was "assigned the task of going through the text of Ockham's questions on the *Sentences*."[68] Lutterell's own case against Ockham was presented to John XXII.[69] His charges include attention to "the role of grace and guilt in human redemption and damnation" in Ockham's commentaries.[70] The case Lutterell makes is fascinating and rich, but here I intend only to note his discussion of the leaden denarius that we have read about in both Aquinas and Ockham. Lutterell defends traditional teaching about the necessity for charity in the gift of eternal life and argues that grace involves the transformation of the human agent as an intrinsic part of the processes of salvation. He thus opposes Ockham's Scotistic belief that divine acceptance entails no such thing, and in doing so he recalls a version of the story about the exchange value ascribed to the leaden denarius by royal will: "But they say that God can accept it as worthy, because a king can establish that a lead penny, so long as it nevertheless carries his image, has the value of a silver penny. Therefore, likewise, God can ordain that a natural work is worthy of eternal life without conferring anything beyond its natural features on it."[71] Lutterell decides that this image is as irrelevant as the argument it represents. He agrees that the royal will can impose value in commercial transactions. But that is not an adequate analogy for salvation as Christians have understood it: "So far as its natural value is concerned, the natural properties of one and another, he cannot establish that one is as valuable as the other—that it is as decorative, as solid, as reflective of the king's crown as the other. Thus, in the case at hand, God can accept an act elicited by purely natural powers by giving eternal life to the agent, but by merit as worthy only if purely natural features can be worthy of eternal life the way Pelagius supposed."[72] Lutterell continues to assert a traditional position concerning "the inherence of the form of charity" as the gift that makes someone loved by God, a gift essential to participation in the divine life.[73] Ockham, as we have seen, habitually deployed the dialectic between God's "ordained" and "absolute" power to assert that with the latter "God can accept someone or some act without any infused charity or grace, and He can not accept someone or some act with such infused charity or grace."[74] This is what Lutterell rightly understood as a break with accounts of salvation developed in traditions that included both Augustine and Aquinas. As Adams observes, "Ockham's differences with Lutterell are absolutely fundamental."[75]

But it was not only by Thomists that Ockham's position in this domain was sharply criticized. Walter Chatton, a fellow Franciscan who had been at the same convent as Ockham in London, opposed the views of Ockham on the relations between divine grace and the gift of salvation.[76] Making substantial use of Augustine, Chatton maintains that Ockham's position on the grace of redemption could well be construed as Pelagian.[77] Charity is the grace that makes people pleasing to God and is a habit of loving God, which is a gift from God poured into the soul. Chatton insists that this position has been handed to us by Scripture, Church, and the saints. And especially relevant among the saints is Augustine "contra Pelagianos in multis libris" (44–45). Chatton emphasizes the role of the Holy Spirit in this gift of grace, which transforms fallen humanity into creatures pleasing to God and, crucially, able to fulfill the commandments with merit (45–46). As Augustine wrote, says Chatton, when God crowns our merits he crowns his gifts; we are justified not through free will ("non per liberum voluntatem") but by grace, a grace that heals the will and enables it to fulfill divine law. We can see Chatton using Augustine to evoke a complex, doubled form of agency, now, in this life (47–48). Chatton also stresses God's revealed promises, that through our redemption in Christ those existing in grace will be counted as worthy to share in divine life.[78] The combination of Christology with divine promise and faithfulness undermines Ockham's theology of grace, divine acceptation, and a freedom in which the dialectic between God's "ordained" and "absolute" power is central. Even if Ockham would have remained unimpressed by such traditional and Christological theology, I am persuaded that we shall see how, and why, Langland did not join him here.

It seems helpful to conclude this chapter with some reflections from Marilyn Adams, one of the most learned commentators on Ockham with abundant sympathy for her subject: "Since worthiness of eternal life is a value dependent solely on God's free and contingent volition, why could God not have legislated that everyone with blue eyes is worthy of eternal life, no matter what he does, just as a king can legislate that anyone who is in a certain room at a given time gets $1,000,000."[79] We are back to the leaden coin and a version of freedom utterly divorced from the specificities of revelation, reconciliation, and promise in Jesus Christ. Adams's reflections on the mode of Ockhamite theology come from full immersion in the Franciscan's commentaries on the *Sentences* and would be extremely appropriate at one of those "modern" disputations that Langland stages. There some of the disputants

> tellen of þe trinite how two slowe þe thridde
> And brynge forth a balled reson, taken Bernard to witnesse
> And putten forth presumpcioun to preue þe sothe.
> Thus they dreuele at the deyes the deite to knowe
> And gnawen god with gorge when here gottes fullen.[80]

CHAPTER 3

Thomas Bradwardine

Reflections on De Causa Dei contra Pelagium
et de Virtute Causarum

Moreover, even if a certain order of causes does exist in
the mind of God, it does not follow that nothing is left to
the free choice of our will [in nostrae voluntatis arbitrio].
For our wills are themselves included in the order of
causes which is certain to God and contained within
his foreknowledge. For the wills of men are causes of
the deeds of men [quoniam et humanae voluntates
humanorum operum causae sunt].

St. Augustine, The City of God, V.9

The point is that here as everywhere, the omnicausality
of God must not be construed as this sole causality. The
divine change in whose accomplishment a man becomes a
Christian is an event of true intercourse between God and
man. If it undoubtedly has its origin in God's initiative, no
less indisputably man is not ignored or passed over in it.
He is taken seriously as an independent creature of God.
He is not run down and overpowered, but set on his feet.

Karl Barth, Church Dogmatics, IV/4, 22

IN THE PREVIOUS CHAPTER I DISCUSSED ASPECTS OF OCKHAM'S
theologizing, which is representative of what was customarily called
"modern" theology in the later Middle Ages.[1] This customary classification seems to have encouraged some contemporary literary commentators to assume that a theology shaped by Ockham gained hegemony
in fourteenth-century England. But such an assumption is simply unwarranted, as William Courtenay showed some years ago.[2] There is no reason to believe that a historically responsible reading of later fourteenth-
century works must interpret them within the paradigms of Ockhamizing
or "modern" theology with their relation to previous theologians, their
categories, questions, and favored solutions. The relevant history suggests that fourteenth-century theology is too heterogeneous and eclec-
tic to allow such homogenizing assumptions to shape any study.[3] This
does not mean that no late medieval writer was decisively influenced by
concerns and arguments of Ockham or Robert Holcot or others called
"modern" theologians, or that theologians were uninterested in the views
of such "moderns."[4] It just means that there are no putatively histori-
cist maps to determine for us what a fourteenth-century theologian must
have thought. Such maps might give us shortcuts that go like this: "Given
the known theological hegemony, Langland's *Piers Plowman* must have
been saying something congruent with what Ockham is taken to have
said about, say, cognition, or justification, or grace, or divine power." Setting aside the grounds for thinking we can have such putatively histori-
cist shortcuts does not entail the claim that the study of history, including historical theology, is simply irrelevant to our understanding of what
a medieval writer was saying. Rather, it reminds us that the role of his-
toriography here is to recover as full an understanding as possible of the
various conversations in which its subjects were immersed, a recovery
that will demand engagement with the practices of its agents and institutions. In fourteenth-century England those pursuing theology (inside or
outside the universities) inherited a strikingly diversified discourse without having to step outside the always developing horizons of what constituted the orthodoxy of a living tradition. This tradition enabled their
thinking, including their critical reflections on past and present teaching. Furthermore we must remember that a historicism driven by a synchronic model of context is never going to be adequate to the study of
Christian writing in the Middle Ages. This is because theologians un-

derstood St. Augustine or St. Bernard or Peter Lombard or St. Thomas Aquinas as contemporary authorities who belonged to contemporary conversations and disputes. They were powerfully present interlocutors, as Bradwardine's *De Causa Dei* copiously witnesses. Furthermore, it seems to me that belief in the communion of saints contributed to this complex sense of presence and absence, of communion in time past, time present, and time future, a communion that resists the synchronic concerns of much contemporary historicism. Of course, such a sense of communion cannot preclude the misunderstanding and inattentiveness to which we are all continuously prone.

It is with such thoughts in mind that I offer brief and partial reflections on Bradwardine's *De Causa Dei contra Pelagium et de Virtute Causarum*. This was completed by the mid-1340s, written both within and outside the University of Oxford.[5] Bradwardine's vast and sometimes remorselessly repetitive work is customarily referred to as Augustinian, an Augustinian turn against the version of divine and human agency in "modern" theology.[6] Bradwardine would have welcomed this appellation, and he constantly turns to Augustine as an advocate for his own arguments on divine agency and human will.[7] Nevertheless the appellation is very misleading. Partly this is an inevitable consequence of the extraordinary scope, variety, and theological range of Augustine's plenitudinous, passionately inquiring work over more than forty years. We recollect extensive commentary on Scripture involving the lasting elaboration of the theology and practice of Christocentric exegesis; profound explorations of a distinctly Christian understanding of conversion, contemplation, and confession; profound, often decisive developments in Christian theology of the Trinity, of grace, of sin, and of Christology; a monumental analysis of pagan culture, religion, and politics set within salvation history; still significant essays in ecclesiology; and abundant sermons and letters addressing different struggles and issues in changing contexts. The identification of Bradwardine's *De Causa Dei* as Augustinian always seems to reduce Augustinian theology to a simple, static scheme of ideas foregrounding omnipresent divine agency with human passivity in the face of grace and predestination. Among literary critics, often committed to a bizarre deployment of the contemporary American vocabulary of "conservative" and "liberal" to late medieval culture, this reductive abstraction of Augustine is called "conservative" in contrast to "modern" theology of the fourteenth century.[8] But even as admiring an engagement with Augustine as Bradwardine's shows how the abstraction of Augustinian ideas on divine sovereignty and human helplessness to be deployed against contemporary opponents could have an outcome that was a mode of theology utterly alien to Augustine. Neither Augustinian nor Ockhamist, *De Causa Dei* is a *tertium quid*. In generating this, Bradwardine illustrates the diversity and eclecticism of fourteenth-century theology: he exemplifies the range of options in Langland's immediate theological culture.

I

While Bradwardine saw his *De Causa Dei* as part of a great battle being fought in his own church, he was convinced that the struggle had a very long history, as we shall see. He himself represents those who offer due worship, acknowledgment, gratitude, and love to God, and he writes for the friends of God on behalf of God (Preface, fol. a1r). His preface tells us that he battles against massed ranks of Pelagians, whom he likens to the prophets of Baal (on their destiny, see 3 Kings 18.40; 4 Kings 10.18–28). Their primary devotion is to an illusory free choice that they defend against the truly free, utterly gratuitous and saving grace of God. This is the foundation of their proud diminution of God's sovereignty and their crazy exaggerations of human autonomy and power. In their delusions they see themselves as Lord and God as their servant. But this madness, in Bradwardine's view, is no longer marginal in the Church. He laments the powerful place achieved by such Pelagians in the modern Church, where almost everybody, he insists, runs after Pelagius into error. He sees himself as part of a tiny remnant of God's servants calling on God to rise up in defense of God's own cause. His preface recounts an enthralling dream vision that symbolizes his identity in the war to which God has called him. He sees himself in a fierce aerial battle with Pelagius. Victory comes to Bradwardine only when he surrenders himself entirely to God's grace. The consequence of this is the violent and total destruction of the enemy (Preface, fols. a1v–b1v).

Bradwardine then traces the genealogy of modern Pelagianism back to Lucifer. This demonic tradition includes the fratricidal Cain and the tyrant Nimrod. Indeed, Bradwardine believes that Pelagianism instigates a tyranny in which its opponents, such as himself (soon to be archbishop. of Canterbury), court martyrdom (Preface, fols. b1v–b2r). This could have opened out some potentially fascinating questions about the politics of the Pelagianism Bradwardine opposes: Could they be more congruent with Nimrod, with tyrannical forms of dominion, than literary scholars customarily assume? But Bradwardine does not follow up such questions. The interests of *De Causa Dei* do not encompass issues of justice and appropriately Christian practice in contemporary or past polities. The difference between Bradwardine and Augustine here is significant and, as far as I am aware, habitually ignored by commentators on Bradwardine's *De Causa Dei.*[9] Of course Bradwardine was not only a university theologian but the confessor and priest of a warrior king, and he celebrated the victories of the English lay elites at Crécy and Neville's Cross in his *Sermo Epinicius,* assuring his powerful compatriots that it is indeed God who gives such military victories. It is not hard to argue that the emphasis on divine agency as against human will or other imagined causes is congruent with a dominant strand of *De Causa Dei.*[10] But just as congruent is the conspicuous lack of Christological reflection. This is particularly striking in that the *Sermo Epinicius* is preached in the face of Christians slaughtering Christians in the wars of Edward III, wars for dynastic power, the politics of honor, and economic profits. Such a lack of critical, Christological reflection on the lust for dominion and the will to kill makes for very sharp contrasts with St. Augustine's *City of God.*[11] But the preface to *De Causa Dei,* as I have indicated, concerns Bradwardine's wars against Pelagius, not the current wars of his earthly sovereign. Here he makes clear that his major concerns are with supernatural and universal causes, God's will, grace, predestination, reprobation, fate, chance, free choice, and sin (fols. b2v–b3r). Only much later in the book will we be told that he himself was once a committed Pelagian, if not a worshipper of Baal.

We reach his conversion narrative in the thirty-fifth chapter of the first book. This chapter is directed "against Pelagius" and argues that grace is freely given by God, not acquired by preceding merits (307–8). Bradwardine confesses that he used to accept philosophic teaching that convinced him that Pelagian positions on will and grace were correct. He tells us that in the school of philosophy where he was studying he heard a great deal about the autonomy and freedom of human agency. Every day he heard that it is equally in our power to do well or to do evilly, to acquire virtues or to acquire vices ("quod in nostra potestate est, operari bene vel male, habere virtutes vel vitia," I.35, 308). Consequently, whenever he heard St. Paul's teaching in church, he rejected it because it exalted grace and disparaged free choice ("gratiam extollentem, & liberum deprimentem arbitrium," 308). He actually believed that Paul had erred from the path of truth (308). Afterwards, although he was not yet studying theology, he experienced a conversion around one of Paul's texts that he had previously rejected. This was a different text from the one famously cited in Augustine's *Confessions* (VIII.11.29), but it also came from the epistle to the Romans: "So then it is not of him that willeth, nor of him that runneth, but of God that sheweth mercy" (Rom. 9.16; *De Causa Dei*, 308). Doubtless Bradwardine intends the Pauline moment of his conversion to recall Augustine grabbing the book of Paul's letters, opening it at Romans 13.13–14, and immediately feeling his heart filled with the light of certainty and all the darkness of doubt dispersed. But the recollection will also bring out some important and symptomatic differences between Bradwardine and Augustine.

Augustine's reading of the verses from Romans 13 is preceded by a long and densely mediated process, mediated by complex webs of people, texts, conversions, and the Church.[12] To this process belongs the moment of clarity around Paul's letter. It is then succeeded by the powerful meditation on memory, God, and the Christian subject seeking God (*Confessions,* X). Here Augustine displays just how the converted and confessing person remains a vastly obscure form of life, an awe-inspiring, infinite mystery, an abyss. Earlier in the *Confessions* he had recounted how he had become to himself "a vast problem" [magna quaestio] (IV.4.9).[13] But his conversion does not result in transparency or mastery. On the contrary, book X echoes the earlier statement: "In your eyes I have become a problem [quaestio] to myself, and that is my sickness" (X.33.50). He confesses that he cannot grasp the whole ("totum") that he is (X.8.15), that self-examination is strenuous labor because he has become a land of difficulty and great sweat (X.15.25). Self-examination is fraught with massive potential for deception and error, for the converted Christian is now acutely aware of "those deplorable blind spots where the capacity that lies in me is concealed from me. . . . What lies within is for the most part hidden unless experience [experientia] reveals it." And experience shows that anyone who changes from the worse to the better "can also change from the better to the worse" (X. 32.48; see, too, X.35.56). Furthermore, the converted Christian finds that the memories of past sinful habits and their delights are still present. Those past compulsions and their pleasures, rejected with such relief and joy in the encounter with Romans 13.13–14, still have a hidden and sometimes not hidden life (X.30.41–41.66). Augustine's intense focus on this opacity and obscurity produces great humility in the face of his own desires. And this is absolutely central to the model he gradually creates for the converted subject. Confession yields acknowledgment that "I am poor and needy" (X.38.63; Ps. 108.22). But the recognition of the minute particulars that lead to this confession, the very displeasure with what he discovers, becomes a liberating acceptance of the path of conversion, which is only consummated eschatologically, in that peace that the eye of the arrogant does not know (X.38.63). With beautiful coherence this meditation concludes by turning to the "true Mediator" between God and humanity, the one who had the power to lay down his life in freeing human beings from the catastrophic consequences of their choices and had the power of taking it up again (John 10.18). Victor and victim, victor because victim, priest and sacrifice, he transforms sinful servants into sons of God. All is "pro nobis" (for us), as Augustine reiterates four times in one short paragraph (X.43.69). And so, because the Word was made flesh and dwelt among us ("in nobis"), neither Augustine nor his readers need despair. For now "pro nobis" (for us) becomes "in nobis" (in us, X.43.69). The appropriate response is to cast all care onto the divine mediator and embrace the sacraments he has bequeathed to his Church: "I think upon the price of my redemption, and I eat and drink it, and distribute it and as a poor man I desire to be filled with it among those who eat and are satisfied" (X.43.70).[14] The richly mediated process of conversion, the opacity of the Christian subject to self-examination, the weight of sinful habit, the liberation of humble acknowledgment, and the gift of the sacrament of the altar: all theology comes from and returns to Augustine's Christology.

Bradwardine's account of conversion is very different. He represents conversion as a sudden and total transformation from being a Pelagian who denied Paul's authority and rejected his teachings on grace to being a Pauline theologian of grace locked in heroic combat with modern

Pelagians. We hear of no mediations, nothing about the role of the Church, nothing remotely Augustinian about the complexities of will, loves, and habits in the converted subject, nothing of the continuities of the past in the present and the force of memory to shake the reformed will and intellect. Most strikingly, we hear nothing about Christology. Suddenly, in a ray of grace, Bradwardine grasped Paul's arguments about the precedence of God's free grace to all good merits. His model of conversion, far from being Augustine's narration, is St. Luke's version of Paul's (Acts 9.1–19).[15] This model of conversion is certainly congruent with his major project. For his great passion is to show God as the first mover and also efficient cause in every movement and to marginalize the role of secondary causes. He is not at all interested in Augustine's extraordinarily nuanced, complex accounts of conversion and continuing resistance.

Later in *De Causa Dei* he offers another narrative of his own experience. This emerges during his treatment of penance, which I will discuss later (I.43). Here he confesses that God has loved him eternally and freely. God has eternally and freely decided to bestow on Bradwardine justifying grace at a time pleasing to God. In that chosen time God freely infuses justifying grace in the unjust Bradwardine to justify him freely, to wash away his injustices freely, to receive and heal him freely, to remove the debt of eternal punishment freely, and to turn it, equally freely, into temporal punishment. Thus the theologian is made a son of the kingdom entirely through God's grace, a gift freely given with which he had nothing to do in terms of preparation or acceptance. The gift worked in him and has filled him with gratitude, love, and blessing to God (406–7). Bradwardine's writing here is suffused with joy as he sees himself exemplifying his book's teaching about divine causality, grace, human agency, conversion, and salvation.[16]

II

Bradwardine himself expresses surprise at the bulk of the first book of *De Causa Dei* (443), but its bulk certainly enables him to indicate his predominant concerns. These center on God's sovereignty, God's freedom, and God's causality of all motion.[17] He emphasizes that divine will is not only the first cause of all things but the efficient cause of everything, moving whatever moves.[18] His aim is to highlight the ontological abyss between the omnipotent God and feeble, dependent creatures. As commentators have observed, Bradwardine's assault on Pelagianism concentrates on this ontological abyss rather than on the consequences of sin for humanity.[19] His emphasis on the universal, efficient causality of divine power was designed to correct Pelagian accounts of human autonomy and freedom. But his approach opened out unintended convergences with the theology he opposed. For Bradwardine's thinking was so overwhelmingly obsessed with divine power and its omnipotent agency that it generated a version of theology undisciplined by a developed Christology and despite its length quite lacking any sustained attention to the fact that orthodox Christians worship the Trinity, together with the consequences of this for Christian theologizing.[20] The ironic result of such an account of God, with its lack of Christology and lack of Trinitarian focus, is that it becomes more congruent with that of those "modern" theologians he sought to crush than with Augustine's theology, which he so often invoked. Not for the last time in this chapter Bradwardine's battles remind me of a situation William Blake describes in *Jerusalem*: "Ah! alas! at the sight of the Victim! & at the sight of those who are smitten / All who see become what they behold."[21]

Setting aside such ironies for a while, I will now return to Bradwardine's treatment of grace. We recall that before his conversion he preferred Pelagius to Paul because the latter seemed to diminish our freedom and power to do well (I.35, 308). He relates how after his conversion he grasped the absolute and exclusive priority of grace. He explicates his understanding of "gratia sola" (I.39, 330) as he attacks a conventional position at the heart of "modern" theology, a position that has been applied to Langland's theology in *Piers Plowman* by numerous scholars.[22] Chapter 39 of the first book of *De Causa Dei* (325–326) is directed against those who concede that while humans cannot merit grace *de condigno* they can do so *de congruo*. This distinction pervaded late medieval theology and was a crucial strand in the attempt of "modern" theology to defend itself against the charge that it had reintroduced Pelagianism into the Church. As we saw in the case of Ockham, the strategy was to concede that humans, by their own natural powers, cannot place God under any obligation to reward them with eternal life. The grace of divine acceptance

cannot be merited in any unqualified sense. The assumed natural goodness and virtues of our works cannot make anyone worthy ("condignus")
of eternal life, cannot make humans merit beatitude *de condigno*. This concession was supposed to safeguard theology from Pelagian exaggeration
of human capacities and their merits. But it was also used to justify another set of claims about human capacity and reward, namely that although our natural powers cannot earn eternal life *de condigno*, God has established a covenant ("pactum") whereby if someone does all she or he
can do ("facit quod in se est") with natural, unaided powers, God will ex-
tend his grace of final acceptance. Thus the human earns eternal life not
de condigno but *de congruo*, and does so in a model fostering the extrinsic understanding of grace discussed in the previous chapter.

Robert Holcot, Bradwardine's colleague in the household of Richard of Bury, bishop of Durham, expresses this position with clarity.[23] In
his lectures on the Book of Wisdom, Holcot stresses that nobody can
merit eternal life through natural goodness, "ex condigno."[24] Nevertheless, people can so merit "de congruo." How can this happen? Because
it is congruent that God, according to his infinite power and the order
he happens to have institutionalized, reward someone who does what
she or he can according to his or her limited ability ("Quia congruum est
quod homini facienti secundum potentiam suam finitam, Deus retribuat
secundum potentiam suam infinitam," 126). In this common enough case
Holcot maintains one can say that our works are condignly worthy of
eternal life although through grace rather than the substance of the act
("condigna vite eterne ex gratia, non ex substantia actus"). This is so
because God has decreed it (126–27). In lecture 117 (on Wisd. 8.19–20),
Holcot repeats the commonplace that we cannot merit first grace condignly ("primam gratiam nullus potest promereri," 391). But if we dispose
ourselves as best we can with our own unaided natural powers ("dispos-
tione naturali") and offer no obstacle to grace through the evil use of our
free judgment ("liberi arbitrii"), then grace will be given to us in response
to a practice recognized by God as meritorious. This merit, Holcot notes,
is congruent rather than condign (391). In lecture 146 (on Wisd. 12.1–2),
Holcot once again considers issues of divine and human agency. He
introduces a "dubitatio," asking whether the grace of the Holy Spirit is
necessarily given to those who do the best they can to prepare themselves for it (492). Holcot acknowledges that God's grace is a gift freely

given out of his mercy. And he considers Jeremiah's figure of God as the potter and humanity as the clay in the hand of the potter (Jer. 18.1–6; see too Rom. 9.20–23). But he also wonders whether it would be wicked for God not to receive those who flee to him and whether those fleeing to God necessarily receive grace. He quotes from Apocalypse 3.20: "I stand at the gate and knock. If anyone opens to me I will come in to him and sup with him." Perhaps it is not by chance that Holcot omits from the scriptural text "si quis audierit" [if anyone hears my voice], for this could open out a complex discussion about those who have ears and will not or cannot hear, a complex discussion about habitual sin and its consequences for will and intellect. Instead of opening such an Augustinian or Langlandian discussion, Holcot chooses to follow up his partial quotation from Apocalypse 3.20 with the statement that the one who opens the door is he who disposes himself by doing that which he can ("iste, qui disponit se faciendo id, quod in eo est, aperit sibi," 492). In a sense, Christ enters the open door "necessarily" and therefore gives grace necessarily. The sense of "necessary" here is God's necessary commitment to his own promise and covenant, his own statute law ("ex promisso suo & pacto, sive lege statuta"). It is God's law and he can change it. He is certainly not obligated outside his freely chosen statutes. Here Holcot again emphasizes that human merit in disposing the self to grace is merit "de congruo," not "de condigno." As for the figure of the potter and the clay, Holcot observes that the comparison with relations between God and humanity does not hold in all respects: there is no covenant ("pactum") between the potter and the clay, while the clay can never merit anything from the potter in any way ("nec de condigno, nec de congruo"). In such ways "modern" theologians confessed that the unaided powers of humans could not elicit eternal salvation, the free gift of God. This confession, they insisted, kept them clear from any Pelagian errors. But while they acknowledged the salvific limitations of our natural powers, they simultaneously maintained that they had been accepted as infinitely worthy by divine statute ("lege statuta").

We have seen this kind of move in chapter 2, and it is one customarily ascribed to Langland in current scholarship on *Piers Plowman*. Bradwardine rightly observes that this position is widespread, and he gives a lucid, very fair summary of it (I.39). Because he considers it to be a Pelagian error he determines to examine it carefully. He thinks that theory is

invented by those who are not content with God's free absolutely unearned grace ("alii non contenti gratia gratis data," 325). They prefer a
market in grace where they can buy what they imagine God sells cheaply,
at a congruent rather than condign price ("volunt quod vendatus a Deo &
ematur ab eis aliquot precio licet vili, congruo tamen ut asserunt, non
condigno," 325). Bradwardine maintains, plausibly enough, that the distinction between merit "de congruo" and merit "de condigno" serves a
theology that enables people to feel confident that they can indeed merit
saving grace by their own powers ("ex solis propriis viribus"). It is thus,
he determines, another facet of the Pelagianism that undermines the
unique and absolute nature of divine causality (325).

Bradwardine affirms against this that only the freely given grace of
charity composes the true virtue whose end is God, whereas the Pelagianism he opposes makes the gift of theological virtues unnecessary.
This is so because according to his opponents we can, in effect, fulfill the
law of love without divine grace, through our natural abilities, a claim
we have seen Ockham defending (chapter 2). The error Bradwardine opposes maintains, explicitly or implicitly, that pagans can also fulfill the divine precepts. Here he addresses an ancient topic that engaged a number
of fourteenth-century writers as it engages many of their modern commentators.[25] Bradwardine's treatment of this complex theological issue
is shaped by his anti-Pelagian mission and his way of conducting theological reflection. He turns to Paul's proclamation that the just live by
faith (328; see, for example, Rom. 1.17, 3.28, 4.5). And whereas he once
doubted Paul's authority, he certainly doubts no longer. Nor does he
doubt that the mature Augustine's reading of Paul is correct (for example,
327–29). The pagans do not live by faith, and it is impossible to please
God without faith. Indeed, the way God has decreed for the human journey to God is through Jesus Christ in the Holy Spirit, the way of charity
celebrated by Paul in 1 Corinthians 13 (328–29). So any virtue not rooted
in charity is only apparently a virtue (329). By grace alone can people truly
do well, and by grace alone are they saved. Nobody can will justly who is
not just, and nobody becomes just except by God's gift. By grace alone
are we saved, and in this our own choice is unequivocally passive ("nihil
eius arbitrio agente," 330). Grace alone justifies. Grace on grace. Grace
alone generates good will and good works (330–31). Logically enough,
he utterly rejects the claim of contemporaries such as Ockham, those he

refers to as "Pelagiani quidam moderni," that people love God above all things and entirely for the sake of God through their own natural powers ("ex naturalibus suis puris potest diligere Deum super omnia gratis proper seipsum," 335). He maintains that the familiar strategy of acknowledging that such love is not meritorious "de condigno" but will certainly receive the grace of final acceptance "de congruo" is a transparently Pelagian one designed to inflate our understanding of our own resources (335, 338–39, 363). At length Bradwardine systematically denies the coherence of the crucial distinction between merit "de congruo" and merit "de condigno" (335–63).

This forceful critique introduces his own theology of predestination. He insists that even if someone is in the greatest charity at a particular moment this will have no happy outcome if such a person is "foreseen" [praescitus], a reprobate destined for the second death. Even in charity such a person is "hated" [oditur] by God as much as one fallen into the deepest sin (338).[26] He invokes Judas, not for the first time. For earlier he has asserted that God never willed to save Judas even when he was behaving virtuously, living in charity and grace ("in charitate & gratia," 248; see 247–48). To Bradwardine the theology of predestination is yet further evidence of the utterly unwarranted nature of the structures built on the distinction between merit "de condigno" and "de congruo."

Although I will return briefly to the issue of predestination, I now wish to follow Bradwardine's elaboration of his version of "gratia sola" in his chapter on the justification of the unjust. As was conventional in medieval theology, the topic "de iustificatione iniusti" is explored within a study of the sacrament of penance and the power of the keys (I.43, 377–420). This is the most obvious place in *De Cause Dei* for a sustained study of sacramental grace and the sources of regeneration bestowed on the Church and its members by the Trinity. Before considering Bradwardine's treatise on penance, I wish to recollect the approach to the Church's sacraments in a great Augustinian theologian who preceded the "moderns" whom Bradwardine seeks to challenge.

St. Thomas Aquinas approaches the sacraments in the third part of the *Summa Theologiae*.[27] They are thus reached only through and after his Christological treatise (III.1–59). Christ is shown as the savior of all, God become man for our salvation. Central to the benefits he brought humankind are the sacraments by which we gain salvation ("quibus salutem

consequimus," III, Prologue). These sacraments are sanctifying signs
that lead humans to God. They are given by God to the Church in forms
especially appropriate for embodied spirits whose knowledge develops
through the mind's relations with the material creation and whose salvation depends on the Word made flesh (III.60.1–6 and III.61.1). Sacraments certainly signify events and doctrine of Christian narratives, but
as the gifts of God they are effective agents in the lives of their recipi-
ents (III.61.1; III.61.4; III.62; III.64–65). Those who participate in the
sacraments are incorporated into the body of Christ. So sacraments both
signify and cause the grace that draws people into the life of the Trinity
through and in the body of Christ, which is the Church (III.62.1–2 and
4). As I observed in the previous chapter, St. Thomas had already outlined
and rejected a "modern" model of a sacrament as in itself a worthless
coin but one that can be exchanged for a large sum of money according
to the king's arbitrary will (III.62.1; III.62.4). There I contrasted Ockham's
espousal of this model with St. Thomas's beautiful image of relations between divine and human agency in the sacraments. Aquinas takes as his
model the power of someone's voice to arouse power, participation, dialogue (III.62.4, ad 1; see too III.64.1). We saw how this provides a profound and symptomatic contrast to the model of a leaden coin, exchange
value in a market, and the arbitrary power of royal authority to fix prices.
Furthermore, St. Thomas's account of the sacraments fills out the Christological commitment of the prologue and structure of the third part of
the *Summa Theologiae*. Time and again he shows how sacramental grace
flows from Christ's life, crucifixion, and resurrection, a grace on which
Christian life depends, both in the Church as a whole community and in
each individual member.[28]

In this sacramental and Christological context Thomas Aquinas himself quotes Paul's insistence that we are justified freely by God's grace
through Christ (Rom. 3.24; *ST* III.62.6, ad 3). The culmination of the sacraments is the Eucharist because it contains Christ himself, the source of
all sacraments. It is the sacrament to which all the others are ordered,
the sacrament of the Church's unity.[29] This is the immediate context for
St. Thomas's explication of the sacrament of penance, which he treats
after discussing the Eucharist and, as I have noted, after a sustained account of Christology. Aquinas shows how penance produces its effect
through the power of Christ's passion (III.86.1, resp.). As in Langland's

Piers Plowman, St. Thomas presents this sacrament as being especially bound up with the virtue of justice, pointing toward the intensely communitarian, social concerns in conventional medieval teaching about confession.[30] In his discussion of the forms of justifying grace in the sacrament he also displays a complex dialectic between divine and human agencies, including the penitent subject and the Church's priest (III.84.1; III.84.5; III.84.8–9; III. 85.5; III.86.4 and 6). Remembering St. Thomas's treatment of the sacraments helps us focus on the traditions Bradwardine inherited and the choices he makes as he considers sacramental grace.

Despite the size of *De Causa Dei* and the substantial length of the chapter on penance (I.63), Bradwardine never offers a sustained or coherent theology of the Church and sacramental grace. His preoccupation continues to be divine agency and his arguments against Pelagians, with reiterated insistence that no kind of meritorious work can precede grace (388–89). God alone can give the necessary grace, not man in cooperation with God ("solus Deus facit, non homo cum eo," 389). Nobody can do penance in a manner acceptable to God without grace; justification is not a do-it-yourself job (397–98, 401–2). Bradwardine has already emphasized this in his tract *De Praedestinatione et Praescientia.*[31] Here he gave concise expression to his understanding of the relations between divine and human agency. The thinking about justification is characterized by a tendency toward a static schematism around a rather simple dichotomy: grace, not contrition, is the cause of justification. Contrition is the consequence of justifying grace (204–5).

One might assume that the brevity of *De Praedestinatione et Praescientia* prevented Bradwardine from exploring agency in a more complex, nuanced way. Certainly its elaboration in *De Causa Dei* offered him apparently unlimited space to enrich his account of God's saving work in relation to human agency and participation in the sacraments. But preoccupied by his battles with "modern" theology and his exploration of God's causality he saw no need for such revisions and increased nuance. He continues to stress that only God can give the grace needed for the fruits of contrition. We must not think of the human person as in any way acting with God ("solus Deus facit, non homo cum eo," I.43, 389). His chapter is replete with supporting citations from Paul, Augustine, and Peter Lombard as he seeks to prove that "modern" theologians have broken with Christian tradition.[32] He is also confident that his arguments about penance are grounded in Scripture. Among his illustrations of this is Luke's story of the woman who has had "a spirit of infirmity eighteen years." Bent down to the ground ("inclinata"), she is unable to look upwards at all. Jesus sees the woman, calls her to him, and says to her, "Woman, thou art delivered from thy infirmity." "And he laid his hands upon her, and immediately she was made straight, and glorified God" (Luke 13.11–13).

This narrative had traditionally been read allegorically, and it is well worth exemplifying the kind of exegesis Bradwardine would know, the kind of interpretive option he inherited. The *Glossa Ordinaria* sees the woman as symbolizing human nature. Her infirmity represents love of earthly things; her inability to look upwards represents her habitual turning away from rectitude of mind. The fact that Jesus sees her, when she herself cannot look upwards, is read as the election of grace: "Praedestinando per gratiam." Jesus calling her represents his teaching. His laying on of hands represents the help of spiritual gifts resulting in her ability to stand upright, to glorify God, and to persevere in good works to the end.[33] Nicholas of Lyra's moral commentary reads the woman as the sinner habituated to inordinate love of the world, hence bent down, "incurvata." He does not mention election but instead sees Jesus's actions and their salvific effects as pointing to the practices of preachers and confessors in the Church. St. Thomas's *Catena Aurea* includes glosses that see the woman's infirmity as representing both original and personal sin, showing the crippling consequences of habitual sin, which binds down the mind and paralyzes the will. Christ's healing miracle symbolizes his salvific mission.[34] The great fifteenth-century theologian and exegete Denis the Carthusian also sees the woman's inability to look upwards as figuring the weight of sin that bends humanity down ("incurvata") into the image of brute beasts, an incurvature against our nature, whose true end is to love heavenly things. Jesus's actions display his compassion and omnipotence. Like Nicholas of Lyra, Denis does not mention election, but his gloss on the spiritual understanding of the narrative does include a comment on Jesus seeing the one who did not see him. This elicits a celebration of the way Christ mercifully saves sinners through a complex and interactive web of mediations. Through inward inspiration, through angelic guidance, through human exhortation, or through other ways,

Jesus calls sinners to himself, to conversion and to worthy penance ("ad conversionem mentalem, poenitentiamque condignam"). After this, Christ pours into the subject confident faith in the forgiveness of sins.[35] Here Denis displays a thoroughly Augustinian understanding of conversion and the divine strategy of mediations, a strategy illustrated in chapter 1 of the present study. What does Bradwardine do with this rich exegetical and theological tradition?

He too sees the woman as the figure of a sinner or human nature. He turns her eighteen-year infirmity into an allegory of humanity before the law, under the law, and in the time of grace (18 = 6 x 3). Burdened with sin, she cannot turn to God (I.43, 391). Bradwardine notes that the woman is not weeping, not asking for Jesus. According to Bradwardine she does not possess any merit. He maintains that Christ's healing miracle demonstrates the working of grace in its absolute gravity and complete independence of human agency (391–92). Once divine grace has healed the woman, she is able to glorify God (as Bradwardine himself does in his joyful confession a few pages later, 406–7). Once healed by Christ, the woman is able to do well ("ad bene operandum," 391). This exegesis certainly has strong affinities with the early medieval *Glossa Ordinaria* (with its gloss on predestination) and also with traditional exegesis of the half-alive/half-dead man ("semivivus") rescued by the Samaritan (Luke 10.25–37), a narrative of great importance in *Piers Plowman* (chapter 4).

Yet these clear affinities also suggest a difference. This relates to the distinctively Augustinian emphasis on mediations to which I drew attention in recounting the exegesis of Denis the Carthusian and that we can also see in Nicholas of Lyra's allegory involving the Church's preachers and confessors. As for the related exegetical tradition around the Samaritan and *semivivus* in Luke 10, there we find that Christology, ecclesiology, and the sacraments are joined in an indissoluble unity.[36] But Bradwardine seems uninterested in these dimensions despite their prominence in traditional exegesis. This is particularly striking because he has chosen Luke's narrative for discussion, chosen it for a treatise on penance, a sacrament involving a contrite, confessing subject in dialogue with the Church's priest, whose office is to listen, to counsel, to absolve, and to determine appropriate practices of satisfaction. Furthermore, it is a sacrament in which the priest's actions and words signify the work of God (see Aquinas,

ST III.84.1, resp.), the God who initiates conversion and justification through a network of actions bequeathed by the divine mediator, Christ.

The difference between Bradwardine's exegesis and the examples I have provided from within his own tradition may seem slight, but it is significant of distinctive features in his theology. For his selection of sacred text and its exegesis are designed to show the irrelevance of *any* action by or in the human subject. From Bradwardine's perspective, the beauty and pertinence of Luke's story are that the figure who represents humanity is absent, as it were, at her own conversion. There is no question of conversion and penance involving processes and mediations, no questions about the community into which the converted person is to continue. Here we do not encounter the inn, the host at the inn, and the command that those at the inn must take care of the rescued person in a continuing process of healing (Luke 10.35; *Piers Plowman,* XIX.65–88).[37] This lack is at least partly due to Bradwardine's conviction that conversion is "immediate," that grace takes away sins "immediately," that grace "immediately" gives us habits antithetical to our ingrained habits of sin, and that all this "immediate" action of grace precedes any sign of contrition whatsoever (402).[38] Bradwardine stresses the absence of any kind of contrition before the subject's conversion through grace. He is confident that one cannot be both in grace and in sin (402). These are the terms within which he wrote about his conversion, as we saw earlier, one apparently without mediations or identifiable processes (I.35, 308). Similarly in the earlier work *De Praedestinatione et Praescientia* he had chosen Luke's account of Paul's conversion (Acts 9) to show how prevenient grace works (203). Bradwardine observes that Paul had been committed to evil when "suddenly" a light from heaven shined round about him. And falling on the ground, he heard a voice" (Acts 9.3–4). In fact Bradwardine only quotes "subito circumfulsit" (suddenly it shone round about) partly because, as was customary, he expects the reader to recall the continuation and partly because what is important to him is the word *subito* (suddenly). This works like *immediate* in the passage I have just been discussing from *De Causa Dei* (402). In Bradwardine's view, the person habitually and compulsively driven to evil action is suddenly, immediately, and decisively converted to glorify God in a new life of total obedience. He finds this displayed both by the conversion of sinful "human nature" in Luke 13 and by Paul's conversion in Acts 9. So Paul himself becomes the model of receiving grace.

Bradwardine had already reminded the readers of *De Praedestinatione et Praescientia* that to challenge the priority of grace is "heresis pelagiana," a heresy that Pelagius himself rejected (203, para. 19).[39]

But if this is Bradwardine's favored model for thinking about the sacrament of penance and justification of the unjust, how does he relate it to his own consideration of St. Peter's conversion in Luke 22.34–62? For here he draws on Augustine's reading, which I discussed in the first chapter of this book (I.43, 395–96).[40] There I showed how Augustine's treatment of agency in the encounter between the sinful human and God offers a subtle and nuanced model of divine and human agency. It is quite distinct from the Bradwardinian model I have been describing. Yet as he considers Peter's conversion, Bradwardine follows Augustine very closely. He notes that Peter's conversion stems from Jesus turning to look at his disciple. Christ's action takes place within Peter ("intus," "in mente," and "in voluntate"). Jesus touches Peter's heart, recollects his memory, and brings him to life with interior grace. This action moves Peter to external tears and the corresponding penitential dispositions (395–96). In this exegesis Augustine offers a way out of Bradwardine's model of conversion and penance, with its tendency to absent the sinner from her or his own conversion and with its propensity to dispense with the culture of mediations developed in the body of Christ, the Church. But the author of *De Causa Dei* decides not to follow the way suggested by Augustine, even though he has chosen to use Augustine's *De Gratia Christi*. It turns out that he is not interested in exploring what the passage displays about the forms of divine agency flowing from God incarnate, from the mediator who has created a community of disciples now fragmenting under violent attack and fear as the divine judge subjects himself to judgment. Nor is Bradwardine interested in taking up Augustine's suggestions about the complex responses of the human subject to the suffering mediator's gaze, responses that involve memory, reflection, and will. As I noted in Bradwardine's treatment of Luke 13.11–13, his dominant aim remains the illustration of his major thesis, the unicausality, the omnicausality, the sovereign and absolute freedom of God. He is not willing to let the potentials of Luke's narrative and Augustine's exegesis, with its complex approach to conversion, interrupt his preoccupations or qualify his own model of agency in conversion. He sees no reason to pursue the processes in which we are formed as habitual sinners who may be converted in ways more akin to those displayed in Augustine's *Confessions* than to those in Luke's version of Paul. Because Bradwardine sees no reason to rethink his model's occlusion of mediation and temporality, his invocation of Augustine generates no concern with the processes of individual transformation and community formation so central to Augustine.[41] This lack of concern is reinforced by his tenacious focus on the Pelagianism he finds pervading "modern" theology and by his primary commitment to eradicating it from the Church. In the treatise on penance in *De Causa Dei* this commitment takes the form of attacking anything that might seem to propose a significant role for human agency, human mediations, and "liberum arbitrium" in the justification of the unjust.

This is perfectly coherent with the book's grand design and its rejection of anything that might seem to sponsor illusions about our ability to earn eternal life "de congruo," through doing that which is within us.[42] While I have drawn attention to some major problems in Bradwardine's model of conversion, problems generated by his major preoccupations, he himself is untroubled by these. He does, however, acknowledge one serious difficulty in his approach. He sees that it could be construed as making the sacrament of penance, and possibly Roman Catholic teaching on purgatory, quite superfluous.[43] How does the future archbishop show that he is not undermining the theology of justification and discipline enshrined in the Church's decision to make annual confession mandatory?[44]

Bradwardine makes it clear that the role of the Church and her sacraments is very limited.[45] God never, in any sense, gives the Church the power of the keys to the kingdom. Nor does God give priests the power to cleanse souls within ("interius," 399). How, after all, can the dead give life to the dead? Once again divine power is immediate, free from mediations. Nor does God follow the fallible judgment of the Church, since God always judges according to truth (I.43, 404–5). So what is the role of the Church and the sacrament she has made mandatory? Bradwardine answers this basic question by citing the story of Lazarus (John 11). Indeed, he turns to this on three separate occasions in his chapter on penance (400, 415, 418–19). On the first occasion he is considering the restoration of the confessed sinner from the death of sin to life. No dead person, he observes, can raise himself to life. Who then raised him? ("Quis eum suscitavit?") The answer is the one who when the stone was taken away cried out, "Lazarus, come forth" (John 11.41, 43). Bradwardine asks what "come forth" means. His response is that he who confesses brings forth what was hidden. He could have cited the second penitential psalm, but does not (Ps. 31.3–5). Such confession, however, depends on the confessing subject being alive. And nobody can be alive without God's call to life. Certainly no free choice, no "liberum arbitrium," can give one life (400–401). In case his Pelagian enemies still resist his argument, he reminds his readers that nobody can justify himself (401).

Before the second appearance of Lazarus in this chapter (I.43), Bradwardine had been reiterating one of his basic themes: the causal priority and precedence of grace, of divine agency (408–14). Turning to the law and practice of penance in the Church, he says that the sacrament is a sign ("signum") that the penitent person is justified ("iustificatur"), her or his sins deleted. But Bradwardine insists that the person's sins have been taken away before confession and so before the priest's absolution—indeed, before any communication with the priest.[46] Confession is made to show penitence and not to obtain pardon ("non ad impetrationem veniae," 414). The Church taught that the sacramental signs of the Old Law were prophetic signs of Christ's work rather than ones that gave sanctifying grace but that the sacraments of the New Law, enacted in the Church, do bestow sanctifying grace (for example, see *ST* III.62). Bradwardine, however, likens the sacrament of penance to circumcision in the Old Law. The latter was given, he says, as a sign of justice rather than a cause of justification ("in signum iustitiae non in causam iustificationis," 414). Similarly, confession to a priest is a sign of pardon already received, not a cause of pardon ("sic confessio offertur sacerdoti in signum veniae acceptae, non in causam remissionis accipiendae," 414). Bradwardine maintains that neither contrition of heart nor confession of mouth in the sacrament takes away sins; only the grace of God does this (414). Nobody, as far as I know, simply denies the decisive role of God's grace in the forgiveness of sins. As St. Thomas recounted the Church's teaching, God alone has the authority to absolve from sin and to forgive sin, but priests do both as ministers because the priest's words in this sacrament work instrumentally through divine power. In this the sacrament of penance is like the other sacraments of the Church: divine power works inwardly in all her sacramental signs (III.84.3, ad 3).[47] So the issue, once again, is how God's grace works in the sacrament, how divine agency and human agencies (plural) work. Bradwardine's commitment here remains, once again, to emphasize the absolute priority of divine agency, which makes of the sacrament a sign of something already done (414). For the second time in the chapter on penance he turns to the story of Christ healing the ten lepers (415; see, too, 404). Luke relates how the lepers beg Jesus to have mercy on them. Jesus orders them to present themselves to the priests, as prescribed in Leviticus 14. Obeying Jesus, the lepers are healed (Luke 17.11–14). Bradwardine characteristically ignores the fact that in Luke's gospel the outcasts call out to Jesus, begging him for help. That is, he ignores the differences between this narrative and the one of the woman who, bent to the ground, did not approach Jesus. Having ignored this difference, Bradwardine concentrates on the way the priests do not heal the lepers but are merely witnesses to a divine healing that has already taken place (415, citing Lev. 14). Christ first heals, "per se," and then sends the lepers to the priests. Their role is to witness the lepers' cleanness. This exactly figures forth the role of the Church's priests in the sacrament of penance (415). As Oberman says: "That which has happened effectively, happens in the Church figuratively."[48] For Bradwardine, this story of the lepers recapitulates the story of Lazarus. After Jesus had raised Lazarus from the tomb he ordered his disciples to loose the cloth that still bound Lazarus's hands and feet (John 11.44). Bradwardine comments that although someone has been freed ("solutus") by God he has yet to be freed ("solutus") in the Church through the priest's judgment. He again insists that the Church's priests function just as did the priests of the Old Law administering the sacraments of the Old Law. This, he declares, is what the Church means by forgiving or retaining sins: judging or showing what God has done (415). In no way is the sacrament actually a divine gift that is a source of grace, a cause of forgiveness and conversion (415). Bradwardine's theology seems to be driven by a scheme that imposes a rather static either/or as it addresses questions about agency in the encounters between God and man in Scripture and the Church. His determination to negate all significant human mediation, including agency embodied in the community of the faithful, the body of Christ, is a profound break with the Augustinian theology he thinks he is defending.

Turning to Lazarus for a third time in the treatise on penance, Bradwardine does so in the context of reiterating his insistence that the grace of justification precedes all stages of the sacrament of penance, while still trying to square his own commitments with the current doctrine and discipline of the Church (I.43, 418–19). Once more he says that his theology of the sacrament is well figured in the narrative of John 11.38–44. Lazarus was dead and buried. The Lord, "per se," first raised up the dead man and then ordered his disciples to unbind him. According to Bradwardine, this clearly demonstrates that those who are dead through sin and brought to life through Christ's grace must nevertheless proceed to oral confession and absolution in the face of the Church ("absolui a vinculo quo apud Ecclesiam tenebatur," 418). This restores them to freedom in the Church Militant (418). We seem to be back in Leviticus 14, but here Bradwardine quotes from part of Augustine's sermons on John 11 (418–19). Augustine had read Lazarus coming forth from the grave in obedience to Christ's call as a figure of confession elicited by the abounding grace of God. He had also taken the command to the disciples ("Loose him, and let him go") as a figuration of the power of the keys bestowed by Christ on his Church (Matt. 16.19). Characteristically, though, Augustine's exegetical sermon includes a densely textured response to the multiplicity of figures, events, and images in the narrative. We are shown the gradual development of addiction to sinful acts; the relation between the Old Law and the New Testament, law and grace, letter and spirit; and the processes whereby faith emerges, groaning, in the sinful subject, a groaning that turns out to be Christ within the subject. What emerges here is a subtle representation of divine agency working "in thy heart" without competition between agencies or a simple either/or.[49] But what Bradwardine wants from Augustine's plenitudinous exegesis and meditation is simply the confirmation that when someone confesses, God has effected this (418). The complexities of agency, mediations, and processes in such an event are not his concern.

He maintains that his approach is not hollowing out the power of the keys given to the Church by Christ (Matt. 16.18–19; I.43, 418–19). The Church's role is to exercise the keys in the forum of the Church Militant. She may also deploy her immense treasury by granting indulgences to mitigate external penance now and in the future, perhaps ("fortassis . . . forsitan," 419).[50] In what seems one of his strongest affirmations of current penitential practices in the Church, he asserts that unless the Christian fulfills the ecclesiastic discipline of oral confession to a priest he puts himself in great danger. Bradwardine again grants that the infusion of grace will already have deleted the Christian's sins before confession; absolution will already have been given without any mediations from the Church. Even so, if the forgiven sinner does not follow the due processes of confession and absolution in the Church, the divinely forgiven sins will return and once again be imputed ("noviter imputantur"). Furthermore, their consequences will be made worse through this contempt for the keys of the Church (419). On the other hand, if the penitent fulfills ecclesiastic discipline, the sacrament of penance will increase the grace already given (419). This suggests that current arrangements in the Church do have divine support, punishing withdrawal of already given grace for those who reject its laws and rewarding increase of already given grace for those who participate dutifully in the sacrament.[51]

But the very terms of this affirmation of the Church's sacrament are symptomatic of a striking transformation and diminishment. We read about reward for following the discipline, punishment for resisting it. But what seems to have been lost here is the traditional understanding that the sacraments are divine gifts for healing us, for cherishing us: gifts for our individual and collective flourishing. Let me return, once again, to St. Thomas. He addresses the question as to whether the sacrament of penance is necessary for salvation (*ST* III.84.5). The necessity he affirms is the necessity for sinners to have sin removed from them if they are to share in friendship with God. Aquinas likens the sacrament to a medicine that heals someone from a dangerous disease. It is a healing medicine because Christ's passion works both in the priest's absolution and simultaneously in the acts of the penitent, who is enabled to cooperate with grace in this healing. Aquinas remarks that, as Augustine said, he who created you without you will not justify you without you.[52] So it is clear, he says, that the sacrament of penance is necessary for salvation after sin, "just as bodily medicine is needed should a man have fallen seriously ill" (III.84.5, resp.). Divine and human agency are characteristically understood to be in no kind of competition while all flows from and draws us toward Christ. In the next question, considering the relations between penance and justice, he argues that while penance is a species of justice it also comprises faith in Christ's passion, hope for forgiveness, and charity: that is, healing virtues that draw a person toward God (III.85.3, ad 4). Above all, in the sacrament, through the sacrament, the sinner's will is transformed. Sin is a turning of the will away from God to lesser, transient goods. In the sacrament the will is converted to God, rejecting past choices that separated the sinner from God (III.86.2, resp.). Such is the healing power of and in the sacrament, such the dialectic of divine and human agency in it.

Reflection on St. Thomas's theology of the sacraments can help us grasp the implications of Bradwardine's treatise on penance. Merely declarative of a prior and totally extrinsic divine art, it no longer belongs to a complex, thoroughly mediated process in which the will is healed while also being present, as an agent, in this process of healing. Recollection of St. Thomas's approach also helps us see how Bradwardine has abandoned Christology in his theory of the sacraments. Given the lack of sustained Christological theology in his work, this is no surprise. But it is, nevertheless, a crucial determinant in his thinking about his Church's sacraments and constitutes a major rupture with the very tradition he thought he was defending against benighted "modern" theologians.[53] These choices, these unselfconscious ruptures with tradition and the centrality of Christology, help to explain an absence that is quite extraordinary in the contexts of devotion in the late medieval Church: the absence of the Eucharist for which the sacrament of penance is a preparation.[54] Irony of ironies, Bradwardine's attack on "modern" theology thus reproduces some key features of that demonic Pelagian modernity: a systematically extrinsic account of grace and an astonishing, systematic sidelining of Christology. Once again I am reminded of Blake, this time of a passage from *The Four Zoas* where the prophet Los tries to restrain Urizen, "the dark Demon," binding him, but with wretched and unintended results: "terrified at the Shapes / Enslaved humanity put on he became what he beheld."[55]

Because Geoffrey Chaucer famously cited Bradwardine in relation to a rather gamesome performance around God's foreknowledge, "necessitee," and "free choys," it is probably necessary to mention Bradwardine's doctrine of predestination here.[56] This does not have the centrality or space in *De Causa Dei* that Chaucer's narrator in *The Canterbury Tales* may have assumed. But it may have played a contributory role in the features I have been discussing. Bradwardine focuses four chapters on predestination (bk. I, chs. 44–47, 420–41). These take up far less space than his treatise on penance or his attack on the theology of merit "de congruo." The most recent and informative study of theories of predestination in the fourteenth century is by James L. Halverson.[57] He offers an extremely important study of Peter Aureol and shows how the theology of predestination fragmented from a thirteenth-century "consensus" into a number of interpretive options to become a sharply debated topic in the fourteenth century. Halverson maintains that Bradwardine's teaching on predestination is traditional, following St. Thomas and rejecting a number of options emerging in the fourteenth century, including the double predestination later articulated by Gregory of Rimini.[58] It is certainly true that Bradwardine observes that traditionally the language of predestination was used only concerning the redeemed (I.45, 421). He also observes that saints and doctors frequently say that God predestined and prepared fire and punishment for reprobates but that he did not predestine sins. Nor, he agrees, did God compel people to sin (422). Yet reprobation is also called predestination of evil ("praedestinatio vero malorum," 421). And he is fixated on Paul's account of God's love of Jacob and hatred of Esau when the children were not yet born (Rom. 9.9–14). This he takes to demonstrate how God elects and reprobates (424). Halverson claims that Bradwardine's doctrine is best construed as belonging to the dominant pre-fourteenth-century teaching that predestination refers to "God's elective purpose to save some individuals" while "reprobation refers to the lack of elective purpose to save others."[59] But it may also be possible to construe Bradwardine as implying a stronger sense of double predestination, one in which God wills certain individuals to damnation ("praedestinatio vero malorum"), and Halverson is probably right when he concludes that "it is impossible to determine Bradwardine's understanding of election" because of unresolved ambiguities in his uses of *nolle, non velle,* and *velle non*.[60] In my view, this lack of clarity is bound up with the approach to divine agency and human agency that I have discussed in this chapter. In Bradwardine's opinion the theologian's resources must be devoted to asserting the absolute sovereignty of God together with its absolute and simple causal priority in relation to the creatures. The nuances of a dialectic between God and the creatures God has created with a potential to love and know God, a potential also to rebel against God and the gifts of grace, do not engage Bradwardine. His polemic against Pelagianism continually sets up one side of a rigid dichotomy. As we have seen, he constantly attacks Pelagian strategies for imagining humans as autonomous, free agents, capable of loving God and neighbor even in their fallen state without divine grace. But in doing so he sets up an utterly passive "liberum arbitrium." A strange model of conversion is entailed in which the person seems absent at her or his own conversion. God's causality, God's agency, seems to be envisaged as divine unicausality in competition with a human agency that must be abolished if divine sovereignty is to be affirmed. What Bradwardine will not imagine is that the Trinity is the source, preserver, and savior of human agency, even in the time of trouble that is history, the time of Christ's reconciling and redemptive work.

CHAPTER 4

Remembering the Samaritan, Remembering Semyuief

Salvation and Sin in Piers Plowman *(the C Version)*

Jesus answered them, "Very truly, I tell you, everyone
who commits sin is a slave to sin. . . . If the Son makes
you free, you will be free indeed."

John 8.34, 36

It is always a mistake to try to establish or understand
the assertion of the bondage of the will otherwise than
christologically.

Karl Barth, *Church Dogmatics,* IV/2, 494

I NOW TURN TO WILLIAM LANGLAND, SOMEONE WHOSE THEOLOGICAL
investigations are pursued in English and in poetry during the second half
of the fourteenth century. His great and lifelong work, *Piers Plowman,*
participates in critical and illuminating conversation with many strands
of its culture, but in this chapter I will address only some aspects of his
explorations of salvation, sin, and agency.[1] These are explicit and major

concerns of the poem. But they are unfolded in a complex work whose processes are thoroughly dialectical. So our reading must recognize how the poem's own processes are intrinsic to the poem's theology. Many positions receive powerful advocacy but are later, often much later, subjected to further interrogation and superseded. Supersession is not, however, the same as forgetting.[2] Furthermore, positions ascribed to Christ or the Holy Spirit have a kind of authority lacking from other figures, although these may be able to foreshadow or articulate what is fulfilled by and in Christ. In a single chapter I cannot offer anything remotely like a full reading of Langland's dense and endlessly wondrous treatment of salvation and sin. Instead I will address a few especially rich and decisive episodes, while seeking to recollect their place in the total process that constitutes *Piers Plowman* in the final version of it left to us.

I

However, before engaging directly with *Piers Plowman* I will sketch the interpretation of sin, grace, and agency in current studies of Langland's theology. The dominant model has emerged out of a debate over whether *Piers Plowman* is "Augustinian" or "semi-Pelagian" and links Langland with the "modern" theology that Bradwardine sought to defeat (see chapters 2 and 3 above). Proponents of the "Augustinian" commitments of *Piers Plowman* tended to have a version of Augustine that was restricted to his emphasis on the ravages of sin and the necessity of grace "to enable man to do good."[3] No attempt was made by these scholars to explore the rich theological contexts to which Augustine's account of sin belonged: its Christology, its Trinitarianism, its ecclesiology. This absence was mirrored in the version of Augustine propagated by those who opposed "Augustinian" readings of Langland's work. The views of the latter have become hegemonic in the field addressed in this chapter, and I shall briefly describe their directions.

In 1983 Robert Adams wrote a substantial essay that was to prove decisive in the debate about whether *Piers Plowman* is an "Augustinian" or "semi-Pelagian" work. This essay maintained that "from one end of *Piers Plowman* to the other" Langland's theology was "semi-Pelagian."[4] Adams found that Langland "strongly repudiates key elements of the authentic Augustinian position," namely "an implicit denial of human responsibility" and an "insistence on mankind's total depravity" (370, 379). In its place Langland emphasizes "the role of free will so far as to overshadow any theoretical statements [a theologian] may make about a need for divine consensus in human decisions" (371). Furthermore Adams, like Janet Coleman, affirmed that Langland "believed firmly" in the "semi-Pelagian" commonplace that if humans do that which is in them they are "guaranteed" divine welcome to eternal life: "facientibus quod in se est Deus non denegat gratiam" [to one who does that which is in him God does not deny grace].[5] This affirmation has become part of the hegemonic "semi-Pelagian" outcome to the debate, and it is reiterated as an unproblematic, lucid theological position to which Langland assented.[6] The dominance of this paradigm encourages literary historians to ascribe to Langland the belief that "the will is responsible for inaugurating salvation" and that "the epistemological center of the poem's theology" shows "the non-sacred beginnings that constitute *Piers Plowman*'s theology of redemption." Within its terms it seems common sense to maintain that a fallen human being can "justify" himself before God, can "through his own initiative reinstate himself in his lord's favours" in a "negotiated atonement" with God.[7]

In this model sin is not seen as habitual opposition to God, as rebellion against divine love for humans, as practices that are overwhelmingly dangerous to others and to self. It is not seen as a force that breaks the bonds of charity and destroys communities. Indeed, it seems not to be of great consequence. But I will show that Langland himself did not subscribe to such a model. On the contrary, his work participates in the one expressed by St. Thomas Aquinas commenting on the letter to the Ephesians. There he tells us that sin is called death because through it humankind is separated from God who is life: "Peccatum enim mors dicitur, quia per ipsum homo a Domino, qui est vita, separatur."[8] Such separation is so catastrophic for humans that its overcoming involved the incarnation of God and the Crucifixion. One might recollect Christ's statement that he gave his life "a ransom [redemptionem] for many" (Mark 10.45). And this brings us to the unconfessed heart of Pelagianism or "semi-Pelagianism": its lack of attention to Christology and the consequences of sin.[9]

One of the central tasks of this chapter will be to challenge the relevance of such a marginalization of Christology in Langland's own exploration of salvation and sin. But I think that it is helpful, given the conspicuous absence of critical engagement with this central issue, to recall an Augustine habitually excluded from consideration by literary historians. This is the Augustine who saw Pelagianism as sidelining Christological and Trinitarian theology in a move that threatened to hollow out Christian faith, collapsing it into a kind of stoicism and a return to a pagan understanding of virtue. Michael Hanby's commentary in *Augustine and Modernity* points us in exactly the right direction:

> To see what the Pelagian controversy is about we must consider *why* Augustine thought Pelagianism should be deemed heretical. Augustine's characteristic rebuttals to the Pelagian position as he sees it support the position argued here: that the Pelagians rupture the unity and mediation of Christ and sacrifice the immutability and transcendence of the Trinity. The first of Augustine's standard responses is Christological. Nature, construed in Pelagian terms, "renders the cross of Christ void." This response takes on added ontological weight when refracted through a second that invokes the gratuity of the Trinitarian economy, "that grace which begins with us is not grace." Together the remarks echo the *De Trinitate*'s understandings of Christ as the visible manifestation of triune love.[10]

I believe that both these responses are thoroughly pertinent to Langland's theology. But here I will briefly follow what Hanby calls the first of Augustine's responses, the Christological, while acknowledging its inseparability from the second, Trinitarian response. Hanby's quotation in this passage is from St. Paul's letter to the Galatians: "I live in the faith of the Son of God, who loved me, and delivered himself for me. I cast not away the grace of God. For if justice be by the law, then Christ died in vain" (2.20–21). But Hanby's quotation is also a quotation from a work Augustine wrote in 415 against the *De Natura* of Pelagius, a work entitled *De Natura et Gratia* (On Nature and Grace). In his *Retractions* (427), Augustine observes that he wrote this book to "defend grace, not as opposed to nature, but as that through which nature is liberated and controlled."[11] In *Nature and Grace* he argued that "if righteousness comes

about through nature, then Christ died in vain," but that if Christ did
not die in vain, as Christians believe, then humanity is justified and redeemed by "the mystery of Christ's blood." In consequence, "We ought
to be afire with a much more ardent zeal that the cross of Christ not be
done away with. But it is done away with, if one says that it is possible
to attain righteousness and eternal life in some other way than by the
sacrament of Christ."[12] To maintain that "without the cross of Christ
a person can become righteous by the natural law and the choice of
the will" is "to do away with the cross of Christ" (see 1 Cor. 1.17) and
to imply that "Christ has died in vain" (Gal. 2.21). The theology here is
congruent with these trenchant reflections in the *City of God* on the situation of humanity, made "in the image of God," made for closeness
to God:

> And yet the mind of man, the natural seat of his reason and under-
> standing, is itself weakened by long-standing faults which darken it.
> It is too weak to cleave to that changeless light and to enjoy it; it is
> too weak even to endure the light. It must first be renewed and healed
> day after day so as to become capable of such felicity. And so the
> mind had to be trained and purified by faith; and in order to give
> man's mind greater confidence in its journey towards the truth along
> the way of faith, God the Son of God, who is himself the Truth,
> took manhood without abandoning godhead, and thus established
> and founded this faith, so that man might have a path to man's God
> through the man who was God. For this is "the mediator between
> God and man, the man Christ Jesus" [1 Tim. 2.5]. As man he is our
> Mediator; as man he is our way. For there is hope to attain a journey's
> end when there is a path which stretches between the traveler and his
> goal. But if there is no path, or if a man does not know which way to
> go, there is little use in knowing the destination. As it is, there is one
> road, and one only, well served against all possibility of going astray;
> and this road is provided by one who is himself both God and man.
> As God, he is the goal; as man he is the way. (XI.2)[13]

If the *City of God* (413–27) was written against "the pagans," it was also
written to correct pelagianizing Christians. Central in this project was the
Christology represented in this quotation, a Christology conspicuously

lacking from Pelagianism or "semi-Pelagianism" but not, I will be show-ing, from Langland's theology in *Piers Plowman*.

II

I will now consider aspects of Langland's own explorations of salvation, sin, and agency. These explorations are shaped by two concerns that are, as I have just pointed out, conspicuously lacking in the recent scholar-ship on Langland's theology: first, Christology, and second, a profound engagement with the consequences of sin, both individually and collec-tively. These concerns are displayed with exquisite beauty in an episode that has been strangely sidelined by those disputing Langland's theology of grace.[14]

The episode is Langland's refiguration of Jesus's parable of the good Samaritan (Luke 10.25–37). The sequence to which this belongs unfolds from Wille's yearning question to Liberum Arbitrium: "'Charite,' quod y tho, 'þat is a thyng forsothe / That maistres commenden moche. Where may hit be yfounde?'" (XVI.286–87).[15] The responses to this question, absolutely central to the fulfillment of the human being, have involved a critique of the contemporary Church, a forceful account of the need for a nonviolent Christian mission, a vision of salvation history, the life of Christ, instruction from Abraham, or Faith, on the Trinity, and instruc-tion from Moses, or Hope, on the divine command of love (XVI–XIX). Wille declares that however puzzling Christian teaching of the Trinity may be, it is easier to accept than the precepts of love conveyed by Moses (XIX.27–47). This is as dangerous an argument for Wille to support as it is understandable. Charity is the love of God and has as its object the final good of human life, eternal happiness, humans becoming "a god by þe gospel" (I.86). But there is a paradox here. Our "kynde," our God-given nature, naturally yearns for a supernatural end beyond its own powers, one that can be attained only by transforming virtues and gifts flowing from Christ and the Holy Spirit. So to achieve their natural, "kynde" end, humans need divine help.[16] Wille's judgment here both reveals his needi-ness and also his dangerous propensity to turn away from his due end even in dialogue with Faith and Hope. At this moment of hope and dan-ger, the disputants see the Samaritan riding a mule with great urgency to joust in Jerusalem.[17] In a wilderness they find a man who has been bound by thieves and left in desolation, utterly helpless, half alive, Semyuief ("semivivo relicto," Luke 10.30). Langland's rendering of Christ's parable emphasizes that this wounded, bound person "ne myhte stepe ne stande ne stere foet ne handes / Ne helpe hymsulue sothly" (XIX.56–57). This figure haunts *Piers Plowman*. Half-alive, half-dead, utterly dependent, Semyuief condenses many moments, moods, and figures in the poem. He is also the kind of haunting presence that many scholars fail to notice. Langland's treatment of salvation, sin, and agency, however, does not encourage us to forget or sideline this figure.

Significantly enough, even Faith and Hope are horrified by the condition of Semyuief. What relation can he have to Holy Church's vision of *deus caritas* (1 John 4.8) and the creature who can become "a god by þe gospel" (I.81–87)? The theological virtues embodied in Abraham and Moses can do nothing. In fear they retreat (XIX.59–64). Wille too can do absolutely nothing.[18] Only Christ the Samaritan, the consummation, source, and end of all virtues, can help Semyuief. He studies the latter's wounds and sees that the man is in danger of death, in need of urgent remedies. So the Samaritan washes Semyuief's wounds with wine and oil, puts balm on him, bandages his head, sets him on the Samaritan's own mule, and leads him to a farmhouse called *lauacrum lex dei* (the bath of the law of God). This is six or seven miles from "þe newe marcat." There he lodges Semyuief. He gives two pennies to the innkeeper for looking after the rescued man, promising that whatever more is needed for medicine he will bring when he returns. With this promise he mounts his mule and hurries off, riding "the rihte way to Ierusalem" (XIX.65–79).

All this is written, to use St. Paul's vocabulary, "by an allegory" [per allegoriam] (Gal. 4.24).[19] In 1951 D. W. Robertson and B. F. Huppé illustrated conventional medieval interpretations of the allegory. The narrative's actions were "explained by Bede," while the "various symbolic meanings of the parable of the Samaritan are well summarized in the *Allegoriae in novum Testamentum*." This commentary "makes clear the general meaning of the parable as it is used in the poem," namely, "the image of God is restored through the charity of Christ."[20] The gloss of Robertson and Huppé is useful, but they were strangely uninterested in either the details of the medieval exegesis or Langland's own allegory. Unlike medieval exegetes, they characteristically have nothing to say about the sacraments and the Church. Some years later Ben Smith enriched their account by using more commentaries, going beyond the twelfth century and tabulating the details of medieval interpretations to show "the dominant emphases." He also paid more attention to "Langland's adaptation of the parable."[21] He noticed how the exegetical tradition stresses that "faith and works alone are insufficient for salvation" since this depends on "the free gift of God's grace brought to man in the person of Christ, typified in the Good Samaritan" (88; see 82–89). This is an important observation in a helpful study. But the role of traditional exegesis is so central in Langland's allegory of the Samaritan and Semyuief that I will recall it here, drawing on some texts that Smith did not use and offering a commentary that reflects the rather different concerns of the present study. Such recollection helps us remember an observation made by Karl Barth: "The atonement is history. To know it, we must know it as such. To think of it, we must think of it as such. To speak of it, we must tell it as history. To try to grasp it as supra-historical or non-historical truth is not to grasp it at all. It is indeed truth, but truth actualized in a history and revealed in this history as such—revealed, therefore, as history" (*CD* IV/1, 157). Of course, as Barth makes clear, this is a very peculiar history, a strange narrative. It is one for which traditional allegory, as Langland so profoundly grasped, can be a most appropriate form.

In his *Catena Aurea* St. Thomas Aquinas glosses the half-dead man ("semivivus") as free will, wounded and unable to return to eternal life. Such a wounded will cannot even rise to seek a physician, "that is, God, to heal him." So God comes to Semyuief, as the Samaritan: "far removed by birth, very near in compassion." Allegorically the Samaritan is both Jesus Christ and, as most exegetes also observed, "keeper" [custos], the keeper of the weak. He comes as the essential mediator and reconciler, bringing oil and wine for the endangered man: respectively pardon given for the reconciliation of mankind and "the incitement to work fervently in spirit," or "the anointing of the chrism" and "sanctification" through the blood of Christ's passion. As for the inn ("stabulum") to which the Samaritan takes Semyuief, this is, as all exegetes agreed, "the Church which receives travelers, who are tired with their journey through the world, and oppressed with the load of their sins; where the wearied traveler casting down the burden of his sins is relieved, and after being refreshed is restored with wholesome food." As for the two pence, their meanings include "the two covenants, which bear stamped on them the image of the eternal King, by the price of which our wounds are healed."[22] This model for thinking about salvation and sin is profoundly Christological, with a strong sense that the consequence of sin undermines the natural, God-given powers of the soul and their due fulfillment, paradoxically, once more, through the gifts of grace.

Nicholas of Gorran, a thirteenth-century Dominican, offers a commentary that in many ways follows the traditional patterns identified by Ben Smith and encapsulated in St. Thomas's *Catena Aurea*. The wounded man is stripped of immortal grace, wounded in all the powers of his soul, and thoroughly enfeebled by the robbers. The Samaritan is Christ, while his merciful actions represent the Passion and Christ's merciful mediation of grace through the Church. The wine, for example, can be understood as the sacrament of the altar, the two pence given to the innkeeper ("stabulario") can be understood as the gift to the Church's prelates enabling them to open out the senses of Scripture. But the robbers are still active, and the Church itself has become a cave of robbers.[23] The immensely popular fourteenth-century commentary on the Bible by Nicholas of Lyra reads the parable as an allegory showing how a sinner is despoiled of grace by demons and wounded in his natural powers. The priest and the Levite are read as bad ministers in the Church ("Ecclesiae mali ministri") who care more for raising money than healing souls. The Samaritan is not only Christ but the preacher and confessor moved by charity to bind up spiritual wounds through wise counsel and to pour in the oil of mercy with the wine of justice. The preacher or confessor puts the wounded person (here a baptized Christian) onto his own beast, meaning that he helps the afflicted not only in mind but also in body ("non solum mente praebet auxilium, sed etiam prout potest corpore"). He leads the despoiled man into the inn, which is the Church, where he is given the good of God's word and the sacrament of the Eucharist ("ubi datur pabulum verbi Dei, & sacramenti Eucharistiae").[24] Like so many others, Nicholas of Lyra is quite clear that the half-dead man represents not only Adam or nonbaptized people but any Christian fallen into sin. The fifteenth-century theologian Denis the Carthusian emphasizes that the figure applies to postbaptismal sin as well as to original sin. For having been reclothed at baptism, we lose these gifts through sin, becoming like Semyuief.[25] In both cases the robbers wound us and strip us, leaving us "as naked as an nedle and noen helpe abouten" (XIX.58).[26] And in both cases the wounded person depends entirely on Christ's incarnation and crucifixion, on his self-emptying journey into this far country, this wilderness where evil powers abound. We should now be clear about an important fact: in choosing this parable with its exegetical traditions, Langland was choosing a story that addressed human catastrophe that pertained to baptized Christians as well as to pre-Christians.[27]

Before returning to Langland's own deployment of these traditions, I will briefly remedy a surprising gap in the discussion of the exegesis Langland inherited. The gap is Augustine's influential treatments of the parable.[28] I do so for two reasons. First, I think it might correct some rather inadequate characterizations of Augustine circulating in disputes between "semi-Pelagian" and "Augustinian" readings of *Piers Plowman* (chapter 1 is also relevant here). Second, Augustine's comments have some illuminating affinities with Langland's setting of the parable. This does not mean, of course, that the poet is "Augustinian," a form of classification that is never going to be unequivocal, given the astonishing scope, fluidity, and quantity of Augustine's writing across a lifetime.

The parable of the good Samaritan often emerges in Augustine's sermons and in his homilies on the Psalms.[29] Here I shall take just two examples, Sermon 131 (preached in 417) and Sermon 156 (preached in 419).[30] Sermon 131 sets out from a New Testament text frequently invoked by Augustine: "No man can come to me, unless it be given him by my Father" (John 6.66). Commenting on Jesus's statement, Augustine observes that faith is a gift. We are drawn to faith through desire, itself a gift. Those who are ungrateful for such a divine gift attribute too much to our wounded nature. Augustine agrees with his Pelagian opponents that prelapsarian people had great powers of free decision making ("magnas arbitrii liberi vires"). But sinning lost these. Here he turns to *semivivus,* the half-dead/half-alive man in the parable. This figuration, in Augustine's exegesis, concerns the Christian present, the baptized Christian. The wounded man is "still being taken along to the inn," he is "still being cured" and has nothing to boast about. Augustine then imagines an objector rather like Wille in Passus XII.59–69. Augustine's objector too protests that baptism has solved the basic problem for Christians: it has decisively remitted their sins. The preacher's response is that while baptism has eliminated inherited iniquity it leaves us infirm, leaves us as fragile, vulnerable creatures. The Samaritan pouring oil and wine into the wounds of Semyuief symbolizes genuine pardon. But such pardon, as Langland's Samaritan makes plain (XIX.86–95), does not eliminate our feeble infirmity. That must be gradually healed in the inn that is the Church, although this process can be securely completed only in our home, the kingdom of heaven.[31] Meanwhile Augustine tells his congregation to accept the cure offered at the inn. But he warns them not to boast of health, for such boasting is a symptom of sickness, the sickness of pride.[32] The argument and exhortation heard by the congregation here matches one in *De Trinitate,* XIV. Considering the reformation of the image of God in fallen humanity, Augustine observes that "this removal does not happen in one moment of conversion, as the baptismal renewal by the forgiveness of all sins happens in a moment." His analogy, as in Sermon 131, is with sickness and healing: "It is one thing to throw off a fever, another to recover from the weakness which the fever leaves behind it; it is one thing to remove from the body a missile stuck in it, another to heal the wound it made with a complete cure. The first stage of the cure is to remove the cause of the debility, and this is done by pardoning all sins; the second stage is curing the debility itself, and this is done gradually by making steady progress in the renewal of the image."[33] Langland writes the parable of the Samaritan and Semyuief to figure forth processes through which the consequences of sin are recognized, forgiven, and gradually healed in that strange history that is the Atonement.

In Sermon 156 Augustine praises the Creator who graciously created human nature without a flaw, giving freedom to his creatures (156.2). But he invites his congregation to recognize the flaws we ourselves have inflicted on this gift. Such recognition will lead to an acknowledgment of our neediness, our need for a savior. "Human nature was capable by free will of wounding itself; but once wounded and sickly, it is not capable by free will of healing itself" [Idonea fuit humana natura per liberum arbitrium vulnerare se: sed iam vulnerata et saucia, non est idonea per liberum arbitrium sanare se].[34] God has sent a doctor, a savior, to cure humans without cost to them. We recollect that neither Semyuief nor anyone but the Samaritan paid the costs of healing. Having cured freely ("gratis"), this doctor astonishingly gives a wage or reward ("mercedem daret") to the person he has cured. Such is God's generosity that he has said:

"Let me cure you and I will give you a reward [mercedem]." We should note how Augustine's theology includes a discourse of payment or reward ("merces" or "praemium") for man; we should never assume that when we encounter such language in Christian tradition we are necessarily encountering "semi-Pelagianism."[35] The savior is the help of the sick, and the reward ("praemium") he gives to those he has cured is to make God himself their inheritance (157.17). Augustine invites his Christian congregation to see themselves as *semivivus,* the man helplessly "lying there, half dead," desperately in need of the "one mediator of God and men, the man Christ Jesus" (Luke 10.30 and 1 Tim. 2.5). In him "God has somehow stretched out his arm to you as a mediator" (156.5). He has also left us medicine: "Grace is a medicine." But we certainly have freedom to be "ungrateful," to reject it. So it seems that grace is *not* irresistible.[36] Contrary to those Langland scholars whose version of Augustine entails denying any place for good works in the process of salvation, Augustine himself continually calls his congregation to practice good works. That is, good works are an inextricable part of a specifically Christian account of salvation, the fruit of charity. As he said in a sermon on the first epistle of St. John: "For many say, 'I believe'; but faith without works saveth not. Now the work of faith is Love." Remember, he says, quoting the epistle of St. James, "the devils also believe" (James 2.19).[37] Augustine asks a question whose force is consistently disclosed in many contexts of *Piers Plowman*: Can we generate such love, charity, from our own resources (156.5)? We have just seen Langland's Wille dismissing the precepts of love carried by Moses/Hope as absurdly unrealistic (XIX.34–47), a judgment that, as I noted, is perfectly intelligible in the face of his and others' experience in the poem. This response actually displays a serious grasp of the demands placed upon Christian disciples by the law of love. Augustine answers his own question about our resources by pondering St. Paul's statement in Romans 5.5: "The charity of God is poured forth in our hearts, by the Holy Ghost who is given to us." Charity, he says, is entirely the gift of God, so much so "that it is even called God, as the apostle John says: *Charity is God,* and whoever remains in charity remains in God and God in him" (156.5; 1 John 4.16; cf. *Piers Plowman* I.79–87). It is Stoics and Epicureans who set "all their hopes of happiness on their souls, by placing their supposed good in their own virtue." But against such delusion Augustine sets the figure of *semivivus:*

"Unless he [Christ the Samaritan] pick you up, you lie there." Neither Stoic nor Epicurean models of human autonomy are adequate to the situation of *semivivus* and those he figures, including, of course, those baptized Christians in Augustine's congregations. Once more Augustine considers objections that his own model of self and grace has passivized the will, meaning that "we are led, acted on, we don't act." Augustine's response is delicate and in one way or another pervades my own reflections on salvation, sin, and agency in *Piers Plowman*:

> Rather, you both act and are acted on; and it is precisely then that you act well, when you are acted on by one who is good. The Spirit of God, you see, who is leading you or acting on you, is your helper in your own action. He gave you this very "helper," because you too have to do something. You must realize what you are admitting, when you say, *Be my helper, do not forsake me* (Ps 27.9 [26.9]). You are of course calling God as your helper. None are helped if they don't do anything themselves. (156.11)

As we found in Augustine's model of conversion (chapter 1), there is neither negation here of all human agency nor a passivization that hollows out human responsibility and will, any more than there is assertion of an independent human autonomy in the making of what Christians understand as a good life, doing well. That which leads us, Augustine continues, is not "the law commanding, threatening, promising," but rather "the Spirit urging, enlightening, helping." He quotes Romans 8.28: "We know that to them that love God all things work together unto good." And he comments: "If you weren't working he wouldn't be working together with you" (156.11). What we encounter here, as so often in Augustine's sermons, is a model of double agency flowing from the gifts of God.[38]

Augustine himself gives the objector in Sermon 156 another chance to criticize his account of agency. The objector says he is prepared to concede that "God's co-operation and God's help" make things easier. He offers the model of wind helping those rowing a boat on a journey that could be completed without such help (156.12). Augustine addresses this line of thought, one to which Langland's Franciscan friars in Passus X are very sympathetic, as we shall see: "That's not what God's help is like, that's not what Christ's help is like, that's not what the help of the Holy Spirit is like. If it's completely lacking, you won't be able to do anything good whatsoever. You can indeed act by your free will without him helping; but only badly. That's what your will, which is called free, is fit for; and by acting badly it becomes a slave" (156.12). That gifts of freedom have been bestowed on us is, for Augustine, beyond question. But we can use these to develop habits that enchain ourselves into the figure of Semyuief. This is the process of habit Augustine described with such force and depth in the *Confessions* (especially in book VIII). It is a process perfectly familiar to the author of *Piers Plowman,* who tracks Wille's abandonment of the virtues in a despair that leads him "into þe land of longynge" (XI.167), compulsively pursuing and consuming objects and people in absolute isolation from any Christian teleology that he wills or thinks (XI.164–95). Such enslavement is condensed into the figure of Semyuief whom Wille encounters later. Augustine reminds his congregation that "without God's help you have free will to act badly; although it isn't in fact free" but rather driven, compelled, cut off from the divine vision, enslaved (156.12). Showing how these teachings emerge from the New Testament, Augustine quotes from John's gospel: "Jesus answered them: . . . whosoever committeth sin, is the servant of sin." As for freedom, Jesus says: "If therefore the son shall make you free, you shall be free indeed." Augustine again emphasizes double agency in the mysterious processes of salvation: "he isn't working together with you, if you aren't doing any work yourself. Understand, however, that you do good things in such a way that the Spirit is your director and helper" (156.13). Returning to the objector who suggested that we should see ourselves as competent rowers in a boat, perfectly able to reach our destination with our own powers but able to reach it more easily with a helping breeze, Augustine tells us what Jesus did *not* say.[39] He did *not* say, "'Without me you can indeed do something, but it will be easier through me,' he didn't say, 'You can bear your fruit without me, but a better crop through me.' That's not what he said. Read what he said; it's the holy gospel, treading on the proud necks of one and all. This isn't what Augustine says, it's what the Lord says. What does the Lord say? *Without me you can do nothing*" (John 15.5). The objector he opposes prefigures crucial aspects of the Ockhamist models discussed in chapter 2. For there we saw the assumption that grace is an extrinsic condition in which God happens to accept the autonomous acts of the human subject. That is why transforming, habitual grace in a life of daily conversion is so alien to Ockham's theology, why he can easily imagine God having decided to dispense with it. This is antithetical to Augustine's understanding of the intimacy and inward delight of divine agency in the disciple's life. He insists that God is never building his temple with "stones which can't move themselves" (1 Pet. 2.5) but that he certainly is building, and with living stones. He continues: "You are being led, but you too must run; you're being led but you must follow; because when you do follow, that will still be true that without him you can do nothing. *Because it does not depend on the one who wills or the one who runs, but on God who has mercy*" (Rom. 9.16 [156.13]). Freedom of the will comes from the charity of God poured into our hearts, and on this he quotes a text to which he so often turns: "The charity of God is poured forth in our hearts, by the Holy Ghost who is given to us" (Rom. 5.5).[40] Such, then, is the outcome of the encounter between the Samaritan Christ and fallen humanity, Semyuief, living under the powers of sin. It is a vision of what Langland's searching Wille has lost and found and lost again and again. In the mode of allegory, deployed with such theological profundity in *Piers Plowman,* "The hint half guessed, the gift half understood, is Incarnation."[41]

I will now return to Langland's refiguration of the parable, although it has never been far away in the preceding turn to exegetical traditions. Once the Samaritan has taken Semyuief to the "grange" and given the host of the Inn, which is the Church, the resources for the man's healing, he rides off to Jerusalem with great urgency (XIX.77–82).[42] Overwhelmed by the plenitudinous charity of the Samaritan, Wille runs after Faith and Hope toward the figure who is their true goal and his, the way and the end (XIX.80–82). Langland does not explicate his theology of grace and human agency here, but he has used the resources of allegory and narrative to illustrate it most evocatively. Wille is certainly acting energetically and freely: "y sewede the samaritaen." Yet his agency has been elicited, drawn forth, lured by the figure of Christ, who appeared in his own time, making time his own. He it is who lifts up Semyuief and brings him into the Church, in a vision that is itself a gift calling for the giving up of the delusive forms of freedom Wille pursued in "þe lond of longyng" in Passus XI. Now he is following the way that will lead through the crucifixion to the harrowing of hell, where Wille hears these

words of Christ's promise, those "secret words" that St. Paul associates
with being "caught up into paradise" (XX.435–42; 2 Cor. 12.4). From
Christ's promise he will be taken back to the Samaritan's insistence that
Semyuief's healing continues in the Church endowed with the transforming sacraments flowing from Christ's blood (XIX.83–95; XXI.149–335).[43]
This, the Samaritan explains, is the only way through the "wildernesse"
(XIX.54, 83–95). As Augustine wrote in another image shared with Langland: "The image [of God] begins to be reformed by him who formed it
in the first place. It cannot reform itself in the way it was able to deform
itself. . . . By sinning man lost justice and the holiness of truth, and thus
the image became deformed and discolored; he gets those qualities back
again when he is reformed and renovated."[44] Langland has Liberum Arbitrium deploy these images and the models of grace and sin to which they
belong. He does so during a highly critical account of the contemporary
Church, maintaining that both secular and religious clergy undermine
the "folk" and their "byleue" (XIX.51–88; see too Liberum Arbitrium at
XVI.242–85). He turns to the image of God in man and the figure of deformed coinage:

> Me may now likene lettred men to a loscheborw oþer worse
> And to a badde peny with a gode printe:
> Of moche mon þe metal is nauhte
> And ʒut is the printe puyr trewe and parfitliche ygraue.
> And so hit fareth by false cristene: here follynge is trewe,
> Cristendoem of holy kyrke, the kynges marke of heuene,
> Ac the metal þat is mannes soule of many of this techares
> Is alayed with leccherye and oþer lustes of synne
> That god coueyteth nat þe coyne þat crist hymsulue printede
> And for þe synne of þe soule forsaketh his oune coyne.
> (XVII.73–82)[45]

One may contrast the two pennies ("two pans") the Samaritan gave to the
Church for the healing of the wounded (XIX.76) and recall Augustine's
observation that the deformed image cannot reform itself. Langland
characteristically develops this figure to display the consequences of sin in
the community, in the Church. The consequences of sin are as collective
as they are individual, forming the community to deform its members.

We have to wait till Passus XIX to encounter Christ as the Samaritan, a wait including Wille's search through the highways and the hedges of that hungry land, the land of longing, a search that took us into the wilderness where the helpless Semyuief lay. This encounter with divine charity supersedes any claims that assumed the ability of humans to do well enough from putatively autonomous resources to make eternal beatitude theirs. Such claims, however unwittingly, make quite unnecessary the death of Christ for the reconciliation of sinners and enemies with God (Rom. 5.5–10). This is so even if the preferred idiom is the kind of contractual language favored by late medieval theologians described in Langland scholarship as "semi-Pelagian." Surely, such claims assume, if we do that which is within us we receive from God eternal bliss, our supernatural end. Characteristically, as we saw above, they maintain that *Piers Plowman* involves "Langland's way of illustrating the current *modern* idiom *facientibus quod in se est deus non denegat gratiam* (to him who does what is in him, God does not deny grace)."[46] But the episode we have just been following corrects all such talk in its devastating figuration of the power we have in ourselves ("in se"), showing it to be enchained and habituated to sin. And I wish to make one further observation about Langland's procedures in this passage, relevant to the poem's Christology: it is through our encounter with Christ the Samaritan that we meet and recognize Semyuief.

Langland discloses this in his allegorical narrative with great care and skill. We need to recall that Wille has just found Faith on a Sunday in mid-Lent, figured by Abraham, and then found Hope, figured by Moses (XVIII.181–XIX.43). Both figures are looking for Christ, who, Faith believes, will deliver us from the power of evil (XVIII.277–85). Wille responds with tears for the consequences of sin symbolized by the imprisonment of humanity in the devil's "pondefold":

> "Allas!" y saide, "þat synne so longe shal lette
> The myhte of goddes mercy that myhte vs alle amende."
> Y wepte for his wordes.
>
> (XVIII.286–88)

As in the liturgy, time present and time past both become present, Abraham's time of waiting and Wille's time of waiting, both now pierced with

recognition of the suffering generated by sinful practices. In this context let us revisit the opening of the narrative about the Samaritan who
fulfills the longings of Faith, Hope, and Wille.

These three travelers suddenly see a Samaritan riding a mule with
great urgency. It turns out that Faith, Hope, and Wille are exactly on the
way the Samaritan has chosen, from Jericho to joust in Jerusalem. But
we certainly never saw Wille choosing any such path as he confessed his
emblematic loss of Liberum Arbitrium (XVIII.178–80).[47] On the contrary, assimilated to the Church's liturgical year, yet without giving this
any overt attention, he has been led by the epistle for "a myddelenton
soneday" (Gal. 4.22–31) to St. Paul's allegory of Abraham and Jerusalem.[48] The text, embedded in its liturgical moment, finds him, comes
alive for him, and draws him into the "way" of the Samaritan (XIX.48),
the way he so desperately needs. This is a delicate, beautiful figuration of
divine grace working through Christ's liturgy, immersed as it is in "al holy
scripture" (XXI.262–73a). Grace leads Wille, apparently looking for the
free choice (Liberum Arbitrium), which has disappeared, in an action
beyond any explicit choice but also one without any crushing of the will,
which continues to search, argue, weep, and long for its fulfillment in
charity (XVIII.1–2). Only *after* Wille has seen the Samaritan, with Faith
and Hope, does he become aware of the true consequences of the violent
activity of thieves in what is now perceived as a "wilde wildernesse."[49]
He discerns a man beaten, stripped naked, and bound so that he cannot
move "Ne helpe hymsulue." This is the man we have been considering,
Semyuief (XIX.53–58). The point I am now adding to the earlier discussion is that only in the light of Christ's way, the way to his "ioust" on
the Cross against the powers of evil, can humans adequately discern the
effects of sin. Through Christ's presence we are enabled to see what has
not been seen in the poem's multivarious, inventive representations of
vice: *semivivus,* in English, *semyuief.* That is, humanity has unmade God's
good creation into a dangerous wilderness in which the very potentiali-
ties of this life are utterly crushed: "he ne myhte stepe ne stande ne stere
foet ne handes / Ne helpe hymsulue" (XIX.56–57). Only the divine vision, the life of Christ, discloses this reality and the need for God's own
journey into the far country where the source of love and life was crucified. In doing so it suggests the limitations of comic and satirical treatment of sins. The episode corrects, places, and supersedes many previ-

ous utterances in the poem, a matter to which I shall turn in a moment. It leaves us with what I have called a haunting image: so *this* is what sin makes of us, this is what sin does to our vaunted powers and autonomy. If we allow ourselves to remember this image and its contexts, it will illuminate earlier sequences and prove relevant to the three remaining passus. But the scholarship on the poem shows how the figure of Semyuief is one that readers, understandably enough, wish to ignore, to repress. As Scripture earlier warned Wille, "*Multi multa sciunt & seipsos nessiunt*" (XI.163).[50] Yet the explorations of *Piers Plowman,* with the theology emerging from them, do not encourage such amnesia. On the contrary, acknowledgment of the figure is inextricably bound up with the way, the mediator between God and mankind: "As God, he is the goal; as man, he is the way" [quo itur Deus, qua itur homo] (*CG* XI.2).

I will now discuss a few of the passages or utterances in *Piers Plowman* that are corrected and superseded by the episode of the Samaritan, Semyuief, and Wille. I select only a few because once the relevant argument has been made and illustrated, exhaustive instantiation would be superfluous in a chapter that has no aspiration to being a commentary on the whole of *Piers Plowman.* My first example comes from two of Wille's instructors, mentioned above, the Franciscan masters in Passus X. Wille has already witnessed the practices of a culture dominated by Mede, attempts at reformation led by Reason, Conscience, and the lay sovereign—attempts that, including his own, are shaped by confession within the sacrament of penance (Prologue–VII). He has also witnessed attempts led by Piers the Plowman to constitute a productive agrarian community that would simultaneously be subject to the labor legislation of the dominant elites and embody Christocentric solidarity with rebels against this discipline.[51] He has also heard about "a pardoun *A pena & A culpa,*" which turns out to be an extraordinarily inventive and enthralling commentary glossing two lines from the Athanasian Creed followed by an unresolved disputation between Piers and a priest (IX.1–296).[52] Wille is left puzzling over the status of his own visions and the relations between virtuous activity, indulgences, papal pardons, divine forgiveness, and salvation (IX.297–352; X.1–7). In this context he meets the Franciscan teachers and begs them for teaching about virtue (X.8–17). Their first response is to assert that their order always embodies virtue. Will objects that this confident claim ignores the human propensity to fall into sin.

The friars are unperturbed by this observation. They readily concede that even steadfast people sin seven times a day. But this concession is glossed by an example. The first part imagines a man in a boat tossed about by wind, water, and the boat's movements. If he tries to stand he inevitably falls. The fallings are, however, without harm or consequence, for he just keeps falling into the boat. Thus it is with "þe ryhtful mannus fallynge" (X.30–41). The second part elaborates the example. Such repeated falling through the temptations of the world, the flesh, and the devil does not entail falling out of charity. For "fre wil and fre wit" apparently never collude with these fallings before temptations but always direct the fallen person to repent "and arise and rowe out of synne / To contrition, to confessioun, til he come til his ende." He never does deadly sin, if he is a "ryhtful" man, however many times he falls (XI.42–55). So sin, however habitual, has no consequences for will and intellect. It can never enchain "fre wil and fre wit." It can never become an impediment to the fallen person (and all the fallen with whom the friars and Wille are concerned here were baptized into "rihtfole" life), never prevent him from rowing "out of synne." Temptations and habitual sin apparently can never persuade a "rihtfole" person to row toward "synne."

The friars forget that when one sins, and sins repetitively, compulsively (seven times a day), one develops habits. The will is not merely an uninvolved spectator in sinful acts. As St. Thomas Aquinas argued, the will directs all other parts of the soul to their due end when the will is subject to God in justice. But disorder in the soul, sin, is the consequence of will turning away from God and wrongly pursuing changeable goods. And sin, he maintained, recollecting the parable of the Samaritan and *semivivus,* diminishes the good of nature, the natural, God-given inclination to virtue.[53] The friars forget that the will, in developing compulsive, sinful habits, becomes an iron chain imprisoning and imprisoned. The responding friar mentions "the fend" but apparently imagines his power restricted to "oure body," forgetting a relevant moment in the *Confessions:* "The enemy had a grip on my will and so made a chain for me to hold me a prisoner."[54] And Langland himself invites us to juxtapose the friars' account of sin and the powers of evil with the figure of Semyuief, whom "theues hadde ybounde," stripped, and made incapable of free agency, leaving him "as naked as an needle and noen helpe abouten" (XIX.54–58). We recall that in the exegetical traditions to which Langland's allegory of the Samaritan belongs "theues" are read as the forces of the devil who strip their victim of the gifts of grace and the virtues.[55] Certainly this fallen man will be rowing nowhere without the Samaritan's presence, sacrifice, and gifts.[56] So even if readers at first overlook the ways in which the Franciscan friars have produced a frivolous and mistaken account of sin in Passus X, the juxtaposition with Christ the Samaritan and Semyuief in Passus XIX should lead the readers back to the earlier passus with a deepened, more adequate grasp of the issues it raised. As the Franciscans' teaching is corrected and superseded (not forgotten), readers are invited to meditate on exactly what was lacking in the earlier instructions and just why, if they did, they found it plausible, even attractive.[57] Dialectical relations within the poem disclose the Christocentric nature of Langland's theology and allegory even as they draw readers toward congruent forms of knowledge about the will, about sin, and about the freedom to do well—that is, so it turns out, to become a disciple of the Samaritan in the "grange" also known as "þat hous vnite, holy chirche an englisch" (XIX.73; XXI.328).[58]

Even figures as devout as Piers give instructions and act in ways that are critically qualified by the episode of the Samaritan and Semyuief. At his first entrance Piers offers to help those who have confessed their sins and have invoked Christ and his mother for "grace to go to Treuthe" but who still have absolutely no idea of "the way" (VII.155–VIII.4). He gives the lost pilgrims directions to Truth (VII.206–12). Then he provides an allegorical map of the route culminating in a promise of the vision of God with an inner Church that will shelter "alle trew" people and give spiritual food to "alle manner folk" (VII.254–60). The resources for Piers's map have been amply described by Elizabeth Salter and others.[59] They are largely commonplaces of Christian instruction in the Middle Ages. But at least in retrospect we should be able to identify some difficulties overlooked by Piers. Although he is addressing Christian pilgrims who have no idea about "the way" and "blostrede forth as bestes" (VII.158–59), Piers seems to assume that they can go on simply by following his instructions, making a beginning that long precedes the arrival of Grace, according to his own map (VII.243).[60] This beginning entails demands that turn out to be far beyond the available resources of fallen humanity: loving God above all else, preferring to die rather than commit any capital sin, loving one's neighbors and never harming them

(VII.205–12). From such a life of virtue, the pilgrims will be on the way to Truth, where the Virgin Mary will open the gates of paradise (VII.243–53). This is a most attractive map, but in the light of the later episode we are compelled to grasp its failings. For it simply assumes the very resources that sinners lack. It assumes their freedom from all the bonds of Semyuief, from the consequences of sinful habits for the dispositions of will and intellect. But, as I have noted, just before Piers issues his map we have been told that these Christians have certainly forgotten "the way" as they "blostrede forth as bestes" (VII.158–66). Piers has forgotten that sin involves an incurvature of the will toward the self, love of self over and against love of God and neighbor. The guide seems to have forgotten the reason for the Samaritan's journey into this land made unfit for human life, his journey to Jerusalem. Although the Samaritan's encounter with Semyuief and the healing processes he offers the man correct such amnesia, Langland has just provided some anticipations that should make readers extremely wary of Piers's confident itinerary. Recall, for example, one of those confessing in the same passus as Piers's map:

> "Y may not stande ne stoupe ne withouten stoel knele.
> Were y brouhte on bed, but yf my taylende hit made,
> Sholde no ryngyng do me ryse til y were rype to dyne."
> A bigan *benedicite* with a bolk and his breste knokkede,
> Raxlede and remede and rotte at þe laste.
>
> (VII.3–7)

Here is another figuration of the consequences of habitual sin: the bondage of the will unable to move on "the way." The plea for blessing collapses into a thoroughly carnal belch that seems a reaction to the speaker's thought of food. Instead of calmly rowing out of sin into repentance, as the friar imagines, the would-be penitent falls into a snoring sleep. So immersed is the speaker in the habits of his sin that he becomes his past and can be named Sloth.[61] Similarly, in the previous passus, a figure sets out for Church to hear mass and to confess, on a Friday. But this journey proves too difficult in the face of his will, his love for ale, hot spices, and the company of the ale drinkers gathered in "betene hous the brewstere" (the house of Betty the breweress). The result is graphically described:

He myhte noþer steppe ne stande til he a staf hadde
And thenne gan he go lyke a glemans byche
Sum tyme asyde and sume tyme arere,
As hoso layth lynes for to lacche foules.
And when he drow to the dore thenne dymmede his yes;
A thromblede at the thresfold and threw to þe erthe.

(VI.403–8; see 350–418)

Once more the figure of sin involves the enchainment of will that Piers's instructions do not acknowledge. As medieval commentators on the story of the Samaritan and Semyuief make clear, such wounding deprivation does not actually annihilate that which makes us human.[62] Although we become the sins we perform, we retain a form of will and "inwit," the potential for repentance (VI.415–40). In acknowledging this, however, we must simultaneously acknowledge that the passage about this sinner began exactly here, with the intention to repent. So we are given a potentiality enfolded in a cycle of relapses that display the chains of the will encumbered in sin. Furthermore, the poet shows us, as we have seen, that even when confession is completed and Repentance's powerful prayer is uttered, the confessed people still lack any sense of how to go on and who "the way" is (VII.120–59). Hearing Repentance's Christocentric prayer, they have neither heard nor understood (see Matt. 13.13–15). They are reconfigured in Semyuief.

The Samaritan's responses to this disaster included the provision of healing "medicyne," the sacramental means of grace bestowed on his Church (XIX.71–77).[63] Yet Piers fails to mention the sacrament of the altar and the bread of life. This omission is complexly related to the manner in which he sidelines the visible Church in his instructions, substituting for it an invisible, inner one.[64] It turns out that Piers has underestimated the neediness of the Christians he addresses, their lack of necessary resources for the journey he outlines. In doing so he has also overlooked their need for the historical community that will recognize that the saints' life is a social one, the City of God.[65]

Both these errors and their relatedness are evident in Piers's attempt to build a Christian polity in Passus VIII (112–340). He wants to preserve a traditional ideal of relations between knights and agrarian laborers while overseeing the new labor legislation imposed by contemporary elites in their own interests. He also wants to mitigate punitive social disciplines by invoking Christian fraternity. And although he has left his body and the remembrance of his soul with the Church (VIII.101–4), and although he asks the knight to protect "holy kerke" (VIII.26), once he begins organizing production and consumption in the community he does not address the Church, an absence quite congruent with the map he provided for lost pilgrims. Langland shows this model running into serious trouble. Agrarian laborers, especially landless ones, reject "þe statuyt," current labor "lawe," disciplinary punishment (such as "stokes"), the knightly enforcer of current legislation, and the overseeing plowman who calls on both the armed ruling class and solidarity in Christ's blood. In response, Piers reinforces some of the contradictions in his position by simultaneously invoking "charite" and punitive hunger as a form of revenge on those who oppose his benevolent rule and knightly power.[66] Despite his appeal to Christian fraternity, Piers never considers the conflicts that vex him in terms such as those disclosed by the Samaritan in his meeting with Semyuief and Wille. As the instructions preceding his map suggested, he assumes that sin does not really have consequences for our resources, collectively and individually. So his angry responses to the angry laborers, despite his charitable commitments, lack any analysis of the role of sin in shaping will, intellect, and politics in the earthly city. Working and organizing work, it emerges, is not a substitute for penitential meditation.[67] Indeed, Piers does not glimpse any issues about the effects of power and political dominion, issues that are soon to be raised by Studie. She observes that dominion encourages selfish accumulation of temporal goods and a distinctively self-aggrandizing version of "Dowel" (XI.61–77). So Piers cannot begin to investigate the chains that might be binding all those involved in the conflicts he seeks to resolve by the force of knightly power and, when that fails, by the punitive discipline of extreme physical hunger. The motives of temporal dominion in the knightly class, in "þe statuyt" of laborers, in the "stokes" (with which the knight "courteisliche" threatens resisting laborers), and in Piers's own role are not made topics of theological reflection. This theological failing leads to an impoverishment of ethical and political analysis, impoverishment that has dismal consequences for practice.

The absence of sustained concern for the Church in Piers's current vision should be seen in this context. Unlike the Samaritan, he does not

see the bonds and wounds of those on the half-acre, does not see the
need for the Church and the sacramental gifts with which she has been
endowed. This is a striking contrast to the office Piers later receives from
the risen Christ in Passus XXI and his activity with the Holy Spirit in dis-
tributing grace to the newly formed community that is also "þat hous
vnite, holy chirche an englisch" (XXI.182–335). Also affording a striking
contrast is the reference Piers does make to the Church as he attempts to
organize agrarian production and consumption in Passus VIII. It comes
when he is first confronted with rebellion from those who "bad hym go
pisse with his plogh" (VIII.149–55). He appeals to the knight, who represents armed power, to take vengeance on these laborers, observing that
"They acounteth nat of corsynge ne holy kyrke dredeth" (VIII.158–59).
Here the Church and its power of excommunication seem reduced to the
ideological and disciplinary apparatus of those who rule the earthly city,
a reduction in which Piers colludes.

This merely helps to confirm what the poem represents as a major
problem in the late medieval Church: that is, its assimilation to the earthly
city. In the Prologue and Passus II–III, this has already been displayed in
numerous ways. Let us recollect a few of these. The Gospel is "glosede"
for material gain; the sacrament of penance is commodified, encourag-
ing sinful practices; ecclesiastic pardons are also commodified, deluding
their purchasers; simony pervades the Church.[68] As that part of the City
of God that is in heaven descends to teach Wille, she asks him if he sees
how immersed people are in the ways, or rather "þe mase," of the earthly
city (I.5–8). Their wills are so devoted to "worschip in this world" that
they consider Christian eschatology a mere "tale" (I.7–9). Although the
Church shown us from the Prologue to Passus VIII legitimizes such worship and the rule of Mede, the layman Piers is, at this stage, unable to grasp
the relevance of this for his own desire to form a distinctively Christian community. This failure undermines his reformation. It is a failure ex-
tensively and energetically corrected by Liberum Arbitrium later in the
poem (XVI.231–XVII.321).

From these theological and political failures emerges the pardon of
Passus IX (B VIII). This has received much discussion, becoming part of
the debates surveyed in the opening part of the present chapter.[69] Such
discussions tend to favor substantive claims about the theology of the
pardon and Piers's response, especially in the B version where he "pulled

it asunder" (B VII.119) in response to the priest's challenge. I think this is
a mistake because the form and content of the passus militate against such
constructions, whether the latter are "semi-Pelagian" or "Augustinian."
As I have shown elsewhere, the passus is compiled of many voices glossing the two-line pardon for 276 lines. These voices pursue issues of immense concern to Langland, especially issues of poverty, mendicancy,
and almsgiving.[70] But they are, nevertheless, in relation to the brief pardon, glosses. We should acknowledge that the very status of the pardon
is obscure. The narrator says that when Truth "herde telle" of the failures to form a peaceful community in Passus VIII he "purchasede" a
"pardon" that remits all the guilt of sin as well as the punishment due to
sin (IX.1–3). For whom is this pardon valid? It allegedly applies to Piers,
his heirs (cf. VIII.80–106), and all who support the social project that
collapsed in the previous passus (IX.3–8). Yet that project, as I have observed, was fraught with inadequacies that were theological and political.
How can the pardon remedy these? We are not shown how it will contribute to converting people, to resolving the serious conflicts around
the justice or injustice of "þe statuyt," or to changing desires shaped by
Mede. But if it does represent divine forgiveness, one would expect a very
distinctive characteristic to be revealed at this point, namely the power of
divine forgiveness to transform the forgiven person. For such forgiveness is a gift from God that, as the Samaritan tells us, heals and frees.[71]
In the Catholic tradition that enables Langland's theology and to which
he contributes, the grace of forgiveness is not only extrinsic but inward
and gradually transforming.[72] Here, however, we cannot say the pardon
is envisaged in this way—certainly not by the priest, who denies that the
two lines of the text Piers has received are a pardon, but not by Piers or
Wille either (IX.281–352; cf. B VII.107–206). Nor is it so understood by
any of the other voices that make up the passus. Perhaps at this stage of
the poem not even Piers clearly grasps what kind of forgiveness people
need. And perhaps this lack of understanding relates to something I observed in the episode of the Samaritan. That is, sinful creatures may fully
grasp the consequences of sin only through the vision and presence of
Christ. It should be very striking that the pardon of Passus IX is not
unfolded in terms of the reconciliation of enemies to God by the death
of Christ, his resurrection, and the gifts of the Holy Spirit, the terms that

will be reached much later and in which Piers will have a significant, transformed role (XIX–XXI).

Furthermore, it is emphasized that the pardon actually consists of
just two lines from the Athanasian Creed (IX.281–88). These lines are
translated into English by a priest who finds "no pardoun" in them
(IX.289–92, 281–82). He draws this conclusion because the two lines
make no mention of forgiveness but only of the supernatural end of
doing good and doing evil. This is certainly not an obvious statement of
forgiveness. Nor is it easily assimilable to the grammar of pardon. After
all, the poem makes clear that humans continually fail to do well and
continue, individually and collectively, to do evil. Humans need the resources of conversion from the latter, resources centered on divine forgiveness, the Samaritan's journey. The pardon thus seems to lack essential elements of a pardon. That does not mean that it is not "in witnesse
of treuthe" (IX.286). Nor does it mean that it is not an enigmatic prefiguration of the pardon that is so powerfully disclosed in the acts of the
Samaritan and the Holy Spirit later in the poem. But the fact that the two
lines in question come from the Quicunque Vult is not sufficient reason to treat the priest's comments, "no pardoun," with condescension,
or worse. For the Athanasian Creed is a painstaking attempt to formalize an Augustinian discourse of the Trinity followed by a similar attempt
to formalize the relations between God and man in "the Incarnation of
our Lord Jesus Christ." It contains just one statement alluding to pardon:
"Who [Christ] suffered for our salvation."[73] This allusion is not elaborated into anything remotely approaching an account of reconciliation,
forgiveness, and the conversion of sinners. Of course, such an absence
is overcome by the creed's place in the Church's liturgy, but that is not
how the priest or reader encounters the two lines taken from it. In my
view the thoroughly inarticulate conflict of interpretations between Piers
and the priest, especially inarticulate in the C version, should be left as the
poet leaves it at this point: unresolved. It is unresolved because all participants in the episode lack attention to the resources that will resolve and
illuminate the enigma together with the struggles that are its immediate
context. These resources are Christocentric: the healing that flows from
Christ and will be displayed at length in Passus XVIII–XXI. This has already been briefly but densely expressed by Holy Churche (I.146–58)

and Repentance (VII.119–50). But in the context we are studying, with its participants' amnesia, the two lines abstracted from the Quicunque Vult and represented as "a pardoun" can at best be seen as an enigmatic prefiguration of these resources, through a glass darkly ("in aenigmate," 1 Cor. 13.12). Wille's puzzlement, together with the scope of his puzzlement, is thoroughly appropriate. And so is his prayer for grace to obey divine teaching in works that will be recognized as such at the Last Judgment (IX.293–352).

This prayer (IX.347–52) relates to an earlier episode added to the C version of *Piers Plowman*. There Wille claims to write as Reason teaches him against "lewede Ermytes" and "lollares," although he is clothed "as a lollere" (V.1–5).[74] But as he wanders down the paths of memory, Reason forces him to look at his own life in the terms he deploys against those he habitually judges as "lolleres" and wasters. Is he himself not also "an ydel man," an abusive mendicant who leads the very "lollarne lyf" that he, with Reason, attacks (V.26–32a)? Wille remembers his youth, his education, and his clerical status. He distinguishes his materially ascetic mendicancy from begging designed to accumulate material goods. He thinks he does fulfill Reason's demand that people serve "þe comune" and, although he himself is extraordinarily mobile, he launches a self-justifying attack against social mobility that undermines traditional social hierarchies (V.35–88; V.20). But Wille's introspective and self-justifying dialogue with Reason in his own memory does not convince Conscience (V.89–91). The result of this challenging encounter with Reason and Conscience is an intense event, a moment of conversion. Roaming in Wille's memory, Reason had suspected Wille of being a waster and "a spilletyme" (V.28). Now Wille sets aside his self-justifications and agrees. He confesses: "and so y beknowe / That y haue ytynt tyme and tyme myspened" (V.92–93). He has wasted God's gifts encapsulated in the gift of "tyme." Such waste involves contempt of grace, the gifts of God. But he shows the virtue of hope, a theological virtue and itself a supreme gift (V.93–101). So whatever he has squandered and rejected, we see that he is still receiving crucial gifts. And hope is inseparable from faith, as Langland shows later in the poem where Wille's meeting with Hope/Moses is preceded by his encounter and searching dialogue with Faith/Abraham (XVIII.181–XIX.26).[75] The theological virtues are gifts that lead the recipient to Christ the giver. So instead of despair as he surveys what seems his lost and wasted time, Wille is able to hope in the one disclosed "thorw wyrdes of grace" (V.98).[76] Drawing on his education in "holy writ" (V.36–37), he recalls two of Christ's parables concerning the kingdom of heaven and the salvation of mankind.[77] He is being drawn, by the grace he prays for, into the divinely given narrative of salvation history. He hears the promise:

So hope y to haue of hym þat is almyghty
A gobet of his grace and bigynne a tyme
That alle tymes of my tyme to profit shal turne.

(V.99–101)

His conversion is thus enabled by the gift of hope in which Wille prays for grace to redeem the sad waste of time, turning all this loss to profit. He glimpses how the divine gifts that he has rejected, "ytynt" and "myspened," "loste and loste" are being given again and again. Encouraged by Reason and Conscience "to bigynne / The lyf þat is louable and leele to thy soule," he is directed to "þe kyrke." There he goes "god to honoure," kneels contritely before the cross, and prays the Lord's Prayer (V.102–8).

Such conversion and confession, however, do not dissolve all the consequences of dispositions cultivated by sinful habits, consequences that include opacity to ourselves, old compulsion, and great inventiveness in our self-deceptions, both collective and individual. The tenth book of Augustine's *Confessions* explored these aspects of the bishop's experience after the account of his conversion in book VIII. And Wille's conversion here will not prevent a long journey "into þe lond of longyng," where the will is driven "by self-love reaching the point of contempt of God" (XI.164–85; *CG* XIV.28). Here he will once more squander the gifts he is being given, becoming to himself, yet once more, a land of famine, a full participant in that city where "vnkyndnesse and coueytise is, hungry contreys bothe."[78] But he will not be abandoned by a Christocentric providence, which draws him, through "tyme myspened," to the tree of Charity and, once again, into the narratives of salvation history of which Christ is the source, key, and goal.

But because Langland's understanding of this goal is profoundly social, his vision of sin is congruently so.[79] For the powers of sin strive to subvert the formation of the community of Christians, the body of Christ, "þat hous vnite, holy chirche an englisch" (XXI.328). In this chapter we have met examples of the poem's treatment of a culture dominated by Mede, the Church's immersion in "þe mase" (I.6) of the world, and the failure to organize a productive, Christian community in Passus VIII. I now want to focus on this aspect of Langland's treatment of sin by considering two episodes. In the first he shows Christians rejecting the supreme gifts of the Samaritan. In doing so they display the transformations of nature, of "kynde," in which the will and desire are turned away from God and toward a catastrophic version of the self and the good.

The episode takes place in the "hous" that Grace has prepared for Piers and his harvest, a house made out of Christ's gifts flowing from the Crucifixion (XXI.317–34). As the culmination of Lenten labors against sin, Conscience invites the Christian community to celebrate a common meal in which all receive the sacrament of the altar, "bred yblessed and godes body þervnder" (XXI.335–87). The Holy Spirit, Grace, "thorw godes word gaf Peres power, / Myghte to make hit and men to eten hit aftur" (XXI.386–87).[80] But this gift never becomes simply extrinsic to the giver, never an autonomous "thing." It calls people to active participation in the life of the giver, the culmination of the virtue of Charity embodied in the Samaritan. And Charity, as we saw both in Langland's treatment of the tree of Charity and in the Samaritan's oration to Wille, is inextricably bound up with the Trinity, the Trinitarian life of God (XVIII.1–176; XIX.96–334; see too XVIII.184–266). It is, St. Thomas argues, a friendship ("amicitia") with God, joining us to God in a manner that entails love of our neighbors and the common good ("bonum commune"), which is God.[81] He observes that the Eucharist is the sacrament of the Church's unity, quoting St. Paul: "We, being many, are one bread, one body, all that partake of one bread and one cup."[82] So Conscience rightly calls Christians to restore the bonds of charity that sin continually destroys and insists that this must be embodied in a practice of restitution and mutual forgiveness (XIX.386–95).[83] But "þe commune" questions Conscience's counsel, which is also obedience to "þe paternoster" (Matt. 6.12; XIX.391–95). The hostile questioning condenses into a manifestation of the consequences of sin permeating the community and its individual members:

"ȝe? bawe!" quod a breware, "y wol nat be yruled,
By iesu! For al ȝoure iangelyng, with *spiritus Iusticie*
Ne aftur Conscience, bi Crist! While y can sulle
Bothe dregges and draf and drawe at on hole
Thikke ale & thynne ale; þat is my kynde
And nat hacky aftur holinesse; hold thy tonge, conscience!
Of *spiritus Iusticie* thow spekest moche an ydel."

(XXI.396–402)

The pursuit of the market's opportunities for some to make money is
paramount and must not be subjected to the qualifications and law of distinctively Christian justice, the fourth and "cheef seed" that Piers sowed
in the making of the Church by the Holy Spirit (XXI.297–311, 405–6).[84]
The brewer's eloquent rejection of divine gifts embodied in the Eucharist
and eucharistic community shows how sin becomes normalized in a society, so much so that its habits change the very nature of individuals: "þat
is my kynde." Such a transformation is as brilliant an image of the power
of sin as Semyuief in its own contexts. But here Langland makes us recognize the profoundly social form of sin, the dominion of sin in the practices of contemporary Christian culture and its conversion of "kynde."
Such a conversion of "kynde" naturalizes conflict, deceit, exploitive competition, and the rejection of those forms of life that Christ's sacraments
compose. In the face of this dominion and its effects, it seems rather frivolous to celebrate doing what happens to be in one, confident that this
will be rewarded by God's grace ("facientibus quod in se est deus non
denegat gratiam"). For unlike the proponents (medieval and modern) of
this cliché, Langland discloses how "the mind of man, the natural seat of
his reason and understanding, is itself weakened by long-standing faults
which darken it. It is too weak to cleave to that changeless light and to
enjoy it; it is too weak even to endure that light. It must first be renewed
and healed day after day" (*CG* XI.2).[85] For this reason the Samaritan trav-
els into the distant country, the "wilde wildernesse" replete with violent
cruelty and fear.[86]

The second episode I wish to consider in relation to Langland's social vision of sin is the Crucifixion (XX.26–94). In Jerusalem, Jesus the
Samaritan will "iouste" against the devil, death, and the false judgment
that would make death rather than life the final word for God's creation

(XX.16–34a). In this setting Langland represents the joust, which is the Crucifixion, as a thoroughly social event.[87] The powers of sin and death are embodied in the empire's judge, "sedens pro tribunali" [sitting in the place of judgment], "crowds," "þe Court," predatory witnesses, two thieves, and violent, unruly officials. All cry out "*Crucifige.*" Christ completes his joust with sin as he is tortured and nailed "with thre nayles naked vpon a rode." The poet emphasizes that this manifests "þe commune lawe" of the earthly city. Like a dying prisoner, the "lord of lyf and liht tho leyde his eyes togederes." This part of the joust concludes with a blind knight being forced to "iouste with iesus." Piercing Christ through the heart, the knight finds that Christ's healing blood streams down his "spere and vnspered his yes," eliciting a passionate, penitential conversion.[88] A whole community and its "commune lawe" embody and enact the power and consequences of sin. But the weakness of God, the divine judge's subjection to the judge and executioners of the earthly city, is also revealed as the power of God.

Langland next moves to Christ's harrowing of hell. Replete with figures, voices, and arguments, this episode includes exquisite celebrations of the reconciliation and redemption of humankind (XX.113–475). The God who is the Samaritan crucified in the earthly city is also the infinite power entering hell. The crucified humanity is exalted. First Langland stages discussion about sin, justice, and divine forgiveness between the four daughters of God, allowing Peace's Christology to resolve the arguments (XX.118–238). She is certain that through the Incarnation and Crucifixion "Crist hath converted the kynde of rihtwisnesse / Into pees and pyte of his puyr grace." The God who "of his gode wille" created all "auntred hymsulue and toek Adames kynde" to inhabit human suffering (XX.185–222, 230–34a). Book, a figure for Scripture, supports Peace's vision, invoking "godes body" (XX.239–68). Next the poet has a group of devils debate the issues of justice, sin, and salvation. They determine that they have no "rihte" over sinful humanity, "no trewe title" but practices based in "treson and tricherie" (XX.274–349a). Here Langland allows them to renounce claims some theologians had made for them.[89] As they do so, the light of glory orders Lucifer to unlock the gates of hell, defended by medieval technologies of war (XX.281–94), whose source is thus revealed. The light is accompanied by a voice of infinite power, the voice of the Creator. This again commands the leadership of hell ("Dukes") to undo the gates so that "Crist may come in, the kynges sone of heuene." With the "breth" of this second command "helle braek with belialles barres" and the gates open wide (XX.270–73, 341–42, 360–65). In this overwhelming action those imprisoned in the darkness of hell see the light of God anticipated and remembered in Repentance's great prayer in Passus VII (119–50). Those who are liberated sing the Agnus Dei, St. John the Baptist's own acknowledgment of Christ (XX.366–69; John 1.36). The stage is set for Christ's magnificent and complex oration, from the depths of hell, on the doctrine of reconciliation (XX.370–446).

Christ declares that he has fulfilled, not destroyed, the law (XX.370–400, 443–44, quoting Matt. 5.17 at XX.395a). Through his journey to the cross, the "lord of lyf" accepted the drink of the "doctour of deth," seeming to die, but doing so for his own drink, love (XX.401–7).[90] And now he still thirsts for human souls, a thirst insatiable through history (XX.408–16). Considering the Last Judgment, Christ lays great emphasis on his fraternal solidarity with humanity, a solidarity that includes profound suffering. The crucified and risen "lord of lyf" says that he would be "an vnkynde kyng" if he did not help his "kyn" in the need under which divine judgment places them. He quotes from Psalm 142 to express this need: "Enter not into judgment with thy servant: for in thy sight no man living shall be justified."[91] He promises that his "rihtwysnesse and rihte" will rule hell and "mercy al mankynde before me in heuene" (XX.417–42a). Reconciliation and redemption: for "al mankynde" or only for "al" whom God exalts to heaven? After all, when Christ has harrowed hell, the devils watch him "lede forth which hym luste and leue which hym likede" (XX.449). Not surprisingly, Christ's statements have led to much discussion about the poem's relations to affirmations of universal salvation.[92] My own view is that Langland leaves the issue of universal salvation open but, like Karl Barth, "with a strong tilt toward universal hope."[93] Most commentators have acknowledged such a "tilt," although some have doubted this. But given God's infinite resourcefulness, the groundless love of such a sovereign creator, reconciler, and redeemer, a vision of the Trinity shared by Augustine, Aquinas, and Langland, to exclude the possibility of universal salvation, to exclude the hope of universal salvation, should not seem compelling. Christ's unequivocal affirmation of his identity with humankind and his promise to be kind rather than "vnkynde" encourage such hope.[94]

But as we ruminate on the whole poem, such hope cannot simply delete the figures that emerge in the next two passus (XXI–XXII), such as the brewer we have just considered. Nor, of course, can hope given by Christ's own work be deleted by human recalcitrance. Yet the poem insists on returning us to a Christian, supported by the Christian "comune" in which he lives, rejecting the gifts of Christ in the Eucharist, rejecting the sacrament of love that joins the participants to the body of Christ. In the brewer we remember hearing someone boasting that his very "kynde" now persists in this rejection (XXI.383–408). Conscience's own response warns that unless "god helpe," the brewer will be unblessed. Unless he repents, in practice, he will be "lost, bothe lyf and soule" (XXI.403–8). Of course, someone might respond that this is another example of an errant conscience claiming that it is not congruent with Christ's oration. But such a response overlooks two important issues. First, the brewer, like many other figures in Passus XXI–XXII, proclaims the solidarities of sin and the tenacious resistance to divine grace. And he proclaims that his own nature is being remade in these solidarities. Second, we should now recall Christ's teaching in the form of the Samaritan. There he warned, without reservations, that human *unkyndenesse* quenches the grace of the Holy Spirit, "godes owene kynde" (XIX.220–26, 255–56). Dives, the rich man of Christ's parable (Luke 16.19–31), was "damned for his vnkyndenesse" to the beggar at his gate (XIX.233–56). Christ then elaborates his account of "Vnkynde cristene men" whose practices undo the works of "kynde." Here he specifies those whose desires lead them to murder. They destroy "lyf and loue, the leye [light] of mannes body," attacking the gift of God given "to reverence with the trinite." The murderer commits the worst of the sins against the Holy Spirit, assenting to destroy "þat Crist dere bouhte." The Samaritan asks how can such a person beg mercy or be protected by mercy when "wikkedliche and wilfulliche" he would destroy ("anyente") mercy? How indeed when the will *becomes* its habits and actions? The Samaritan does not believe that Charity will "louye þat lyf þat loue and Charite destruyeth" (XIX.257–78). This is not Christ's final word in *Piers Plowman*. But it is certainly offered as Christ

teaching Wille. And it is congruent with the representation of the brewer
and others who reject sacramental gifts of Christ and the Holy Spirit in
Passus XXI–XXII. For what this poetry forces us to acknowledge is
the enchainment of the will in practices that systematically reject the love
of God and neighbor.

At the end of his oration in hell, with its hope for "al mankynde,"
Christ binds the strong man who had bound Semyuief (XX.446;
XIX.54–58; see Matt. 12.29).[95] But the hope of universal salvation in the
infinitely resourceful love of the Trinity coexists with what in the poem's
vision comes to look like an inexplicable mystery but one Langland insists on representing. This mystery is the strange possibility that even
when humans are offered the gifts flowing from the crucified "lord of
lyf" (XX.403) they may reject these gifts. In doing so they reject the invitation to the great "mangerye," the ineffable banquet, and they refuse
the wedding garment they are given (XII.46–47; Matt. 22.1–14).[96] Langland's theology thus presents the coexistence of a great hope that divine
forgiveness will include "al mankynde" together with a sustained display
of the compulsive tenacity of sin, individual and collective, its capacity
to reject the grace of Christ. In reflecting on Langland's vision of this coexistence, I have again come to see a convergence with Karl Barth's
consideration of the doctrine of universal salvation, a question that of
course belongs to eschatology.[97] Barth discusses the threat under which
our sinister practices place us. Can we assume that the outcome of this
dangerous situation will be determined solely by divine deliverance? If
we can do so, this is entirely "the unexpected work of grace and its revelation on which we cannot count but for which we can only hope as an
undeserved and inconceivable overflowing of the significance, operation
and outreach of the reality of God and man in Jesus Christ." Does God
"owe" eternal felicity to those persistently rejecting the gifts of salvation?
The Samaritan's lesson to Wille, thinking of murder, thinking of Dives,
denied this. We recollect how even the divine resources bestowed in the
Church will not help the "vnkynde" because "vnkyndnesse" quenches
the Holy Ghost. The Samaritan invokes the bridegroom's terrifying judgment on those without the oil to light lamps at the wedding: "Amen I say
to you, I know you not." This leaves the door to the wedding "shut."[98]
The Samaritan's denial of divine obligation to humanity in its contempt

for grace makes us consider with great care our participation, individual and collective, in the practices of "the rulers of the world of this darkness . . . the spirits of wickedness in the high places" (Eph. 6.12). Barth himself similarly denies that in the face of evil we can simply assert universal salvation as a necessary consequence of the cross and resurrection of Christ. He observes, "We must not arrogate to ourselves that which can be given and received only as a free gift" (IV/3, 477). And received: we remember Langland's brewer and his "commune" rejecting the body of Christ, along with the massive support for Anticrist in the next passus (XXII.53–71, 110–14). But Barth also argues that "there is no good reason why we should forbid ourselves, or be forbidden, openness to the possibility that in the reality of God and man in Jesus Christ there is contained much more than we might expect and therefore the supremely unexpected withdrawal of that final threat, i.e., that in the truth of this reality there might be contained the super-abundant promise of the final deliverance of all men" (IV/3, 477–78). It seems to me that the coexistence of the strands identified above in Langland's theology, centered in Christology, is being affirmed by Barth, with the hope grounded in a "truly eternal divine patience and deliverance" to a universal reconciliation:

> If we are certainly forbidden to count on this as though we had a claim to it, as though it were not supremely the work of God to which man can have no possible claim, we are surely commanded the more definitely to hope and pray for it as we may do already on this side of the final possibility, i.e., to hope and pray cautiously and yet distinctly that, in spite of everything which may seem quite conclusively to proclaim the opposite, His compassion should not fail, and that in accordance with His mercy which is "new every morning" He "will not cast off for ever." (Lam. 3.22–23, 31 [IV/3, 478])

It is fitting that after the harrowing of hell angels hymn the reconciliation, Justice and Peace kiss, Truth sings the Te Deum Laudamus, Love celebrates the joy of life in unity, and Wille awakes on the morning of Easter as people "rang to þe resureccioun" (XX.450–68).[99] Joining cross and resurrection, he calls his wife and daughter:

"Arise and go reuerense godes resureccion
And crepe to þe croes on knees and kusse hit for a iewel
And rihtfollokest a relyk, noon richore on erthe.
For godes blessed body hit baer for oure bote
And hit afereth the fende, for such is þe myhte
May no grisly goest glyde þer hit shaddeweth."

(XX.470−75)[100]

As I have noted, Langland allows the hope for universal reconciliation through cross and resurrection to coexist with counterpossibilities. He does not seek to harmonize or resolve an eschatological question now. He waits, in hope, in a theological vision of salvation and sin that is thoroughly Christocentric. Whatever the state of Wille's disintegrating body, whatever the state of the Church seemingly dominated by forces welcoming "þat fende," Wille is commanded to remain in the Church and there to pursue the life of Christian discipleship. He obeys unquestioningly (XXII.58−73, 183−213). Here he finds in a very hard time, and against most appearances, the life of "vnite" (XXII.213). Here too, at last, he finds what Reason and Conscience had exhorted him to follow: "The lyf þat is louable and leele to thy soule" (V.102−4). Led by the visions of Christ, in the midst of the apparently successful attacks of "þat fende," he has found the treasure hidden in the field, although the field and the treasure may be very different from anyone's expectations (V.94−98a). The poem ends with Wille in the Church and Conscience searching for Piers the Plowman and Grace (XXII.380−86). Such searching seems to be a gift of the Grace for whom he searches. Here it is appropriate to recall Augustine's prayer at the end of his own great exploration, *De Trinitate*. He prays to the Trinity for "the strength to seek, having caused yourself to be found and having given me the hope of finding you more and more."[101]

III

I have concentrated on Langland's Christology and his treatment of sin's consequences, individual and collective, paying attention to the poem's dialectical form. These explorations are certainly capable of much more elaborate instantiation. But they must suffice for the present. However, the debate I traced in the opening section of this chapter persuades me to address an episode that has been widely taken to be a particularly ir-refutable example of Langland's "semi-Pelagianism." This is the brief episode of Trajan.[102] In my view there has been a tendency to abstract this moment from the process to which it belongs, thus giving it a kind of autonomous authority. I shall try to avoid this tendency because it goes against the grain of the dialectical relations that the poem creates and that constitute *Piers Plowman*. Such reading against the grain would neces-sarily distort our understanding of the minute particulars that compose the episode, whose existence is not at all autonomous.

Scripture confronts Wille with a "sarmon" whose "teme" is from one of Christ's parables of the kingdom, the marriage feast of Matthew 22. What Wille hears is that many ("multi") were invited to the feast but that when they arrived the porter opened the gate and secretly pulled in a few ("pauci"), leaving the rest to wander away (XII.45–49). Derek Pear-sall notes that the "version" of the parable Will ascribes to Scripture "eliminates" the part that shows people rejecting the king's invitation. The effect, he says, is to stress "the idea of the pre-election of God's grace, and raises again (cf. XI.208), more acutely, the problem of predestina-tion."[103] Pearsall's observation helps us attend to what Wille overlooks in Christ's parable. Had Wille paused to consider conventional exegesis, he would have found strands of interpretation that link the parable to the Incarnation, to ecclesiology, to the sacraments of the Church, and to faith. Nicholas of Lyra, for example, reads the wedding feast as the sacra-ment of the Eucharist, while Nicholas of Gorran sees the nuptial as rep-resenting the union of divine and human nature in the Virgin's womb, the union of Christ and the Church, "a great sacrament" begun at the Cruci-fixion (Eph. 5.25–32), and the union of wisdom with the faithful soul. He also treats the dinner prepared by the king as the mystery of the Incarna-tion. The king calls all to enter the Church, good and bad, but some lack the necessary wedding garment, which is charity.[104] It is not surprising that Wille's truncated version of Christ's parable terrifies him. His re-sponse is to dispute with himself about his personal election or reproba-tion. Although this is a serious mistake, driven by panic, Wille does turn to the Church and his reception of the sacrament of baptism (XII.52–53).

As Christ the Samaritan later insists that nobody is saved without the blood of Christ and the baptismal sacrament, this is potentially a promising move (see XIX.81–91), especially as Wille remembers that "crist cleped vs alle," not just a few (XII.54–57). Indeed, he remembers that in calling all people Christ "bad hem souke for synne saue at his breste / And drynke bote for bale" (XII.56–57). His memory thus foreshadows Christ's recollection of the Crucifixion as he frees the souls locked in hell, promising that his grace will grow wider and wider:

> For y þat am lord of lyf, loue is my drynke,
> And for þat drynke today y deyede as hit semede.
> (XX.403–4)

These are the only sources for any Christian talk and hope about emancipation from sin, death, and hell, as *Piers Plowman* makes absolutely clear.[105] That is why, as his response to Christ's parable appreciates, Christ's invitation is also a command (XII.55a–57), albeit one that people can disobey. But despite anticipating aspects of Christ's later oration that I addressed above, Wille's panic drives him into some theologizing whose inadequacy is amply revealed within *Piers Plowman*. Instead of following the paths the poem will take, into the narratives of human bondage and Christ's battles with the powers of sin, he expropriates Christ's gifts from their contexts, maintaining a position unknown to orthodox traditions of Christian teaching, namely that baptism isolated from the actual life of the baptized person guarantees the vision of God, the bliss of eternal life. Wille asserts that Christians, however disobedient to Christ's precepts and however impenitent, simply cannot be separated from final salvation in the City of God. At worst, he says, they will burn in purgatorial fires till Judgment Day (XII.58–71).[106] Wille claims that baptism makes a person into God's bondman and thus securely bound to God's saving lordship (XII.60–71). Christology and the evangelical narratives of salvation are abandoned. So is all conception of divine forgiveness as a transforming gift. Wille forgets the most pertinent figure of bondage in Christ's own teaching, one soon to be dramatized in the encounter with Semyuief: "whosoever committeth sin is a servant of sin" [omnis qui facit peccatum, servus est peccati] (John 8.34). He forgets that the "wages" [stipendia] of sin are death, whereas life everlasting is the gift

("gratia") of God in Christ (Rom. 6.23). He has also forgotten the intimate relations between baptism, the cross of Christ and the Resurrection, forgotten that justification is inextricably bound up with conversion
into the practices of a new life.[107] So he forgets that baptism entails stripping off habits of the "old man" and cultivating new ones according
to the image of God in Christ, a process whereby the bondman of sin
becomes a child of God.[108] He even forgets that he himself has experienced how the sinful acts of the "old man" become habitual chains.
Panic generates amnesia and manifold errors. Scripture seeks to encourage the trembling Wille by agreeing that divine mercy is certainly able to
amend all sin. But instead of returning to Christ's parable of the kingdom
that so disturbed Wille, she quotes from Psalm 144: "His mercy is over all
his works" (XII.74a). We should not wish to be justly charged by Conscience with the sound reasons he deployed against Mede for ignoring the
contexts of scriptural quotations (III.484–500).[109] So let us consider the
contexts of her quotation here. The previous verses in Psalm 144 remind
us that rejoicing in God's gracious, patient mercy goes with rejoicing in his
power and justice (Ps. 144.1–8). Continuing to celebrate God's mercy,
fidelity, and generosity, it concludes: "The Lord keepeth all them that love
him; but all the wicked he will destroy. My mouth shall speak the praise
of the Lord: and let all flesh bless his holy name for ever; yea, for ever
and ever" (Ps. 144.10–21). Grace and judgment are inseparable, offering a
pertinent topic for Wille's rumination at this point. But instead of continuing to explore the resources of Scripture in Christ's parables and the
psalms, the dialogue between Wille ("mysulue," XII.51) and Scripture is
interrupted. The voice of someone allegedly "broken out of helle" immediately dismisses "bokes" in a direct response both to Scripture, the revealed word of God in the "bokes" of the Church, and to Scripture's
quotations from her "bokes," Gospels and psalms (XII.75). The dismissive voice resembles Rechelesnesse in his sinful "rage" as he challenged "clergie" and "scripture scornede" (XIII.129–30), but it belongs to
Troianes, or Trajan. His opening dismissal of Scripture is not propitious.
The author of Scripture is God ("auctor sacrae scripturae est Deus"), and
the gift of divine revelation, including Christ's teaching, is given in canonical Scripture.[110] Furthermore, the revelation of God's word, as Wille
experiences, is an event, an action. In this even the Word forms listen-
ers into hearing agents who become the community of the Church (see

XVIII.125–294; XIX.48–336; XXI.177–334, 381–90). Despite this un-propitious entry, which should not be ignored, I incline to accept the apparently unanimous view that Trajan's breaking out of hell is not like that of Milton's Satan in the second book of *Paradise Lost* but rather in accord with the text referred to in the B version of this episode (B XI.161, deleted from C XII): that is, the "legenda sanctorum."[111] Nevertheless, the initial assertion that he was "broken out of helle" invites some obvious questions. Why was he in hell? How had he "broken out?" Trajan's answer to the first question is that he was "dampned to dwellen in hell" because he lacked baptism (XII.77).[112] This answer is supported by Christ in the form of the Samaritan. He teaches that absolutely nothing can save humanity without baptism in the blood of Christ, incorporation in the body of Christ (XIX.80–85). As my discussion of Christ's oration in hell made clear, this teaching coexists with one whose inflection may seem significantly different. In hell Christ proclaims a divine mercy constraining divine "ire" and a promise to be "merciable to monye of my halue bretherne" (XX.430–36). This promise is certainly a source of great hope. But it also leaves us with the word *monye,* not all, just as Christ takes "which hym luste" from hell leaving behind "which hym likede" (XX.430–36, 449). So we have no warrant to foreclose eschatological questions by guaranteeing ourselves universal salvation. The poem casts no doubts on Trajan's clear answer to the first question. His answer to the second question (how he broke out of hell) is less clear.

Having confessed that he was damned to hell, he claims that his virtues, virtues formed according to pagan "lawes," were able to snatch him from hell (XII.78–81). He does not pause to wonder how, if this is indeed the case, he was ever condemned to hell. Instead he chooses to proclaim his virtues. He describes himself as "a trewe knyht" who always practiced "werkes" of "love and leaute" and "soethnesse" according to his pagan "lawes" (XII.76, 80–82). Not for him any sympathy with Jesus's statement that "None is good but God alone" (Luke 18.19; see B X.447a), or with the pagan Cato's view, quoted by Reason: "Nemo sine crimine vivit" [Nobody lives without misdeed] (XIII.212). So he shows no glimpse of understanding how inveterate, habitual faults shape individual and collective lives, a shaping powerfully displayed in *Piers Plowman.* And if he could be saved by a form of life totally independent of Christ's incarnation and the body of Christ, contrary to Christ's teaching in *Piers Plowman* (XIX.83–95), why was he ever "dampned to dwellen in hell"? And, again, if this was the case, its consequences had been made utterly clear by St. Paul: "If justice be by the law, then Christ died in vain" [Si enim per legem iustitia ergo Christus gratis mortus est] (Gal. 3.21). But in fact "all" are under sin and "by the works of the law no flesh shall be justified" (Rom. 3.9, 20).[113] As the Lord's Prayer or Pater Noster taught, everybody needs to pray for the gift of forgiveness every day: "Forgive us our sins" [Dimitte nobis peccata nostra] (Luke 11.4). Trajan, however, never acknowledges that he has ever sinned, let alone that he has experienced the dominion of sin in human life. His breezy confidence makes the figure of Semyuief as superfluous as Christ's priestly journey into the distant land where he endured crucifixion. Trajan may be freed from hell, but he has certainly not yet begun to reflect on the Christian gospel and Trinitarian faith so central to *Piers Plowman*. Not surprisingly then, he apparently knows no gratitude to Christ, the one mediator of God and mankind.[114] There is no good reason to confuse this disposition with Langland's theology as it unfolds in the totality of his poem.

Although Trajan does not relate his salvation to the one who died "for our bote" (XX.473) and harrowed hell, he does say more about how he "was broken out of hell." He says that "a pope," St. Gregory, knew that this pagan was "dampned to dwellen in helle" despite his good works. Weeping at this judgment, the pope willed salvation to the pagan's soul. "God of his goodnesse ysey his grete will" and responded by granting his "bone," thus saving Trajan (XII.81–86). Yet even this part of Trajan's answer to the second question (how he broke out of hell) does not confirm claims about the ability of his pagan forms of life and law to save him.[115] On the contrary, it undermines them. But this does not give Trajan pause for reflection, and he concludes his self-justification with a reassertion of claims quite unsupported by the story he himself told: "Loue withoute lele bileue and my lawe rihtful / Saued me" (XII.87–88). As we have seen, the end of his form of love and law was actually hell. Ruminating on this, we do well to remember this "lawe" and its contexts. Trajan, after all, was an emperor, a Roman emperor. He was an integral part of a people ("populus"), a commonwealth ("res publica"). And we can recollect Augustine's definition of a "people": "the association of a multitude of rational beings united by a common agreement on the objects of their love." We thus understand the identity of a people, he says, by looking at what it loves (*CG* XIX.24). And Rome certainly belonged to the earthly city, in its loves, systematically disobeying the divine command that sacrifice (the act designed to unite people to God in holy fellowship) should be offered only to the one God in three persons. The consequence was a culture and religion based on an ontology of violence and embodying a pervasive love of dominion tempered, temporarily and at best, by a love of worldly glory.[116] Although Trajan offers no reflections on these matters, they are relevant to his confident claims about his love and his law, claims profoundly criticized by Liberum Arbitrium, "cristes creature," "in cristes court yknowe wel and of his kynne a party" (XIV.165–70; see XVII.125–321).[117] Doing that which was in him and his culture, however lovingly and lawfully in its terms, had led to hell. St. Gregory's tears and "bone" (prayer) flow from a grasp of this reality coexisting with the hope of salvation he has learned in the Church where he is pope, successor to Piers, himself endowed by Christ (XXI.182–90).

I began my discussion of Trajan by suggesting that his jaunty confidence in the needlessness of the revealed word of God in Scripture, one that foreshadows Rechelesnesse's similar dismissiveness (XIII.129–30), was not propitious. So it has proved. Despite his sojourn in hell and his miraculous delivery, he has no sense of human frailty, of human neediness, of human dependencies. Above all, and most bizarrely in terms of the poem in which he appears, he has absolutely no sense of any need for forgiveness, let alone of a community embodying forgiveness. There is no indication that he could join Wille's contemplation of human suffering:

> "Allas!" y saide, "þat synne so longe shal lette
> The myhte of goddes mercy that myhte vs alle amende."
> Y wepte for his wordes.
>
> (XVIII.286–88)

Nor does he show any inkling of the grateful, joyful humility that Wille manifests after witnessing Christ's crucifixion and harrowing of hell in the passage from the end of Passus XX quoted above (XX.470–75). Nor does he display any sign of the compassionate solidarity with humankind so central to Christ as Samaritan, in the Crucifixion and in his oration in hell. This is the compassionate solidarity invoked by Piers in his attempt to build a Christian community in Passus VIII: "hit are my bloody bretherne for god bouhte vs alle" (VIII.216). In fact his speech shows a striking lack of humility, a lack of any understanding of the need for reconciliation with God. The absence of even a hint of Christology or Trinitarian faith in his words suggests he still knows nothing of God's own humility, nothing of God taking the form of a servant "mankynde to saue / And soffred to be sold to se þe sorwe of deynge" (Phil. 2.5–11, with XX.217–24).[118] But *Piers Plowman* teaches us to recognize such lacks together with their human consequences. Langland's theology should never be identified with the lacks in Trajan's brief account of his salvation.

On the contrary, Trajan's statements must be understood as a moment, a fragment in a much larger, dialectical process. The latter is certainly constituted by such moments, but it also constitutes their meaning as they are superseded in the totality to which they belong. This process will overcome the isolation of Trajan's own story from the Word made flesh and reconfigure it with a meaning it still lacks. Trajan's confident declaration is subjected by Langland, though not by all his readers, to a later discussion by Liberum Arbitrium that I have just mentioned. There "cristes creature" (XVI.165–70) and teacher of Jesus (XVIII.137–41) draws out the catastrophic consequences of religions that invent a false mediator, "a false mene" (XVII.258). However "rihtfole" within the norms of their culture, however monotheistic, their adherents cannot love God "aryht" and inevitably "lyuen oute of lele byleue." The outcome is a lack of "lawe" and lack of "leute" (XVII.252–59, 150–62). As much as Augustine, Langland insists on humankind's need for the one true mediator, fully divine and fully human, in a divinity revealed as Trinity.[119] So the episode of Trajan should be understood as pointing beyond itself to the later Christological and Trinitarian narratives.

IV

I will conclude this discussion with Langland's brief and final mention of Trajan. This occurs during Ymagenatyf's conversation with Wille in Passus XIV. Ymagenatyf is the power of the soul that receives sensible forms on which the higher powers work. Through Ymagenatyf Langland enables Wille to review a number of disputes and topics on his journey toward his encounters, much later, with the tree of Charity, Abraham, Moses, and Christ.[120] One of Ymagenatyf's tasks is to defend the role of learning and "clerkes" against vehement attacks by Rechelessnesse and Wille (XIV.99–102; XIII.129–33), himself a frustrated clerk (V.35–108). This defense is also relevant to Trajan's dismissal of Scripture's books that I have already mentioned. Ymagenatyf argues that "a kynde witted man" cannot be saved without "clerkes" guiding him to Christ's treasure, the grace bestowed in baptism (XIV.50–57). Indeed, "clergy is cristes vycary to conforte and to cure; / Bothe lewede and lerede were lost yf clergie ne were" (XIV.70–71; see too 72–88a, 99–130).

Whatever the merits of his defense of "clergy," Ymagenatyf's own theologizing can be bizarrely idiosyncratic and blandly unaware of the anomalies it generates. This is especially so in the context from which he invokes Trajan, namely the story of the thief who "hadde grace of god a gode fryday" (XIV.131; cf. Rechelesnesse, XI.252–61, 275–312). In Luke's gospel one of the robbers crucified with Jesus prays that Christ will remember him when he comes into his kingdom. Jesus replies: "I say to thee, this day thou shalt be with me in paradise [in paradiso]" (Luke 23.42–43). Christ's unconditional grace and promise of paradise to the converted robber makes Ymagenatyf very uncomfortable.[121] He acknowledges that "god is ay gracious to alle þat gredeth to hym / And wol no wikkede man be lost bot if he wol hymsulue" (XIV.133–34, citing Ezek. 18.26–28). But he is convinced it would be thoroughly unreasonable (XIV.148) of Christ to give such unearned gifts to people like the crucified robber. So he glosses Luke's gospel. The robber "hadde heuene," as Jesus promised, but he is there without any "hey blisse" (XIV.135). Once in heaven, the robber remains an isolated beggar, "as a soleyn by hymsulue and yserued on þe erthe." He is eternally segregated from the communion of saints, both from "seynt Iohan and oþer seyntes" and from "maydenes," "martires," and "mylde weddewes" (XIV.135–44). Furthermore, because the man redeemed by the "grace of god" (XIV.131) has been a thief, he "is euermore in daunger" of the death penalty from "þe lawe" (XIV.145–46). Ymagenatyf is sure that it would be "no resoun ne riht" to serve a saint "and suche a thef togyderes" (XIV.147–48). The whole gloss on the Gospel displays a truly dire failure to grasp the implications of Christ's open table, his commitment to "publicans and sinners," his declaration to elites that "publicans and harlots shall go into the kingdom of God before you" (Matt. 9.11; 11.19; 21.32). *Piers Plowman* places such glossing, unequivocally, as failure.[122] Ymagenatyf's gloss also shows extraordinary disregard for Christian teaching on the communion of saints. Belief in this communion is affirmed in the Apostles' Creed ("Credo . . . Sanctorum communionem"). As St. Thomas says, commenting on this creed, "all the faithful are one body" and "the good of one is communicated to another" (see Rom. 12.5). The good of Christ, he continues, "is communicated to all Christians, as the wisdom of the head is communicated to all the members." Indeed, Christ's merits are communicated to all in this communion.[123] And that embraces the part of the communion still immersed in history. But in Ymagenatyf's teaching, the communion of saints, including its eschatological life, has been disintegrated and atomized.

Into this wayward teaching Ymagenatyf introduces the figure of Trajan. He asserts that because Trajan was a "trewe knyhte" he was not lodged deep in hell. He imagines that Christ therefore "hauede hym lihtliche out" (XIV.149–50). This strange imagining, so far removed from the poem's vision of the harrowing of hell in Passus XX, quite occludes Gethesmane and the Crucifixion. It also splits these off from the harrowing of hell, unlike Langland's writing in Passus XX. But what really preoccupies Ymagenatyf is still the redeemed robber and his putatively marginal place in heaven. He now asserts that as Trajan was not deep in hell, so the robber is not secure in heaven. In fact he is at the "loweste" point of heaven where "wel losliche he lolleth" (XIV.149–52a).[124] The term *lolleth* does significant and strange work here. It echoes the line preceding Ymagenatyf's version of the redeemed robber. There he had been approvingly ruminating about clerical privilege that saved literate criminals from being hanged at Tyburn where "lewede theues ben lolled vp" (XIV.129–30). The echo ("lolled," "lolleth") thus brings a hint of Tyburn into Christ's paradise, corroborating Ymagenatyf's view, mentioned above, that the robber imparadised by Christ is still a potential subject to the death penalty under the "lawe" (XIV.145–46a).[125] This imaginative teacher is quite untroubled by casting such a shadow into the heaven to which Christ brought the crucified robber.

Ymagenatyf turns once again to Trajan. Reflecting on God's grace, he hopes for the salvation of non-Christian "clerkes" such as Socrates, Solomon, and Aristotle (XIV.194–98). Like Trajan, Ymagenatyf is content to invent, at this point, a form of salvation without Christology, a readiness quite alien to Langland's theology as it unfolds in *Piers Plowman*. He also simply deletes the role of St. Gregory. Wille, however, still brooding on baptism and apparently unpersuaded that Trajan offers a pertinent model of salvation, questions Ymagenatyf's hope for the salvation of his non-Christian "clerkes" (XIV.199–201). In a passionate response Ymagenatyf insists that the just man ("iustus") shall be saved, invoking Trajan as his example: "Troianes was a trewe knyhte and toek neuere cristendoem / And he is saef, saith the boek, and his soule in heuene" (XIV.202–6). It is striking how much more enthusiastic Ymagenatyf is in asserting the salvation of a just pagan emperor than that of the crucified robber who confessed Christ and received Christ's own promise. This seems the product of an imagination under the sway of worldly power, imperial or knightly, an imagination, in this matter, alien to evangelical narratives, such as Luke's.

Ymagenatyf then picks up a prominent strand from Trajan's story. The "treuth" that saves is allegedly practiced in accord with the particular "lawe" of any culture, so long as the subject believes that there is no better "lawe." Ymagenatyf says that the "trewe god" certainly approves "trewe treuthe" defined in this thoroughly relativistic manner (XIV.209–12).[126] This position generates some fascinating and important difficulties. Although Ymagenatyf himself is unable to notice these, I will briefly follow his commendation of "clergy" as "cristes vycary" (XIV.70) by turning to St. Thomas Aquinas.[127] During his treatise on law in the *Summa Theologiae*, St. Thomas asks whether law makes men good (*ST* I-II.92.1). He answers that good law should indeed lead its subjects to virtue, making them good. It directs people to the common good regulated according to divine justice. However, St. Thomas raises a critical issue: sinful laws and sinful legislators. The latter can make laws that serve only their own material interests and oppose divine justice. He shows that such sinful laws will make people "good" only in relation to that particular polity. He considers the case of a band of robbers with its own laws prescribing what constitutes a "good" robber (*ST* I-II.92.1, resp.).

Pursuing the insights this example elicits, we can see that non-Christian "lawe" celebrated by Ymagenatyf and Trajan could belong to a wider community than a band of robbers. It could constitute a society organized around the worship of Moloch and the sacrifice of children. Or it could constitute a genocidal Nazi society. A "good" citizen formed in such a culture is likely to follow the given laws as the best available, a view instilled in the citizen from cradle to grave, a view enmeshed in every practice. He will become habituated in evil dispositions and actions. He will have a host of "good" reasons for crushing any opponent of the city's law. And so a "good," law-abiding citizen becomes a wicked person living a life shaped by mortal sin. These reflections remind us, as *Piers Plowman* often does with great force, how sin can be simultaneously individual and collective. Ymagenatyf has no sound reason to be confident that "trewe god" would praise such "good" citizens or that they deserve eternal salvation for following their culture's perverse "lawe" (XIV.209–14; XII.80).

Certainly this is not the view that emerges later in the poem when Wille encounters "cristes creature," Liberum Arbitrium (XVI.165–70), the figure who takes Wille to the great vision of salvation history in the tree of Charity (XVIII.1–178).[128] As I noted above, in discussing his correction of Trajan's assertions, he brings together Christology and ecclesiology; salvation is inseparable from the one true mediator, Jesus Christ, the way to participation in the life of the Trinity. Hence his commitment to Christian mission and the nonviolent conversion, "littelum and littelum" (XVII.318), of those nurtured in religions that imagine "a fals mene" between God and humankind (XVII.258; see XVII.125–321). Unlike Ymagenatyf, Langland will not allow us simply to ignore St. Paul's observations to those "senseless" and "bewitched" Galatians: "if justice be by the law, then Christ died in vain" (Gal. 3.1; 2.21). Trajan's declamation and Ymagenatyf's "hope" in "a corteyse more þen couenant" will be corrected and fulfilled only in the one who as God is the goal and as man is the way ("quo itur Deus, qua itur homo").[129] Unlike semi-Pelagianism or neo-Pelagianism or Pelagianism or liberal inflections of these, Langland's theology has Christology at its center, together with all that the Crucifixion discloses about the power and horizons of sin. In Passus VII, in his priestlike role, Repentance foresaw and remembered:

Ego in patre & pater in me est et qui me videt videt & patrem meum &c;
And sethe in oure secte, as hit semed, deyedest,
On a friday in fourme of man feledest oure sorwe:
Captiuam duxit captiuitatem.
The sonne for sorwe þerof lees siht for a tyme.
Aboute mydday, when most liht is and mel tyme of sayntes,
Feddest tho with thy fresshe blood oure forfadres in helle:
Populus qui ambulabat in tenebris vidit lucem magnam &c.
The lihte þat lup oute of the, lucifer hit blente
And brouhte thyne yblessed fro thennes into þe blisse of heuene.
A synful marie þe sey ar seynte marye þy dame
And al to solace synfole thow soffredest it so were:
Non veni vocare iustos set peccatores &c.
And al þat mark hath ymade, Matheu, Ion and lucas
Of thy douhtiokest dedes was don in oure sekte:
Verbum caro factum est.

> (VII.128a–40a; see, for the Latin quotations,
> John 14.9–10; Eph. 4.8; Isa. 9.2;
> Matt. 4.16; Matt. 9.13; John 1.14)

CHAPTER 5

Sin, Reconciliation, and Redemption

Augustine and Julian of Norwich

And God made man also upright, with the same power
of free choice, an animal of earth, yet worthy of heaven
if he adhered to the author of his being, but by the
same token, destined if he abandoned God, for a misery
appropriate to his kind of nature.

Augustine, *City of God,* XXII.1

For if, when we were enemies, we were reconciled to God
by the death of his Son, much more, being reconciled,
shall we be saved by his life.

Rom. 5.10

JULIAN OF NORWICH IS PROBABLY THE MOST WIDELY READ AND
admired writer from fourteenth-century England. Not only is she read,
taught, and written about in university departments of English, theology,
and religion, but she also has a substantial following outside universities

among Christians. There is an Episcopalian Order of Julian of Norwich, her works have been published in many modern translations, at least four Web sites are devoted to her, and, as her most recent editors note, "her cell is a stop on many a devout bus tour."[1] Indeed, on the cover of this edition the current archbishop of Canterbury observes that Julian's *Showings* "may well be the most important work of Christian reflection in the English language." This accords with views he had expressed many years earlier in *The Wound of Knowledge*: "She is a theologian of extraordinary intuitive resource" who displays "the essentially 'kenotic' character of the divine," and "she deserves to stand with the greatest theological prophets of the Church's history."[2] Such admiration for Julian is given with very good reasons. The longer version of her *Showings* is an extraordinarily powerful work of Christian theology, meditation, and devotion. Julian receives a "revelation" (2/285) from Christ and is drawn into an extensive, searching dialogue with him. Tenaciously searching, formidably intelligent, thoroughly learned in the traditions of the Church, she is enabled to explore, and often to explore critically, central strands of Christian teaching. The book is suffused with a joy and a generosity that truly display just what it might be to have heard that "God hath reconciled us to himself by Christ; and hath given us the ministry of reconciliation" (2 Cor. 5.18). Julian also writes with exquisite beauty in a capacious form that involves dialogue, disputation, vision, meditative reflection, dazzling imagery, and one of the most complex, inventive passages of allegorical writing in medieval literature. Not surprisingly, her work has received abundant and varied commentary.[3]

My own concerns in this chapter are limited to aspects that have preoccupied me throughout the present book: theologies of agency, freedom, and sin. I am certainly not attempting a reading that addresses all Julian's immensely rich explorations or all her often brilliant rhetorical strategies. But, limited as they may be, my concerns were also as much Julian's as Langland's or those of other theologians studied in these pages. Indeed, most commentators on the *Showings* address its teachings on sin because the question "What is synne?" (11/336) is a major topic in Julian's inquiries. Her answers to the question have elicited immense admiration in recent scholarship. Characteristic is the judgment made by Denise Baker in her distinguished work on Julian's theology: "While she affirms her submission to church teachings, she nonetheless presents a solution to the problem of evil that interrogates the retributive premises of or-thodox theodicy."[4] She does so, Baker argues, by offering "an alterna-tive" to Augustine's teaching on sin, the will, and salvation. This "alter-native" overthrows Augustine's "judicial paradigm" and his allegedly "legalistic definition of sin" with its "punitive" God displaying "malevo-lence toward sinners." The outcome is "her critique of the medieval ide-ology of sin."[5] Augustine is allegedly shown to have been wrong to think that sin is an act of "free will," "the deliberate violation of divine in-junctions," and Julian, in showing Augustine's mistakes, was correcting the medieval Church, which "attributed evil to the free will of creatures, either angelic or human, who deliberately chose to disobey God."[6] How-ever one evaluates Baker's reading of Augustine, her book was a major contribution to the understanding of Julian's *Showings* as a work of pro-found theological seriousness engaged in a critical dialogue with Augus-tine. Julian's interlocutor was, in Langland's figuration, one of the four "stottes" (horses) given by Grace to the Church "to harowen" what the evangelists had plowed in cultivating God's field. Augustine, Ambrose, Gregory, and Jerome teach the faith, harrowing holy Scripture with har-rows formed out of the gift of revelation, which is both Old and New Testament inseparably bound together (XXI.263–74).[7] By following Baker's invitation to examine that which Julian corrected, we may be able to sharpen our perception of what Julian actually did and with what consequences. And because Augustine has been woven into the present book he makes an appropriate interlocutor in its final chapter. Here I shall revisit Augustine's exegesis of humanity's first disobedience and the fruit of that forbidden tree as revealed in the history of the two cities.[8] This episode is an essential moment in Julian's *Showings* and one studied in the third part of the chapter.

I

Let us begin by recalling how the *City of God* returns to the story of the Fall and its implications for us in relation to the origin and end of two communities.[9] These two communities are two cities, known as the city of God, or Jerusalem, and the earthly city, or Babylon. These communi-ties are ordered by different forms of love. The earthly city is "created by self-love [amor sui] reaching the point of contempt for God, the heavenly city by the love of God carried as far as contempt of self. In fact the earthly city glories in itself, the heavenly city glories in the Lord" (XIV.28). Since we are constituted as social beings, our loves are inextricably bound up with our social practices. The earthly city, contemptuous of the God revealed in Scriptures and through the one mediator (XI.2), is dominated by the lust for dominion ("dominandi libido dominator"), loving its own power embodied in its powerful leaders (XIV.28). The loves fostered in the earthly city tend to turn fraternity into fratricide, recapitulating the story of Cain, who founded the first city (XV.1). We should recall that earlier in the *City of God* Augustine had written a sustained and often brilliant analysis of the politics, culture, religion, and structures of feeling cultivated in the earthly city and its supreme exemplification in Rome (I–V).[10]

One important fact should already be emerging from these recollections of the *City of God,* a fact systematically overlooked in Baker's rather dismissive talk of the "juridical" and "legalistic" nature of Augustine's theology of sin and salvation (67), namely that in the lives of social beings for whom the due end ("debitos fines") is social (XIX.5), love and justice, or injustice, are inseparable. So in the *De Trinitate* Augustine makes the following observation:

> But when the devil became a lover of power through the vice of his own perversity, and the betrayer and attacker of justice, and since in this respect men also imitate him so much more, in proportion as they set aside or even hate justice and strive after power, and as they either rejoice in acquiring power or are inflamed with the lust of it, it pleased God that for the sake of rescuing men from the power of the devil, the devil should be overcome not by power but by justice, and that men too, by imitating Christ should seek to overcome the devil not by power but by justice. (XIII.13)[11]

Our loves, like the devil's, are inextricably bound up with justice or injustice, individually and collectively. As Augustine wrote in *Nature and Grace* (70.84): "Hence, the beginning of love is the beginning of righteousness; progress in love is progress in righteousness; great love is great righteousness; perfect love is perfect righteousness" [Charitas ergo inchoata, inchoata justitia est; charitas provecta, provecta justitia est; charitas magna, magna justitia est; charitas perfecta, perfecta justitia est].[12] Charity and justice are, once, again, inseparable. In *The Spirit and the Letter* (36.64), Augustine states that this is explicitly affirmed by Jesus Christ in his summary of "all the law and the prophets":

> Someone might suppose that we lack nothing with regard to the knowledge of righteousness [ad cognitionem justitiae], since the Lord summed up and shortened his word upon earth [Rom. 9.28] and said that the whole law and the prophets depended on two commandments. He did not fail to state them and did so in plain language. He said, *You shall love the Lord your God with your whole heart and your whole soul and your whole mind* and *You shall love your neighbor as yourself* (Matthew 22.37, 39). What could be truer than that, when we have fulfilled these, we have fulfilled all righteousness [impleri omnino justitiam].[13]

But while we sinful creatures have to cultivate love in forms of justice directed to the final good, we must now confess, and hope to sustain, more a practice of mutual forgiveness than perfected virtue (*CG* XIX. 27). So love and the pursuit of justice, together, foster communities dedicated to embodying forgiveness.[14] Such are the constituents of what Baker dismisses as Augustine's "juridical paradigm" (67), constituents forgotten in many accounts of his theology. With this brief attempt to recollect some central aspects of Augustine's teaching, I will turn back to the *City of God*.

In the present contexts we should remember that Augustine precedes his account of the Creation and the Fall by addressing the sources of Christian theology. These are, he stresses, the revelation of God to the prophets, later through Christ, God incarnate, and after that "through the apostles, telling men all that he decided was enough for man." God also founded the Scriptures that are gathered in the Church as canonical. The Scriptures, he writes, are of the most eminent authority ("eminentissimae auctoritatis"), and we trust them in "those things which we need to know for our good, and yet are incapable of discovering by ourselves" (*CG* XI.3: see XI.2–4).[15] Christian doctrine depends on God's self-revelation handed on in Scripture, and this is the point from which St. Thomas's *Summa Theologiae* sets out (I.1.1–10).[16] And as Robert Jenson observed in his *Systematic Theology*: "Throughout Scripture, the central moral and historical category is 'righteousness.' Since Israel's God is invested in Israel's community, her righteousness consists in faithfulness to that community; thus righteousness in Israel's Bible is the vigor of the entire network of communal relations within which participants divine and human live. Nor are these relations external; precisely as relations, they constitute the quality of the persons. Scripture's many words for sin are mere contraries of 'righteousness' and denote one or another betrayal of community."[17] Sin is "what God does not want done," rebellion against God (see, e.g., Ezek. 20.1–31), but Jenson rightly observes that this is also rebellion against the community's hope and its flourishing.[18]

Before Augustine addresses human sin he considers the angels, those who belong to the city of God and those who once did but now do not (*CG* XI.9, 33; XII.1, 6). The latter sinned and so abandoned God, as Scripture recounts (XI.33; 2 Pet. 2.4; Matt. 4.9). Those who had been created good chose to reject the community that loves the creator of this good, and in doing so they founded the earthly city (XII.1). Individual identity is complicatedly but empathically social, a central fact in Augustine's theology of fall and redemption, a subject touched on in chapter 1. The good angels' wills and desires constantly hold to the good that is common to all ("in communi omnibus bono"): that is, to God. Other angels, however, mysteriously delighted in their own power. They thought they were made solely for their own good. In this disposition they fell from the supreme, beatific *common* good to what they grasped, illusorily, as their own exclusive *private* good ("a superiore communi omnium beatifico bono ad propria defluxerunt").[19] They chose to be "self-sufficient for their own felicity, and hence would forsake their true good" (XXII.1). For the creatures' true ecstatic freedom and final good is thoroughly social, a common life (XXII.30). Sin, as the *City of God* had already displayed with painful clarity in its long account of Rome (books I–V), is an activity that shatters the bonds of charity and substantive commitments to the good of others, to the good that is common to all whose source and end is God. This, as we saw in the previous chapter, is a vision powerfully embodied in *Piers Plowman* but one also taught in late medieval instructions on the sacrament of penance around the obligations of restitution.[20]

Augustine's statement on the fall of the angels echoes what he had written in his "literal" interpretation of Genesis (*De Genesi ad Litteram*).[21]

In book XI, he joins two texts of Scripture: "The beginning of all sin is pride" (Ecclus. 10.15) and "The root of all evils is avarice" (1 Tim. 6.10). Avarice is identified as a product of the will to dominion and a love for one's own property. Augustine states that in Latin the adjective *private* qualifying property suggests "loss rather than gain in value: every privation, after all, spells diminution." The ironic outcome is that "the very means by which pride aims at preeminence serve to thrust it down into sore straits and want, when its ruinous self-love removes it from what is common to what is its own property" (XI.15.19). The devil's pride, "his twisted love of self," is also avarice, the love of his own personal power, "a rejection of the bonds of holy companionship." Charity, in contrast, "does not seek her own" (1 Cor. 13.5): that is, it "does not rejoice in private preeminence and superiority" (XI.15.19). Here, too, Augustine sees "two loves," one of which is holy, communitarian, and directed to the source of life, the other one of which is unholy and private ("privatum"). The determination to set aside the common good is a determination to set aside justice, obedience to God, and peace with one's fellow creatures in a quest for self-gratification and dominion over others (XI.15.20). These "two loves were thus first manifested in the angels" and showed "the two cities, one of the just, the other of the wicked" (XI.15.20). As I observed in the first chapter of this book, conversion will always entail a conversion from one community to another, from one set of relationships with God, neighbors, and self to another, from one form of love and life to another. None of this means, for Augustine, that conversion simply deletes "the old man"; it simply deletes habitual desires and memories shaped in the earthly city, in rebellion against God.[22]

In the *City of God,* Augustine also ascribes the source of the angelic fall from the common good to a putatively private good in the will. The angels who reject the commonality of love in the city of God are not compelled to do so by nature or fate. Indeed, their ability to choose is a sign of the greatness and praiseworthiness of the nature with which the creatures were endowed. This remains so even when the will chooses a version of its own good in rebellion against its own final good (XII.1). Such an act of will exemplifies what he had already argued about evil, namely that evil is a willed rejection of participation in the eternal light whose consequence is the deprivation, the lack, the loss of good. Evil is the privation of good in an act of will (XI.9; XI.22). Augustine's teachings about evil as privation become orthodox commonplaces in Christian tradition, ones that Julian herself espouses. But it is clear that in this model of privation the role of the will in evil is not negated. On the contrary, it is central. The will itself makes an act evil ("Quid est enim quod facit voluntatem malam, cum ipsa faciat opus malum?" XII.6).[23] Angels and humans are creatures who love and who define themselves by the form and goal of their loves. But this gift of freedom can be lost in its very exercise. The *Confessions* generates a web of narratives driven by the hungry love of the subject who is constantly, restlessly loving to love but choosing that which enchains the will in troublesome and increasingly compulsive acts. Such is the bondage of the will (*Confessions*, III.1.2; VI.12.21; VIII.5.10–12). Both in the *Confessions* and in the *City of God* Augustine argues that if the will (human or angelic) turns away from God to the self envisaged as a "private," autonomous center of desire it simultaneously deprives itself of the power to love anyone other than itself. This turns out to be a form of desire that is catastrophic for self and others: evil. In these acts the will abandons justice—toward God, fellow creatures, and the self.

With this extensive prelude in place, Augustine is ready to focus on human sin and human death. God created humans to be united by origin, likeness, and the affection of kinship (*CG* XII.22). They were called on a journey that would culminate in community with angels and immortal joy without any intervening death (XII.22).[24] But this blissful way to a blissful end depended on forms of love toward God that constituted obedience. If humans were to recapitulate the use of free will displayed by those angels who chose to reject God and the common good, if they were to use the gift of free will proudly, that is, in self-loving choice of the "private" against the community, then the consequences of such agency would be catastrophic. The biblical term for that catastrophe was "death" (XII.22; XIII.1–16; see Gen. 2.17, 3.3–4). However polysemous the saga of Genesis 3, we can be in no doubt that human flourishing demands obedience to the divine precepts. In this story of creation, sinful fall, divine judgment, and divine care for the fallen foreshadows the story of the covenant between God and Israel in the Old Testament. Like the history of God and Israel, Genesis 1–4 elicits a Christocentric, prophetic allegory pointing to the new covenant, to the reconciliation between God and fallen humanity in the mediator Jesus Christ.[25]

Some aspects of the human fall in Augustine's exegesis come into extremely interesting dialogue with Julian's treatment of this event in the *Showings* (especially *CG* XIII.13–15, 21; XIV.1–28; XV.1). His account shows that, in many ways, the human fall recapitulates the fall of the angels already discussed. He analyzes the way in which the Fall is presented in Scripture as an act of will, an act of love directed toward what was judged to be its own pleasure and power, a choice made against commitment to God and fellow creatures, both future and present (XIII.13–14). From the misuse of free choice ("a liberi arbitrii malo uso") followed a "chain of disasters" (XIII.14). In this decisive act Adam and Eve are at one, equally free, equally willing, and equally responsible (XIII.13; see XIII.13–15).[26] Augustine emphasizes that the human will "takes the initiative" and that initiative is to forsake God "in disobedience." In doing so, the soul forsakes the source of its life; the consequence is death (XIII.15; Gen. 2.17).

Augustine quotes from the passage in which Adam and Eve, having eaten the fruit of the forbidden tree, perhaps imagined as a shortcut to deification (Gen. 3.5–6), hear the voice of the Lord. They hide from God: "And the Lord God called Adam, and said to him: Where art thou?" (Gen. 3.8–9). Augustine's comment on this haunting moment points toward the humans' excitement in plotting their elevation and the consequent inattention: "Obviously God was not asking for information; he was rebuking Adam; and by the form of the rebuke he was warning him to take notice where he was, in that God was not with him" (*CG* XIII.15). God is admonishing Adam ("admonens") to recover the kind of attention that is one of the first casualties of self-will. In such excited acts of putatively self-gratifying will we become inattentive to the complex circumstances of our choices, inattentive to their diachronic implications and to the network of relations (present and future) in which they are performed: freewheeling presentism. Augustine's allegorical exegesis then brings home the force of the divine admonition. He reads the story as a prophetic representation of salvation history. It figures forth the ways in which God, through the mediator Christ, with his Church and Scriptures, will bring supreme good out of the destructive self-love of human agency (XIII.21). The tree of knowledge, in this allegorical exegesis, can be understood as "the personal decision of man's free will" [proprium voluntatis arbitrium] (XIII.21). The humans have taken their own judgment ("proprium. . . arbitrium") and tried to make it an exclusively private ("proprium") issue.[27] It turns out that such absolute privatization is not possible for human beings without dire consequences.

In book XIV, Augustine develops his theological, philosophical, and psychological reflections on the two cities whose history he is writing (*CG* XIV.1; XIV.28). He expands his account of the Fall that Julian, too, will address in *Showings,* chapter 51 (see *CG* XIV.11 and 13). Once more, Augustine focuses on the ways in which evil acts are generated by evil acts of the will. He now takes up Christ's statement that "the evil tree bringeth forth evil fruit" (see Matt. 7.16–20) and likens the defective wills of Adam and Eve to the evil tree bearing evil fruit. The human couple in the scriptural narrative are given true freedom of will: that is, freedom from compulsive servitude to the habits of sin. But in their attempt to assert that freedom as an autonomous, private good they lose the gift of freedom they were exercising and enslave their divided souls to inner anarchy. Augustine quotes Christ's words in John 8.36: "If the Son sets you free, then you will be truly free," that is, "truly saved" (XIV.11). So God's will to reconcile humanity to God informs both creation and fall. In affirming this Julian follows a core component of Christian theology and liturgy.

But having treated the will of Adam and Eve as one in his analysis of the relation between the will's choice and evil action, Augustine then follows the narrative of Genesis and apostolic commentary to distinguish different motivations in the choice against the city of God. Eve, he observes, accepted the serpent's statement as true (Gen. 3.4–6; 1 Tim. 2.14). Adam did not (1 Tim. 2.14). Like Milton after him, Augustine identifies Adam's reason for disobeying God as the refusal "to be separated from his only companion, even it if involved sharing her sin" (*CG* XIV.11; *Paradise Lost,* IX.952–59). The consequence was that both "were taken captive by their sin and entangled in the snares of the Devil" (XIV.11). This entrapment, entanglement, and captivity of the will is displayed with immense power in Augustine's *Confessions* (VIII.5.10–12; see, too, X.30.41, X.31.44–32.48). Yet the humans had hoped to create a space in which they could plot together and with a slippery, twisting trickster to reject God's covenant and to invent a narrative of autonomous agents possessing the fruits of the earth in a freedom answerable to none. This is a striking image of central features in the earthly city, one whose polity, ethics, and religion Augustine had displayed in books I–V of the *City of God* and would return to in book XIX.

Augustine's account of human sin includes a virtue and a vice that are conspicuously absent from Julian of Norwich's *Showings*. The virtue I have in mind is obedience and the vice disobedience. Both have been encountered in the foregoing commentary, but in book XIV of the *City of God* Augustine pauses over obedience and disobedience. Chapter 13 begins with an analysis of pride as the beginning of every sin, following the lines we traced earlier from the *Literal Meaning of Genesis*, XI.15.19 (Ecclus. 10.15). But the self-pleasing will of pride, committed to abandoning God and existing in itself ("esse in semet ipso"), ironically misses the plenitude it aims at and draws near to the nothingness out of which it was created. True enough, in the liturgy we are exhorted to lift up our hearts, but not to oneself, which is pride, but to God. And this proper exultation, says Augustine, is obedience (XIV.13).

In modern liberal societies it is hard for many to imagine how obedience could be a virtue; on the contrary, it tends to be regarded as a mindless or malevolent subjection to tyranny. There can be no question that obedience has indeed been put to such uses time and time again. But any distinctively Christian obedience would have to be worked out along lines set by "Peter and the apostles," who said: "We ought to obey God, rather than men" (Acts 5.29). Augustine was fully aware that Scripture and many Christian traditions taught that the love of God, which generated obedience to the precepts and covenant, simultaneously demanded disobedience to certain authorities and commandments in the earthly city. This, he stressed, would often lead to hatred of Christians in the earthly city, assaults, and persecutions (*CG* XIX.17).[28]

But the disobedience displayed in Genesis 3 bears no relation to such lovingly obedient disobedience to the authorities, religion, and culture of the earthly city. Augustine seeks to elaborate his understanding of Christian obedience: "God's instructions demanded obedience, and obedience is in a way the mother and guardian of all the other virtues in a rational creature, seeing that the rational creature has been so made that it is to man's advantage to be in subjection to God, and it is calamitous for him to act according to his own will and not to obey the will of his Creator" (*CG* XIV.12). For Augustine, as for Langland or Julian, God is love (1 John

4.7–13). Satan is the tyrant consumed by the lust for dominion (XIV.11). Here the language of obedience is to bolster his own power. But God's call to obedience to the precepts and covenant is for man's final flourishing in the city of God. Furthermore, in seeking a way to bring good out of apparent catastrophe, God chose to embody obedience as a virtue inextricably bound up with divine love and human salvation: "For let this mind be in you, which was also in Christ Jesus: Who being in the form of God, thought it not robbery to be equal with God: But emptied himself, taking the form of a servant, being made in the likeness of men, and in habit found as a man. He humbled himself, becoming obedient unto death, even to the death of the cross" (Phil. 2.5–8). Ringing, too, in Augustine's ears were many similar statements by Paul, such as this one: "For as by the disobedience of one man, many were made sinners; so also by the obedience of one, many shall be made just" (Rom. 5.19). His thinking about obedience and disobedience was shaped by texts such as these and Jesus's own fusion of love and obedience: "If you love me, keep my commandments" (John 14.15; see, too, 15.10).[29]

In this light I will now return to Augustine's comments on pride and sin in his treatment of Genesis 3 (*CG* XIV.13). I noted how he showed the ways in which the will to autonomy and the abandonment of God draws humanity toward nothingness. Such is the teleology of disobedience. But contrary to Satan's promise (Gen. 3.5), humans "would have been better able to be like gods if they had in obedience adhered to the supreme and real ground of their being, if they had not in pride made themselves their own ground" (XIV.13). In choosing to be self-sufficient, humanity "defects from the one who is really sufficient for him." Evil is thus when "man regards himself as his own light, and turns away from that light which would make man himself a light if he would set his heart on it" (XIV.13). Thus Augustine answers the question that so preoccupies Julian of Norwich's *Showings*: "What is synne?" (11/336).

But before turning to Julian I wish to consider one other feature of Augustine's reading of Scripture around humanity's fall into sin. I think it helps us attend more closely to some of Julian's choices and their consequences. This feature is Augustine's sense that Scripture discloses a richly textured human drama. William Babcock describes this well. In book XIV of the *City of God,* the action of Adam and Eve "took place in and through a complex set of circumstances involving the interaction of a variegated cast of characters."[30] Augustine's attention was drawn to the human responses to God's question about their new avoidance of God and their new shame: "And Adam said, 'The woman, whom thou gavest me to be my companion, gave me of the tree, and I did eat.' And the Lord God said to the woman, 'Why has thou done this?' And she answered: 'The serpent deceived me, and I did eat'" (Gen. 3.12–13). In a dazzling, extended psychological and theological exploration, Milton drew out the resentments, hostilities, and evasions in this moment of fallen history (*Paradise Lost,* IX.1046–1189, X.103–62). Augustine's comments on what he notices are sparse in comparison with Milton's, but they are congruent. He finds the couple's response to God's questions even more culpable than the initial acts of will that culminated in the rejection of God and the covenant. For both humans "search for an excuse" even when their sins are manifest. In Augustine's view, this is the work of the pride that has decided to set God aside. It is pride, he writes, that "seeks to pin the wrong act on another; the woman's pride blames the serpent, the man's pride blames the woman." Nowhere is there any acknowledgment that each of them has chosen against God. "There is not a whisper anywhere here of a plea for pardon [petitio veniae], nor of any entreaty for healing" (*CG* XIV.14). There is no recognition that in the midst of abundant life they have chosen death (see Deut. 30.19). Pride involves an incurvature of the soul on itself; this diminishes a person's perception of reality, of others, and of the gifts received. So it makes for overwhelming ingratitude (XIV.15). As Augustine analyzes the consequences of such turning against the source of life, such disobedience, he characteristically describes them in a manner that is both inner and outer, both individual and collective (e.g., XIV.15–28). We are thus ready to encounter fratricide, martyrdom, and the founding of the Church (Gen. 4).

Book XIV concludes with the reflection on what we have been shown in the opening chapters of Genesis. Scripture has shown us

> that the two cities were created by two kinds of love: the earthly city was created by self-love [amor sui] reaching the point of contempt for God, the Heavenly City by the love of God carried as far as contempt of self. In fact, the earthly city glories in itself, the Heavenly City glories in the Lord. . . . In the former, the lust for domination lords it over its princes as over the nations it subjugates; in the other, both those

put in authority and those subject to them serve one another in love, the rulers by their counsel, the subjects by obedience. The one city loves its own strength shown in powerful leaders; the other says to its God, "I will love you, my Lord, my strength." (*CG* XIV.28)

This quotation brings me to the boundary of this *excursus* into Augustine's reading of the Fall in sacred Scripture. But I will draw some further reflections on what follows Augustine's reading of the saga in Genesis. Books XV–XVIII address the history of the two cities. This is the history of the covenant, salvation history as disclosed through the sacred Scriptures of the Old Testament. The sequence reminds us, if we needed reminding (as Manichees and Marcionites did), that Christianity is unintelligible without God's covenant with Israel, the people chosen by God to be "a priestly kingdom and a holy nation" (Exod. 19.16), that olive tree into which Christians are grafted (Rom. 11.24). History is an inescapable aspect of the covenant. We do well to remember that Augustine earlier recounted how he had not been able to contemplate conversion to Christianity until Ambrose's exegesis showed him how to read the Old Testament. Figural interpretation was a decisive discovery that led to his understanding of how the law and the prophets, with historical narratives concerning Israel, were integral to the Catholic faith. This did not bring him into the Church, but it was an important part of the processes of conversion.[31]

II

Julian of Norwich confesses that she, like all humans, will continually sin and do many "evylles" (37/436; 46/492). We are all sinners (80/712). She also emphasizes that sin is darkness impeding the vision of God and the sharpest scourge that can afflict any "chosyn soule" (72/663; 39/449). Sin is "alle that is nott good" and "the uttermost trybulation" that Christ suffered for us (13/405). Such statements seem unequivocal support for Denise Baker's judgment that despite her critique of Augustinian theology Julian "subscribes to a thoroughly Augustinian understanding of human peccability" (74).[32] According to Baker, Julian "repudiates the Pelagian belief that salvation is a reward for good works and the more prevalent semi-Pelagian notion that her own effort to do her best initiates God's gift of justifying grace" (74). Julian combines a "thoroughly Augustinian" understanding of human sinfulness with an equally thorough rejection of what Baker calls "the orthodox medieval solution, first proposed by Augustine, to the problem of evil" (67), a solution bound up with "the medieval ideology of sin" and "Augustinian theodicy" (68; see, too, 69, 74). Baker apparently finds no problems in this combination. But I am convinced neither that such a combination is coherent nor that Julian actually did develop "a thoroughly Augustinian understanding of human peccability." I outlined the latter in the second part of this chapter and in the previous chapter on *Piers Plowman* explored a model of sin's consequences that is congruent with Augustine's. Here I will consider Julian's answer to a question that she places at the heart of the *Showings*: "What is synne?" (11/336). What does it mean to confess, "I shalle do ryght nought but synne" (36/436) while simultaneously teaching that I have "a godly wylle that nevyr assentyth to synne" (37/443)? What are the implications of correcting the story of Genesis 3 so that it now denies that Adam turned against God's covenant and denies that humanity chose to reject God's word? In considering Julian's answers to these questions, I will be exploring their implications for the Christian theology of salvation history, free choice, will, and responsibility.

I set out with comments on the place where Julian's visions and dialogues with Christ themselves begin: Golgotha.[33] Her representation of the Crucifixion is replete with writing of extraordinary subtlety, conceptually and imagistically, but as I have written about this elsewhere, I will now limit my comments on her treatment of this event to one observation: namely, that in her long and detailed meditations on the Crucifixion (chs. 4–26), Julian deletes all the human agents and human institutions (religious, political, judicial, military) involved in killing Jesus Christ.[34] In doing so, she necessarily sets aside the sacred narratives that display these agents, their motives, and the processes culminating in the judgment and crucifixion of Jesus.[35]

Julian's decision to eliminate the human agents and institutions responsible for condemning Jesus to death transforms the event of the Crucifixion in ways that are very far-reaching. Her choices systematically desocialize and depoliticize the Crucifixion. The grammar of the sequence sometimes registers the deletions on which it is composed. For example:

"I saw the reed bloud rynnyng downe from vnder the garlande. . . right as it was in the tyme that the garland of thornes was pressed on his blessed head" (4/294). The passive voice, "was pressed," acknowledges that someone was pressing the thorns into Jesus's head, but it occludes the agent. This grammatical form accords perfectly with the deletions in question. A similar effect is achieved by Julian's choice of nominalizations in her description of the Passion. She tells us she saw "dyspyte, spyttyng, solewyng and buffetyng, and manie languryng paynes, mo than I can tell, and offten chaungyng of colour" (10/324). The processes by which evil is constituted and enacted, by determinate agents, working in determinate institutions, are occluded. This is characteristic of Julian's vision, and the implications of such grammar will emerge in the ensuing discussion.

The work done by this grammar can be brought out by comparing the narratives of the action in the gospels of Matthew and John. First from Matthew 27.27–31:

> Then the soldiers of the governor, taking Jesus into the hall, gathered together unto him the whole band. And stripping him, they put a scarlet cloak about him. And platting a crown of thorns, they put it upon his head, and a reed in his right hand. And bowing the knee before him, they mocked him, saying: Hail King of the Jews. And spitting upon him, they took the reed and struck his head. And after they had mocked him, they took off the cloak from him and put on his own garments and led him away to crucify him.

Second, from John 19.1–6:

> Then therefore Pilate took Jesus and scourged him. And the soldiers platting a crown of thorns, put it upon his head: and they put on him a purple garment. And they came to him and said: Hail, King of the Jews. And they gave him blows. Pilate therefore went forth again and saith to them: Behold, I bring him forth unto you, that you may know I find no cause in him. Jesus therefore came forth bearing the crown of thorns and the purple garment. And he saith to them: Behold the Man. When the chief priests, therefore, and the servants had seen him, they cried out, saying: Crucify him, crucify him.

Pilate saith to them: Take him you, and crucify him: for I find no cause in him.

In both narratives the agents who crown Jesus, mock him, and assault him are identified. They are the soldiers of Rome acting under the command of the Roman governor. Jesus is identified as Jewish and mocked as such ("Hail, King of the Jews"). We are also told that the representative of imperial power sees no reason to kill this man but that the "chief priests" and their servants demand his death, by crucifixion. Theology is inseparable here from a thoroughly political narrative. Jesus is confronting a concentration of political, military, and religious powers, the powers who have found his ministry an intolerable challenge. Matthew, in the same chapter, also says that the religious elite "persuaded the people" to threaten a riot unless this man was condemned to death (27.20, 24). Religion and politics, elites and "the people," are bound together in this event and the culture in which it was made. Langland's meditation on the Crucifixion is far more compressed than Julian's and offers a comparison that brings out the latter's choices well.

In *Piers Plowman* Langland figures the Crucifixion as a strange and densely populated joust. As we saw in the previous chapter, Jesus is a knight without spear, without spur, barefoot, riding an ass, and armed with vulnerable *humana natura,* his divinity hidden. The joust is in Jerusalem and involves both human forces and the fallen demonic powers encapsulated in the fiend. The scene is explicitly a trial (invoking Matt. 27.19):

> Thenne cam *Pilatus* with moche peple, *sedens pro tribunali*
> To se how douhtyliche deth sholde do and demen here beyre rihte.
>
> (XX.35−36)

Jewish leaders and Roman "iustice" act against Jesus: "And alle þe Court on hym cryede *'crucifige'!*" (XX.37−38). In this context Langland has the officers of human justice taking "kene thornes," making a garland from these, and setting this "sore" on Christ's head, an act that runs into the Crucifixion itself (XX.47−59). The brief sequence compels reflection on the politics of the earthly city and its forms of justice. We witness the assimilation of God and God's covenant to the contingent self-interests of political factions united in the lust for dominion. Because the judgment is against the one who embodies Justice, the only ultimate Judge, Langland elaborates the texture of painful ironies in the gospels, ironies centered on religion and justice in the earthly city, its agents, and institutions. The ironies are also haunted by the return of the unjustly condemned one in the power and glory of that divine love that is inseparable from justice and truth, a return prefigured in the harrowing of hell with which Langland follows the scene of the Crucifixion (XX.115–475). Langland thus gathers up the poem's pervasively and densely specified understanding of sin. In individual *and* collective choices we compose evil societies in which sinful actions, disobedience against God's covenant with humanity, and unkindness to our neighbors become normal.[36] Sin is shown to be both personal and transcending the personal: it generates solidarities and produces consequences whose legacies far exceed the intentions and actions of the immediate agents. That is why St. Paul declares that all, Jews and Gentiles, are under the dominion of sin (Rom. 3.9; 11.32). As Augustine often sought to show, human rebellion against God—that is, sin—transforms the gift of our powers into compulsive, tyrannical, and lordless forces likely to destroy others and ourselves.[37]

But the lust for dominion, the fantasies of autonomy involved in sin, also have designs upon God. If such humans consider divine action they are confident that they can set the terms that define it. So Langland has the officials of justice taunt Christ on the cross:

> Yf thow be Crist and kynges sone come adoun of the rode;
> Thenne shal we leue that lyf þe loueth and wol nat late the deye.
>
> (XX.55–56)

Following the gospels (Matt. 27.39–43; Mark 15.29–32; Luke 23.36–37), Langland thus displays the consolidation of sin in taunts that recapitulate the demonic temptation that Jesus had already overcome at the beginning of his ministry: "Then the devil took him up into the holy city and set him upon the pinnacle of the temple, And said to him: If thou be the son of God, cast thyself down, for it is written: *That he hath given his angels charge over thee, and in their hands shall they bear thee up, lest perhaps thou dash thy foot against a stone*" (Matt. 4.5–6; see similarly Luke 4.9–10).[38] Sin, collective sin, institutionalized in the earthly city, blinds all the agents in this collective act from even the merest hint of a perception that Christ's refusal to come "adoun of the rode," the refusal to terminate their own practices of torture at their derisive command, could be an act of God. After all, it is characteristic of the earthly city that it worships God or gods who can be manipulated or controlled to sustain the city's lust for dominion, its victories, and its own form of peace (*CG* XV.7). How unimaginable that God would take the form of a servant who "humbled himself, becoming obedient unto death, even to the death of the cross," actions related to "the disobedience" that made "sinners" (Phil. 2.5–11; Rom. 5.17–19).

Langland's grasp of the social nature and catastrophic consequences of sin, the shaping of people's most intimate lives by the habitual practices of the earthly city, was often shared by late medieval dramatists as they performed the events of the Crucifixion. Indeed, they could do so with a scope, detail, and insistence that forced their audience to recognize themselves as the laity and clergy of the town that had become the polity crucifying Christ. In the East Anglian N-Town playing of the Passion, for example, the sequence of events leading to the Crucifixion are represented in thoroughly communal and political terms. A group among the religious leadership finds Christ a dangerous threat to their power. They are especially vexed at his preaching to the people and the following he draws. Dangerous to them, Christ must be dangerous to God. The contemporary paradigm in which this confrontation is grasped and played is that of the persecution of heretics. Ananias declares that as judge of the law he is expert at discerning heretics and giving them due judgment. Taking counsel from theologians, he decides to involve the secular arm, "temperal jewgys," and to follow the practices of the English Church in its persecution and execution of those it deemed to be heretics. So the charges become heresy and sedition. Christ is both "an eretyk" and "a tretour" to the lay sovereign. One of the punishments considered is the appropriate contemporary punishment for someone who combines challenges to both sources of power in the earthly city of England: hanging, drawing, and burning. The play concentrates on this conjuncture throughout the Crucifixion.[39] The York Corpus Christi plays offer an even richer, more densely textured version of the earthly city and the forms of life that organize and kill Jesus Christ. The plays display individual and collective agency, individual and collective choices, in such a way as to show us how our city, our institutions, and our practices constitute forms of life in which demonic evil can be habitualized, made part of an ordinary working day. There is no need to elaborate these reflections on the York plays and their relationship to their culture and its politics, lay and ecclesiastical, because this has been studied in exceptional depth by Sarah Beckwith in *Signifying God*.[40]

Recollecting such contemporary meditations on the Crucifixion can help us identify the choices Julian makes and the options she rejects.[41] Her choices extract the Crucifixion from the earthly city and its agents. Nobody is actually responsible for organizing the event, for torturing and killing Jesus. Nothing compels our recognition that the city where this happens is ours, these judges ours, these torturers ours, these sane workmen dutifully solving the technological problems of crucifixion ourselves in our crafts and fraternities. True enough, Julian once tells us that she sees "a fygur and a lyknes of our fowle blacke dede, which that our feyre bryght blessed lord bare for our synne" (10/327–28).[42] But this "fygur" is not unpacked. The relationships between "our fowle blacke dede," the Crucifixion, and just how, or why, Jesus "bare" our sins in this condemnation are not specified. Such specification could go down the different paths chosen by Langland or by the authors of the N-Town or York plays. But Julian rejects such options and immediately tells us that this vision turned her attention to Veronica's handkerchief: "It made me to thynke of the holie vernacle of Rome, which he portrude with his one blessed face, when he was in his hard passion, willfully goyng to his death, and often chaungyng of coloure, of the brownhead and the blackhead, rewlyhead leenhead" (10/328).[43] Instead of meditation on the agencies that constitute sin, specifically in relation to the Crucifixion, Julian turns to an aestheticizing contemplation of the wounded body that I have analyzed elsewhere. This strategy deliberately resists conventional affective identification, but it also prevents the kind of specification of sin and its culture that I have just illustrated.[44] Someone might object that this kind of specification would be irrelevant to Julian since she is alluding to the source of all sin, to original sin symbolized as "our fowle blacke dede." But such an objection overlooks the fact that precisely what a theologian means by original sin and its consequences needs explication: the term does not have its meaning written across its face. Nor does its invocation tell us how it informs our actions, or which of our actions it does inform and with what consequences. Nor does its mere invocation explain why

Christ is being crucified in Jerusalem. Because Julian herself grasps the force of these questions, she defers her answers to them until chapter 51. She presents that long chapter as the way Christ "answeryed in shewyng full mystely" (51/513) her questions about sin and the marked tensions between what she sees and the "comyn techyng of holy church" (50/511). I shall discuss this answer below, but before doing so I will mention a fascinating aspect of the way Julian envisions the Crucifixion. This is her decision to omit Jesus's cry of dereliction from the cross: "My God, my God, why have you forsaken me?" [Deus meus, Deus meus, ut quid derelequisti me?] (Matt. 27.46; Mark 15.34; Ps. 21.2). In *Powers of the Holy* I compared Julian's remarkable meditation on the Crucifixion with more conventional late medieval approaches. There I discussed the fact that in her meditation Jesus does not die: "And right in the same tyme that me thought by semyng that the lyfe myght no longer last, and the shewyng of the ende behovyd nydes to be nye, sodenly I beholding in the same crosse he channgyd in blessydfulle chere. The channgyng of hys blyssed chere changyd myne, and I was as glad and mery as it was possible. Then brought oure lorde meryly to my mynd: Wher is now any point of thy payne or of thy anguysse? And I was fully mery" (21/379).[45] This ecstatic moment allows the contemplative to circumvent Christ's death, to experience the joy of those disciples who encountered the risen Christ on Easter Sunday without experiencing their own utter dereliction, their own sense of abandonment by him whom they had abandoned. So we can see why Julian deletes Jesus's own cry of abandonment. The decision not to draw attention to this absence in her vision is also perfectly coherent. But in the context of a sustained, detailed, and loving meditation on the Crucifixion, what are the implications of this deletion? The question remains, for me, an open one. Yet I suspect that the implications have bearings on Julian's understanding of sin. For Christ's cry of dereliction expresses something of what it means to say he bore our sins.[46] Perhaps its deletion may tend to mitigate the consequences of sin despite Julian's attention to the crucified body, an attention that is aestheticized with astonishing rhetorical strategies.[47] This would be congruent with the related decision to rewrite the saga of the Fall and its traditional theological interpretation, a decision I shall discuss below. For the moment, however, I will stay with some other issues concerning the treatment of sin and agency in the *Showings*.

Julian presents her central puzzle about sin in terms of God's omni-presence, omnicausality, and predestination. God "is in althyng," "doth alle that is done. . . be it nevyr so lytyle," and foresees everything "fro withouȝt begynnyng"(11/336–37; 11/340–41). If God is "in" all and "doth" all, "What is synne?" (11/336). One could begin to address this question by reflecting on the narratives of Scripture, or by drawing on available theological discussions of secondary causes, or by considering how God causes our free choice. But Julian takes none of these paths. Instead, she reiterates that "our lord god doth all . . . ther is no doer but he," and she hears God saying, "I am in all thyngs. See, I do all thyngs" (11/338, 340). But she is confident that God "doth no synne" (11/338). She then answers her question ("What is synne?") with a negation: "synne is no dede" (11/338). In doing so, she draws on the well-known argument that sin is privation. Augustine had developed this as part of his own lib-eration from the Manichees' teaching that evil is a substance (*Confes-sions,* III.7.12; VII.5.7; VII.12.18; VII.13.19). With help from Plotinus, he concluded that "the evil into whose origins I was inquiring is not a sub-stance, for if it were a substance it would be good" (VII.12.18).[48] So Ju-lian: "I saw nott synne, for I believe it had no maner of substannce, ne no part of beyng" (13/406).[49] Her claim that "synne is no dede" and is nothing, "no part of beyng," might call forth similar objections to those St. Anselm had considered when he himself was pursuing the line that "sin and injustice are nothing" in his work *Virgin Conception and Origi-nal Sin.*[50] Having mentioned that "injustice has no being" and that "evil is nothing" but the lack of the good a being should have, Anselm says there are some who respond as follows: "If sin is nothing, why does God pun-ish man for sin, when nobody ought to be punished for nothing" (6). Anselm's reply is that God "rightly punishes sinners not for nothing but for something." What is that? It is the sinner's denial of due honor in the order of divine justice (6).[51] But Julian neither considers this objection nor uses Anselm's reply. This is unsurprising because she rejects Anselm's traditional and liturgically embedded views on the punishment of sin-ners.[52] Nevertheless, Julian's attempt to apply a familiar Augustinian argu-ment about evil is done in a context fraught with difficulties for a Chris-tian theologian. Perhaps I can identify this most clearly by turning back to the *Confessions.*

There we find that Augustine combined the argument that evil is privation of being with a sustained exploration of wickedness. This displays how, although he did not find "a substance," he did discover "a perversity of will twisted away from the highest substance, you O God" (*Confessions,* VII.16.22). Earlier in this chapter I recalled Augustine's reading of the Fall saga in Genesis 3, and there we glimpsed his rich elaboration of the human will in rebellion against its divine source and completion, the will rejecting the divine covenant. But Julian combines Augustine's arguments about evil as privation with a doctrine that is incompatible with Augustine and Augustinian traditions of Christianity. For Julian never represents sin as "a perversity of will," as rebellion against the grace of God, as disobedience to God's gift of covenant. Correspondingly, she does not acknowledge the way we form habits that enslave us in the earthly city, individual and collective habits of will and intellect that bind us in iron fetters composed out of practices we have chosen, making for us a law from "the violence of habit" (*Confessions,* VIII.5.10–12; see Rom. 7.22–25). She seems to reject Augustine's vivid grasp of the formation and power of sinful habit: "The consequence of a distorted will is passion [ex voluntate perversa facta est libido]. By servitude to passion, habit [consuetudo] is formed, and habit to which there is no resistance becomes necessity. By these links, as it were, connected to one another (hence my term a chain), a harsh bondage held me under restraint" (VIII.5.10). Julian's dismissal of such theological and psychological analysis relates to what Denise Baker calls Julian's "optimistic anthropology" (78). Although I began this section of the chapter with quotations exemplifying Julian's declarations about the pervasiveness of sin and its power to impede the vision of God, it remains true that she also insists sin is no deed (11/338). But can I, who "shalle do ryght nought but synne" (36/436), do what is claimed to be no deed? Can we have "vyscious pryde" (28/409–10) without the will being curved in on itself in rebellion against God? Does such "vyscious pryde" immersed in "the veyne glorye" (28/409) of the earthly city not generate habits of sin, iron fetters binding the will? Are we not here in a domain of inquiry that might link the agencies involved both in the saga of the Fall, culminating in fratricide, and in the crucifixion of Christ? Are we not compelled to follow an Augustinian understanding of "a perversity of will twisted away from the highest substance, you O God" (*Confessions* VII.16.22), the will tracked through the history of the covenant in Scripture? Julian does not think so. Instead, she produces her own doctrine of will in defense of her rejection of Augustinian theology in this field.[53]

This doctrine maintains that "in every soule that shalle be savyd is a godly wylle that nevyr assentyth to synne, nor nevery shalle" (37/443).[54] Yet, we remember, I certainly sin (36/436). I sin; but simultaneously I myself retain a will that never assents to what I actually do, never even colludes with my own actions. What exactly does Julian envisage in this claim? Her explication is concentrated in four chapters (37, 45, 53, 58), and I shall follow her argument in detail.

Her first move is to set up a scheme in which the human soul has two distinct wills: (a) the "godly wylle," which we have just encountered; and (b) the "bestely wylle" (37/443). These two wills apparently exist in what she calls two parts of the soul: (a) "the hygher party" and (b) "the lower party" (37/443). In (a) she claims that evil simply can never be willed: "it may nevyr wylle evylle." Indeed, in (a) "good" is always willed (37/443). In chapter 37 she is as silent about what the "bestely wylle" actually does as she is about its origins. I will take up this issue later. Here, I recall her statements that God "doth alle thyng, be it nevyr so little" and is "in althyng" (11/336). But at this point she does not confront the "bestely wylle" with her earlier statements about God's agency and her questions about sin. Nor does she explain the relations between her doctrine and relevant scriptural narratives. However, the next chapter (38) may cast some light on the doctrine we are following. Julian *conflates* sin with "payne," without a remainder (38 and 40/458). This proves to be an important decision. It facilitates her wish to set aside the issues of will, of choice, of sin as a chosen separation from God, and of the social consequences of sin. For, all too obviously, many forms of suffering and pain are constantly inflicted on humans who have made absolutely no acts of will, not the slightest choice. Innocents suffer. But, plainly enough, it does not follow that all suffering is uncaused by human acts of will, uncaused by sinful individual and collective choices. It seems that Julian's conflation of sin and suffering has the rhetorical effect of assimilating sin to causeless, unwilled suffering. And as we have just seen, an individual's sin is indeed unwilled by the "godly wyll in the higher party" of the soul (37/443). There are striking non-Christian antecedents of this always unfallen "godly wylle," one that is never separated from God, whatever the sinner's beastly lower part of the soul may choose. For example, in his *Enneads* Plotinus maintains that wherever it sinks, a part of the human soul continues to dwell "in the Intellectual Realm" and continues in unbroken contemplation.[55] Whatever the embodied Socrates may do, for example, the higher part of his soul remains in the "Intellectual Realm": "that is to say, the individual soul has an existence in the Supreme as well as in the world," and this existence changelessly participates in the divine (V.6.1; see too VI.9.10). As John Kenney observes, in contrasting Augustine's understanding of contemplation with Plotinus's, "contemplation reveals to Plotinus the soul's intelligible and unfallen, undescended self in the eternal world of being."[56] Whatever her sources may have been, an issue irrelevant to my present inquiries, this is where Julian's contemplation has led. For Plotinus and Julian there is a higher part of the soul that never falls but continues its divine contemplation, even though the fallen part of the soul is quite unaware of this.[57] It is not at all clear to me that such a version of the soul and ontology is compatible with Christian teaching (embodied in liturgy, sacraments, Scripture, and tradition) about God, creation, sin, and redemption in Christ through the Holy Spirit.

Be that as it may, Julian goes on to assert that "synne shalle be no shame" to sinners. In fact, it will be "wurshype to man" (38/445). Sin is certainly suffering: sins are "ponyssched with dyvers paynes." But sins will also be rewarded with heavenly joys, "for theyr victories, after as the synne haue ben paynfulle and sorowfulle to the soule in erth" (38/445; see, too, 39/452–53). This is an original approach to sins' victories: it is a striking contrast to Paul's statement that "the wages of sin is death" (Rom. 6.23). Once again, Julian's argument is facilitated by the rhetorical fusion of unwilled suffering and sin. There is still no specification of sin. We are led to see it as a suffering that is "no shame" and will be rewarded in heaven as suffering endured (38/445). This assertion is grounded in God's love of "the soule," and the rewards are eschatological. But it seems not to be a statement exclusively about the eternal election and consummation of humankind in Christ. For Julian tells us that when sins of holy people are recalled in "the chyrch on erth" the sins are "to them no chame, but alle is turned them to worshyppe" (38/446–47). Here she must be talking about (b), "the lower party" and the "bestely wylle" encountered in chapter 37, because (a), "the hygher party" with the "godly wyll," never sins and never assents to sin. Among the figures invoked to illustrate this teaching is David from "the olde lawe" (38/446). Julian chooses to ignore the particularities of his sins and the ways they are treated "in the chyrch on erth." Instead, she merely asserts that they are "no chame" but only "worshyppe" (38/446–47). In exploring Julian's procedure here and her doctrine of sin, agency, and will, it is helpful to remember how David's sin is actually represented in Scripture (2 Kings [2 Sam.] 11–12).

David sent his soldiers, under Joab's command, to attack the Ammonites and besiege Rabba while he remained in Jerusalem. One afternoon when he was walking on the roof of his palace he saw from there a woman washing herself, "and the woman was very beautiful." David made a decision: he would find out who the woman was. "And it was told him, that she was Bethsabee the daughter of Elias, the wife of Urias the Hethite." He then made another decision: he sent messengers to Bethsabee, and they brought her to him. The narrative relates that "he slept with her." She returned home having conceived. When she discovered this, she "sent and told David." In response, he ordered Joab to send Urias back from the army. The chapter then describes David's attempts to get Urias to stay the night at home with his wife Bethsabee. But Urias slept outside the gates of the king's house. Frustrated in his plan, David asked Urias why he had not gone home. Urias responded as a devout and loyal soldier following the form of consecration and sexual abstinence once practiced by his king (see 1 Kings [Sam.] 21.5): "The ark of God and Israel and Juda dwell in tents, and my Lord Joab and the servants of my lord abide upon the face of the earth. And shall I go into my house, to eat and to drink and to sleep with my wife? By thy welfare and by the welfare of my soul I will not do this thing." David's conscience was untouched by this reply. His response was to feed Urias and get him drunk. But Urias still did not go home, choosing instead to sleep "on his couch with the servants of his lord." Far from being reminded of the covenant and the commandments, David now planned to have Urias killed. He sent his loyal follower back to the army with a letter to Joab: "Set ye Urias in the front of the battle, where the fight is strongest: and leave ye him, that he may be wounded and die." Urias was duly killed. David married Bethsabee, "and she bore him a son." The chapter (1 Kings [Sam.] 11) concludes with an unequivocal judgment: "This thing which David had done, was displeasing to the Lord." But this is not the end of the story. The next chapter opens with an equally unequivocal statement about divine agency: "The Lord sent Nathan to David." God's prophet told David a moving story about two men living in the same city, one man exceedingly rich, one exceedingly poor. The rich man plundered the only and cherished possession of the poor man. David responded angrily to this injustice and cruelty: "The man that hath done this is a child of death." But he failed to see how the story displayed and judged his own sin, how he stood under the condemnation he himself had uttered. So Nathan applied the parable directly: "Thou art the man." He went on to recollect God's graciousness to David and mediated God's question: "Why therefore hast thou despised the word of the Lord, to do evil in my sight?" [Quare ergo contempsisti verbum Domini, ut faceres malum in conspectu meo?]. David's "evil" was further specified: "Thou has killed Urias the Hethite with the sword; and hast taken his wife to be thy wife; and hast slain him with the sword of the children of Ammon." Nor did the prophet conclude with this memorial. He told David that the "evil" he had willed against the covenant would have further, terrible consequences. David now confessed: "I have sinned against the Lord" (2 Kings [Sam.] 12.1–13).

The narrative Julian invokes specifies "sin," "evil," and agency in ways that her own allusion deletes. In the Scriptures, David is shown to will adultery and murder. He is not ignorant: he knows the covenant, the commandments, and the sacred history to which he belongs. His own judgment of the tyrannical rich man in Nathan's story depends on this knowledge. The text shows how sin and evil are rebellion against God's grace, God's word. Thus Nathan's charge that David has despised the word of the Lord ("contempsisti verbum Domini"). This is the "contempt for God" that Augustine identified as intrinsic to the self-love ("amor sui") fostered by the earthly city (CG XIV.28). David's confession acknowledges this: "I have sinned against the Lord." The text is extraordinarily resistant to Julian's Plotinian scheme of two wills, one of which never assents to sin. There is no hint anywhere that David, in one of his wills, never assented to the choices of his "bestely wylle." Nor is there any hint of an invitation to develop a language in which we would conclude that "synne is no dede" (11/338). Nor are David's sins recounted in a manner that would allow "the chyrch on erth" to claim that these sins were "no chame" to David but only "worshyppe" (38/446–47). Indeed, such a reading would involve a strange failure to recollect the penitential psalms, especially Psalm 50 [51], read in the Church as David's repentance of the sin we have just been following in 2 Kings [2 Sam.]: "Wash me yet more from my iniquity, and cleanse me from my sin. For I know my iniquity, and my sin is always before me. To thee only have I sinned and have done evil before thee: that thou mayst be justified in thy words, and mayst overcome when thou art judged. . . . For behold thou hast loved truth: the uncertain and hidden things of thy wisdom thou hast made manifest to me. . . . Deliver me from blood, O God, thou God of my salvation: and my tongue shall extol thy justice" (Ps. 50.4–6, 8,16).

Augustine's sermon on this psalm begins by recalling the narrative I have been discussing. The psalm and the Book of Kings, he says, both belong to "canonical scripture, both are accepted by Christians with unhesitating faith." The story tells us what we must avoid and what we must do "if we have slipped into sin." Contrary to Julian's view, Augustine says that the "sin" of David is "proclaimed in church" precisely as sin. The fall of David calls Christians to recognize their own fragility and to avoid temptations. It also awakes the fallen to acknowledge the gravity of their situation without despair and recklessness. David's psalm calls sinners to participate in his penitent tears and to hope for forgiveness. Augustine notes that David, unlike Paul, "could not say, *I acted in ignorance* [1 Tim. 1.13]. He knew very well how wrong it was to lay hands on another man's wife, and how wrong it was to kill her husband." So Christians who acknowledge that they too have sinned knowingly can hope, with David, that God will wash away the deep stains of sin. Unequivocal acknowledgment is crucial. So Nathan elicits recognition from the willful amnesiac and draws forth confession. Augustine then turns to Christ's forgiveness of the woman taken in adultery (John 8.4–11). Here I will leave Augustine's characteristically Christocentric reading of Psalm 50.[58] His teaching, like that of the texts he explicates, sees the "worshyppe" entirely given to the God who challenges, forgives, and transforms sinful human agents. Together with "the chyrch on erth" and Psalm 50, he sees "chame" as a necessary moment in this process, a moment of recognition both about what the sinner had willed and whom the sinner had rejected in that sinful action.

On one occasion Julian herself does turn to the orthodox understanding of the sacrament of penance. We are told that the "holy gost
ledyth hym to confession, wylfully to shew hys synnes nakydly and truly
with grett sorow and with grett shame." The penitent must follow the
"penannce for every synne enjoyned by his domys men [confessor]."
Such is "the lyfe of holy chyrch" (39/449–50). She does not comment on
the relations between this avowal of "shame" and the Church's alleged
remembrance of the sins of penitent, converted sinners, as "no chame"
but only "worshyppe" (33/446–47). But even here she insists that while
the penitent experiences "shame" God "beholdyth synne as sorow and
paynes" and in his love "he assignyth no blame" (39/452). This recapitulates her earlier declaration that she "saw nott synne" as it "had no
maner of substannce" but could only be known by "payne," for which
God shows "no maner of blame" (27/406–7). Once again, the will to
sin, the choices against divine grace, are assimilated into the language of
"payne," of suffering, for which there is no "blame." It seems to me that
the strategy here systematically diminishes human responsibility for evil
and, equally systematically, banishes the discourse of divine justice as
though this might be in conflict with divine love.[59] Such a strategy will have
striking consequences for any doctrine of reconciliation. I am thinking
of its impact on teaching such as the following: "When we were enemies,
we were reconciled to God by the death of his son" (Rom. 5.10). But I
address this issue later.

Julian's insistence that in God's eyes there is no "blame" for sin returns her to ontological claims about the two parts of the soul, each with
its will, parts I annotated above as (a) and (b). We recall that the higher
part (a) is always united to God with a will that never assents to sin. Only
the lower part (b) has a "bestely wylle" (37/443). Chapter 45 elaborates
these claims. Julian now describes the higher part (a) as "oure kyndely
substance." This is "evyr kepte one in hym [God], hole and safe, without
ende" (45/486). God only judges us in this higher, unfallen, always sinless
part, which is always united to God (45/486–87). Insofar as God takes
note of the "bestely wylle" she has mentioned earlier it seems he must
have done so entirely in the mode of pity for the suffering of the sinful person. That is why she is so confident that God ascribes "to vs no
maner of blame" despite her careful acknowledgment that this is not
the view of "holy chyrch" (45/487–88). Indeed, she aligns the Church's

teaching with the lower part of the soul and her own vision with the higher part (45/488). She concludes chapter 45 by reiterating that this higher part, our natural substance ("kindely substannce"), is now blissfully "in god," has been since its creation, and always will be (45/489). Our higher part, our natural substance, has never turned from God and is thus not a subject of salvation history, not in need of reconciliation and redemption through Jesus Christ. Here is the Plotinian turn.

What about the lower part of the soul? This is described as "oure channgeable sensualyte" (45/486). It seems to be the aspect of the person that is a social being in historical relations with other humans and the natural world. It is the part that human judgment addresses, "outward" being (45/486). And it must be the part of humans that is a subject of salvation history, the part in which the "bestely wylle" (37/443) exists. Does Julian then identify rebellion against God, contempt of God, and disobedience in this lower sphere of the soul? It seems not. For the words "channgeable sensualyte" do not direct us unequivocally to human will, free choice, and action informed by rational (or irrational) intentions. They can pertain to modes of being and changes that humans share with mice, rats, and cats. When such locutions are used in descriptions of human action, they may be used to imply action not informed by rational choice and will: for example, the familiar denial of responsibility in statements such as "I do not know what came over me," or "Stuff happens." Let us look a little more closely at the grammar in Julian's text. In the higher part, (a), there is never any assent to sin but rather perpetual union of our natural substance to God. Here there is simply no trace of temptation to wrongdoing. Julian then asserts that God's judgment of humanity is made entirely in relation to this impeccable life. Hence, and despite whatever happens in the "channgeable" sphere, (b), her "revelation" is that God assigns "no maner of blame" (45/487). She recognizes human judgments in the lower realm (b), and she claims that where these are "hard and grevous" Jesus reforms them by mercy and grace through his passion and so brings this lower judgment to "ryghtfulnesse" (45/486–87).[60] So Jesus brings lower judgments, emerging from "oure channgeable sensualyte," into God's unblaming gaze on humankind's sinless natural substance. But this says nothing about the motives, contents, and consequences of sin. So nothing is said about how sinners became sinners in need of forgiveness through "his blessyd passion" (45/486–87).

One is left with a haunting question: What has been done that makes the Crucifixion a fitting and liberating response?

Whatever difficulties it generates, however incongruous with what she has been taught by the Church, Julian continues to proclaim her doctrine of the two wills, the two parts of the soul, and to proclaim that divine judgment considers only the "kyndely substance" that has allegedly never assented to sin and has always "kepte one in hym, hole and safe," in blissful union (45/486, 489). She is convinced that the "answere" God gives to her puzzles about sin (45/488; 51/513) does not call for any revision to this doctrine. In chapter 53 she reiterates her teaching that in all who are finally saved there always remains "a godly wylle that nevyr assentyd to synne ne nevyr shall" (53/555). Furthermore, this will "is so good that it may nevyr wylle evyll, but evyr more contynnuly it wylleth good and werkyth good in the syght of god" (53/555). This statement draws on a conventional model of the beatific vision of the redeemed. The transcendence of the possibility of further sin is an eschatological gift flowing from the work of Christ and the Holy Spirit. But Julian has projected this eschatological gift across the totality of human existence in such a way as to dissolve temporality and the complex actions of salvation history disclosed in Scripture. Not only is the human soul made by God, according to Julian, it is "made of god" and is always "knyte to god," always "onyd to the maker, whych is substanncyall kynde vnmade, þat is god" (53/558–59; see, too, 58/582). Is such an ontotheology and anthropology compatible with scriptural accounts of the history of the covenant, a history including narratives such as that of David considered above? Is it compatible with traditional affirmations of human freedom, rebellion against God, and reconciliation between God and man (for example, Ezek. 20.4–44; Rom. 5.10, 17–19)? These must remain open questions until we have studied chapter 51.

Before doing so, however, I wish to offer one further observation about Julian's teaching on the unfallen will, a will apparently quite distinct from the "bestely wylle" that commits "many evylles" (37/443; 46/492). I have become intrigued by a strange, and as far as I know, unnoticed link between this doctrine and one that emerges in Augustine's *Confessions*. When he was in Rome Augustine still associated with "those false and deceiving Saints," the Manichees. Following their teaching, he confesses, "I still thought it is not we who sin, but some alien nature [aliam . . . naturam] which sins in us" (V.10.18). The consequence of Julian's teaching on the sinless, unfallen will of the one who sins is congruent with the Manichean belief that Augustine recalls. Augustine says that this belief made him think that when he had done something wrong he remained "free of blame" [extra culpam]. He observed the sin as caused by something accompanying him while he felt that he did not sin and remained unstained by the enacted sin (V.10.18). Whatever Julian's intentions may have been, her teaching about a will that is untouched by the sin performed by the sinner takes her toward the position Augustine had held as a Manichee, a position he found to be both psychologically implausible and incompatible with Christian teaching and practice.[61] It encouraged him to think that however sinful his acts might seem, he himself was not really a sinner and so did not need to confess to God (V.10.18). For Julian, all sin happens externally to the "godly wylle," which is always united to God and never assents to sin (37/443; 45/486). Sin just happens. It "fallyth to þe agaynste thy wylle" (82/717).[62] In such a perspective the sinner's "godly wylle" remains absent from the sinner's acts, much as it had done in the ontology of Manichean Augustine.[63] I appreciate that the convergence between Julian's doctrine of the two wills and aspects of the latter is nothing Julian would have welcomed. But even the most brilliant and devout theologians are capable of generating ideas whose implications have not been worked out and are in contradiction to other strands of their theology.

Perhaps Julian's observations that humans are not blamed by God for their sin and therefore not forgiven by God should also be understood in relation to such unexamined implications. She announces the former on a number of occasions (for example, 27/407; 39/452; 45/487; 82/717–18). Its rationale is the doctrine we have been tracing, that we have a will that never assents to sin and is always united to God. In God's sight at least, there is no need for "forgevenesse" (46/493). In his "curtesy" God forgets our sins, repented in the Church, and wants us to do the same (73/670; see 668–70). Julian is obviously, here and elsewhere, trying to counteract what she took to be punitive standards in her Church's treatment of sin and penance, ones that perhaps lacked adequate focus on God's love. But such statements run against the centrality of divine judgment and forgiveness in both Old and New Testaments as well as throughout the Church's liturgy:[64] hardly news to Julian, of course, who often comments on the sharp tensions between the teaching emerging from her revelation and the teaching of the Church.[65] These were tensions she hoped to supersede through chapter 51 but if not there then when the book she had begun would, by God's grace, be "performyd" (86/731).

Chapter 51 holds a special place in the answers Julian received to her tenacious inquiry into the theology of sin and the related questions I have been pursuing. " I nee had no nother answere," she had said, "but a marvelous example of a lorde and of a seruannt, as I shall say after" (45/488). So to this answer, "in shewyng full mystely" (51/513), I now turn. This "example" revises the saga of the Fall in Genesis 3. It is an extraordinarily complex passage of allegorical writing and theological reflection, one that has engaged some of the most distinguished commentators on the *Showings*.[66] My aims are certainly not to offer a comprehensive reading, and I make no attempt to address all its strands. I explore aspects of Julian's "example" that are most relevant to the issues I have been following, namely issues concerning human agency, freedom, responsibility, and sin, as these are intrinsic to any distinctively Christian doctrine of reconciliation and redemption. I began the present chapter by recalling how Augustine addressed the saga of the Fall and also how recent criticism has celebrated Julian's rejection of Augustinian theology in this sphere. My responses to Julian's inventive correction of Genesis 3 continue the dialogue between her text and the Augustinian starting point from which I, like Julian, set out.

In the first narrative of chapter 51 the servant "that was shewed for Adam" (51/519) is unequivocally represented as "reverently redy to do his lord's wylle" (514). Receiving his lord's command, the servant not only obeys but obeys with great zeal, "in grett hast for loue to do his lordes wylle" (514–15). In his zealous, obedient love the servant falls: "he fallyth in a slade [valley]" (515). Through this unambiguously faultless fall the servant becomes extremely miserable. He becomes unable to look upon his loving lord and in this misery loses the good of intellect (515–16, 522). His condition tends toward that of Langland's Semyuief, discussed in the previous chapter. The latter, however, belonged to a familiar allegory of sin and its catastrophic consequences in the bondage of the will, enslavement from which Christ alone could free mankind through his works and through his gifts to the Church (*Piers Plowman*, C XIX.48–95).

Julian's "example" rejects this tradition. Instead it insists that neither disobedient will nor rebellious free choice is involved in the fall of Adam. The servant did nothing against God's will. Julian emphasizes that he is "as good inwardly as he was when he stode before his lorde, redy to do his wylle" (516). Yet once more we hear that where the Church perceived ingratitude, disobedience, and consequent reproach there is actually no kind of "blame" (516). This vision of Adam's fall puzzles her (519). But she is unwavering in her conviction not only that fallen humankind is blameless but that God applauds the servant's "good wylle" in the Fall and determines to "reward" him for his unmerited suffering (517). In "an inwarde goostely shewyng" it is revealed to her that the reward for the Fall is endless bliss in excess of what the servant would have received "yf he had nott fallen" (518). So Julian presents a thorough rewriting of the tradition's account of *felix culpa* celebrated in the mass on the evening of Holy Saturday (Exultet) and beautifully articulated after the confession of the sins in *Piers Plowman* (C VII.120–31). We are now given *felix* with absolutely no trace of *culpa*. In doing this, Julian has broken with a tradition that is not only "Augustinian" but embedded in Scripture and liturgy.[67]

Julian continues to stress her conviction that the figure of blameless, faultless Adam in her version of Genesis 3 represents "how god beholdyth alle manne and his fallyng" and how God unambiguously approves the will of falling and fallen humanity: "For his wylle I saw oure lorde commende and aproue" (522). Suffering, with which sin is once again totally identified, is caused by our innocent failure to see God's love and our own good will (522). Just as *felix culpa* is rejected for *felix* without *culpa,* so the language of sin is utterly transformed. Having strenuously denied the remotest source for *culpa* in fallen humanity, Julian then writes that God "beholdeth vs in oure synne" (523). In the context she has so carefully established, sin now does not mean rejection of God, rebellion against God's loving precepts, disobedience to the grace of the covenant, and wickedness to neighbors. Rather, it means suffering that happens through zealous and unambiguous obedience to God's command. We see why she finds it appropriate to talk of "synne þat fallyth to þe agaynste thy wylle" (82/717). We also see a feature I remarked earlier, her tendency to swallow up the language of sin in a discourse of suffering: suffering, that is, with no source in a will rebelling against God's love and covenant, suffering rather on the model of a child whose learning to walk necessitates, despite total parental care, some falling (61/602–3). No wonder there is no trace of a divine *no* to our sin. One can see how Julian has gotten here, and I have been following some of her paths. But in response to the contexts she has woven for the language of sin, which she continues to use copiously enough, my response can be encapsulated in a phrase from Wittgenstein's *Philosophical Investigations*: " A wheel that can be turned although nothing else moves with it, is not part of the mechanism."[68]

Having rewritten the saga of Adam's fall in Genesis 3, Julian doubles the fall of sinless but now suffering (and so, in her language, sinful) mankind. She does so with the incarnation of Jesus Christ as the servant (51/523–25; Phil. 2.5–11). Given the subtlety of Julian's allegory and the compassionate love that suffuses every sentence of her *Showings,* an exegete raising the questions that preoccupy my own reading risks being both leaden-footed and wretchedly unappreciative. Despite these risks, I want to add some further questions that have emerged in my reflections on her theology of sin and agency as they return to haunt her treatment of the Incarnation in this long and central chapter. If the appropriate model for humankind's fall is Julian's, then how does the appropriate divine response entail the crucifixion of Jesus Christ rather than the appearance of a sage teaching enlightenment to humans who have, after all, never rebelled against divine love and the covenant but rather tripped up while lovingly obeying the divine command? How do we get from Julian's model to the crucifixion of the Son of God with which the *Showings* set out? How could we get from Julian's version of sin to the collective evil and violence against God and humanity embodied in the Crucifixion? How could God's good creatures become subjected to the power of injustice, destruction, cruelty, and death, to the history against which the Old Testament prophets so continually protest and that are displayed in the Crucifixion? Consider the following meditation on the Crucifixion: "And you, when you were dead in your sins and the uncircumcision of your flesh, he hath quickened together with him, forgiving you all offences: Blotting out the hand-writing of the decree that was against us, which was contrary to us. And he hath taken the same out of the way, fastening it to the cross" (Col. 2.13–15). Recalling my earlier observations on Julian's treatment of the Crucifixion, one response is that we never do get here. As I showed, Julian's own treatment of the Crucifixion eliminates the human agency and collective social practices making this event.

Another response is that if we were to get here that would go completely against the grain of the narratives and theological exegesis offered in chapter 51 and earlier. Indeed, talk of cities and communities in the *Showings* is directed to the city within the individual soul that is God's "dwelling place" (51/525; see chs. 53–55).[69]

As Julian doubles her narrative in chapter 51 to encompass both Adam and Christ, she continues to emphasize Adam's virtue as an obedient, devoted laborer (530–31; see 523–31). When the innocent servant falls, "Goddys son fell with Adam in to the slade of the meydens wombe" (533–34; see 514–15). Denise Baker maintains that the identity of human servant and "Goddys son" is an "ontological union."[70] This would certainly be congruent with Julian's account of the higher, godly, and always unfallen will that is always united to God. But whether Julian is postulating the kind of "ontological union" Baker describes or whether she is thinking more in terms of the figurative ways in which Langland relates Piers and Christ in *Piers Plowman,* we encounter some fresh difficulties here.[71] Having emphasized that mankind has done nothing blameworthy, Julian now says that Christ fell with Adam "for to excuse Adam from blame" and to take on "all oure blame" (534–35). The work's tenacious emphasis on no sin, no blame, has become blame, indeed a blame that leads to hell (534). Julian is responding to pressures exerted by conventional soteriology in the Church: Christ entered the earthly city to rescue humans from the catastrophic consequences of sinful choices, individual and collective. These consequences are displayed in the Crucifixion. Julian has made a transition from emphatically asserting that there is no blame to acknowledging such blame as leads to hell. But how can this be done with any semblance of coherence is not made a topic for reflection in the *Showings.* Nevertheless, I intend to make it just such a topic because this will cast light on Julian's theology of human agency and of the Incarnation.

Despite her conventional talk of blame and hell in chapter 51, Julian is not abandoning her position on the blamelessness of Adam and "all mankynde that shall be savyd" (537). She is still assuming one of the doctrines I have discussed at some length, namely her doctrine that our souls have a higher and lower part with two distinct wills (chs. 37, 45, 53, 58). The higher, we recall, is "oure kyndely substance, wych is evyr kept one in hym [God], hole and safe, withoute ende" (45/486). Here is that

"godly wylle that nevyr assentyth to synne, nor nevyr shalle" (37/443).
The lower part is "oure channgeable sensualyte," where we find "a bestely
wylle. . . that may wylle no good" (45/486; 37/443). This scheme explains
how Julian could imagine the transition in question. A "bestely wylle"
takes mankind on a blameworthy path to hell, while the "godly wyll" remains absent from this journey, "hole and safe" in unbroken union with
God, blissfully free from blame and the sufferings of human history.
So the task is to get the lower part of the soul back to the higher part
dwelling in God. This is accomplished by the Incarnation. Christ "oure
moder" in the Trinity (54/563) becomes "knytt to oure kynde, whych is
the lower party in oure flessche taking" (57/577–78). He thus unites our
fallen, "channgeable sensualyte" with our always unfallen "kyndely substance, whych is evyr kept one in hym [God]" (45/486). She reiterates this
in chapter 58: "the seconde person [of the Trinity], whych is oure moder
substanncyally the same dereworthy person is now become oure moder
sensuall" (585).[72] And so the lower part of our soul is "onyd to oure substance" (58/586). In this model of redemption it is clear that only "the
lower party" of the soul and its "bestely wylle" need the saving ministry
of Christ. Here the problems in Julian's account of human agency and
responsibility generate serious difficulties for the doctrines of reconciliation and Christology.

But we still do not know what the supposedly "bestely wylle" has actually willed and done that is so blameworthy. There is no indication that
it is disobedient and rebellious to the source of its life. On the contrary,
as we saw in discussing chapter 51, Genesis 3 is corrected to eliminate all
suggestions of this kind. We certainly know that when mankind experienced the unequivocally innocent fall of chapter 51 suffering ensued. But
this was a fall without any trace of unloving rejection of divine grace. At
no point is there the slightest reason for thinking that such poor creatures could have become "enemies" of God (Rom. 5.10), let alone those
who would kill each other and also the son of God. True enough, in
chapter 51, unlike her earlier extended vision of the Crucifixion, where
Christ does not die (21/379), Christ is "sleyn" (51/542). But once more the
agents, agencies, and motivations are not identified, let alone explored.
Just how and why the human beings of Julian's "example" of the Fall
should exercise their gifts and their freedom to torture and crucify Jesus
is never even acknowledged as a question, let alone explored. Yet again

there seems to be a lack of theological resources to recognize social sin, to recognize how we make the earthly city a place where evil becomes normalized. Such a lack is part of the problems intrinsic to Julian's account of human agency, responsibility, and sin. She continues to occlude our will to seek autonomy in relation to God. Compare Jesus's own haunting parable of the lord and his rebellious tenants: after the latter have killed his messengers the lord sends his son, saying, "They will reverence my son." But the tenants react differently: "This is the heir: come, let us kill him, and we shall have his inheritance" (Matt. 21.33–39). Julian systematically ignores our freedom to disobey the covenant offered by the source of life, to destroy others and ourselves, individually and collectively, as we strive to shore up the power of the earthly city we inhabit. This occlusion is congruent with her elimination of the rich texture of the saga told in Genesis 3, one carried into Augustine's exegesis from which this chapter began. Through the talking serpent, Scripture displays a call to disobedience, a call to exercise a version of freedom that sponsors a form of selfhood and privatization elaborated in the *City of God*. Julian's theology does not, probably cannot, address collective life and its domination by will and power alienated from God and the covenants. It cannot address the stuff of the earthly city. Perhaps someone might suggest that Julian's orientation toward the eschatological peace beyond history accounts for the features I describe. But such an orientation is foundational to Augustine's *City of God*, to its understanding of peace, and to most Christian theology.[73] Indeed, Christian eschatology often elicits very sharp questions about the uses of freedom, decision, and responsibility in human communities. In this connection one could well recall Jesus's own story of the Last Judgment (Matt. 25.31–46), together with its powerful dramatization in the York Corpus Christi plays. Julian's eschatological vision does not account for these characteristics.

Her hollowing out of the language and theology of sin, together with her treatment of human agency, has a series of consequences that unravel central strands of the Christian doctrine of reconciliation. It is in this context that we should also reflect on the way she sets aside the history to which I have drawn attention throughout this chapter, namely the history of the covenant, God's relations with Israel, a history of God's faithfulness, mercy, and judgment in the face of human unfaithfulness and repentance. Perhaps this setting aside is encouraged by the decision to figure Adam's fall and Christ's incarnation as simultaneous in chapter 51. Be that as it may, it seems appropriate to conclude this chapter and its concerns with a statement from Karl Barth's *Church Dogmatics*: "The atonement is history. To know it, we must know it as such. To speak of it, we must tell it as history. To try to grasp it as supra-historical or non-historical truth is not to grasp it at all. It is indeed truth, but truth actualized in a history and revealed therefore as history" (*CD* IV/1, 157).[74] Thus it must be known with the human agency, freedom, and catastrophic consequences of sin woven into a history in which "God indeed was in Christ, reconciling the world to himself" (2 Cor. 5.19).

NOTES

LIST OF ABBREVIATIONS

The following are abbreviations for series names that are used in the notes and bibliography:

EETS   Early English Text Society
PL   *Patrologiae Cursus Completus, Series Latina,* 221 vols., ed. Jacques-Paul
       Migne. Paris, 1844–91. Cited by volume and column numbers.
WSA   Works of Saint Augustine: A Translation for the 21st Century

PREFACE

The epigraph is taken from William Langland, *Piers Plowman: The C Version. Will's Vision of Piers Plowman, Do-Well, Do-Better, and Do-Best,* ed. George Russell and George Kane (London: Athlone Press, 1997).

1. Quotations from the Bible in this preface are from *The Holy Bible, New Revised Standard Version* (Cambridge: Cambridge University Press, 1997).

2. William Shakespeare, *Measure for Measure,* 2.2.71–75, *The Riverside Shakespeare,* ed. G. Blakemore Evans (Boston: Houghton Mifflin, 1974). Subsequent citations to this work are given in the text.

3. For very different attempts at this, compare Eric L. Saak, *High Way to Heaven: The Augustinian Platform between Reform and Reformation, 1292–1524* (Leiden: Brill, 2002); Risto Saarinen, *Weakness of the Will in Medieval Thought from Augustine to Buridan* (Leiden: Brill, 1994); William J. Courtenay, *Schools and Scholars in Fourteenth-Century England* (Princeton: Princeton University Press, 1987), ch. 10; Heiko A. Oberman and Frank A. James, eds., *Via Augustini: Augustine in the Later Middle Ages, Renaissance and Reformation* (Leiden: Brill, 1991).

4. This occlusion is perhaps partly due to the bizarrely reductive version of Augustine propagated by D. W. Robertson and his followers in a once influential school of "historical criticism," a version simply accepted by the school's opponents.

5. See Thomas Aquinas, *In Oratorionem Dominicam Videlicet "Pater Noster" Expositio,* in *Opuscula Theologica,* ed. R. A. Verardo, R. M. Spiazzi, and M. Calcaterra, 2 vols. (Rome: Marietti, 1954), 2:221–35, para. 1066 (p. 228). Here he observes that we must note how doctrine, Christian teaching, is given to us through a particular mode of talking, in the minute particulars of language to which we must, as he goes on to demonstrate, pay careful attention ("Notandum autem, quod ex modo loquendi datur nobis doctrina"). The demonstration he offers here concerns relations between divine and human agency, drawing both on the Lord's Prayer and on St. Augustine's homilies on John's gospel, a demonstration whose guidelines I have sought to follow in my own exploration of Augustine in chapter 1.

6. For an excellent example of such a survey, see Courtenay, *School and Scholars;* for one with more doctrinal interests, see Jaroslav Pelikan, *Reformation of Church and Dogma (1300–1700)* (Chicago: University of Chicago Press, 1984), chs. 1–2. Given the role of Scotus in developing a form of voluntarism that often challenges St. Thomas explicitly, and given his role in some recent grand narratives of Western culture, he would obviously feature in such a survey. For an example of the place of Scotus in some recent grand narratives, see Catherine Pickstock, *After Writing: On the Liturgical Consummation of Philosophy* (Oxford: Blackwell, 1998), 121–40; John Milbank, *The Word Made Strange: Theology, Language, Culture* (Oxford: Blackwell, 1997), ch. 2. I have found the following particularly relevant in thinking about this version of Scotus: Bernardine M. Bonansea, "'Duns Scotus' Voluntarism," ch. 5 in *John Duns Scotus, 1265–1965,* ed. John K. Ryan and Bernardine M. Bonansea (Washington, DC: Catholic University of America Press, 1965); Richard Cross, *Duns Scotus* (Oxford: Oxford University Press, 1999); Olivier Boulnois, *Être et representation: Une généalogie de la métaphysique moderne à l'époque de Duns Scot, XIIIe–XIVe siècle* (Paris: Presses universitaires, 1999); André de Muralt, *L'unité de la philosophie politique de Scot, Occam et Suarez au libéralisme contemporain* (Paris: Vrin, 2002), especially 14–16, 29–37, 71–76.

7. Here I reiterate observations made in the preface to David Aers, *Sanctifying Signs: Making Christian Tradition in Late Medieval England* (Notre Dame: University of Notre Dame Press, 2004), ix–x.

8. This is the place to acknowledge how my thinking about the practices of critical writing from within a living polysemous tradition such as Christianity has been profoundly influenced by the work of Alasdair MacIntyre;

here the most relevant books are *Three Rival Versions of Moral Enquiry* (London: Duckworth, 1990) and *Whose Justice? Which Rationality?* (London: Duckworth, 1988).

9. Bob Dylan, "Beyond the Horizon," *Modern Times* (New York: Sony BMG Music, 2006).

Chapter 1.   Augustinian Prelude

The epigraph is from Sermon 227, in Augustine, *Sermons,* trans. Edmund Hill, 10 vols., WSA, pt. 3, vol. 6 (Brooklyn, NY: New City Press, 1990–95).

1. From the immense storehouse of scholarship on and around Augustine, the following are works that I have found especially helpful in writing this chapter: Robert Dodaro, *Christ and the Just Society in the Thought of Augustine* (Cambridge: Cambridge University Press, 2004), "Augustine's Secular City," ch. 14 in *Augustine and His Critics,* ed. Robert Dodaro and George Lawless (London: Routledge, 2000), and "Eloquent Lies, Just Wars and the Politics of Persuasion: Reading Augustine's City of God in a 'Postmodern' World," *Augustinian Studies* 25 (1994): 77–138; Pierre-Marie Hombert, *Gloria Gratiae: Se glorifier en Dieu, principe et fin de la théologie augustinienne de la grâce* (Paris: Institut d'études augustiniennes, 1996); R. A. Markus, *Saeculum: History and Society in the Theology of St. Augustine* (Cambridge: Cambridge University Press, 1970); Michael Hanby, *Augustine and Modernity* (London: Routledge, 2003); John Milbank, *Theology and Social Theory: Beyond Secular Reason,* 2nd ed. (Oxford: Blackwell, 2006); Oliver O'Donovan, "The Political Thought of the *City of God* 19," *Dionysius* 11 (1987): 89–110, decisively revised in *Bonds of Imperfection: Christian Politics Past and Present,* by Oliver O'Donovan and Joan Lockwood O'Donovan (Grand Rapids, MI: Eerdmans, 2004), 48–72 (all further citations are to the revised version); James Wetzel, *Augustine and the Limits of Virtue* (Cambridge: Cambridge University Press, 1992); John P. Kenney, *The Mysticism of Saint Augustine: Rereading the Confessions* (New York: Routledge, 2005); Rowan Williams, "Politics and the Soul: A Reading of the *City of God,*" *Milltown Studies* 19/20 (1987): 55–72. Whereas the title might suggest otherwise, I have not found help for my own concerns in Karl Morrison's essay on Augustine's *Confessions* in his *Conversion and Text: The Cases of Augustine of Hippo, Herman-Judah, and Constantine Tsastos* (Charlottesville: University Press of Virginia, 1992), "Case I: Augustine of Hippo's *Confessions.*"

2. *Concerning the City of God against the Pagans,* trans. Henry Bettenson (London: Penguin, 1984); for the Latin text I use *De Civitate Dei,* ed. B. Dombart and A. Kalb, 5th ed., 2 vols. (Stuttgart: Teubner, 1993). I have also consulted *The*

City of God against the Pagans, trans. R.W. Dyson (Cambridge: Cambridge University Press, 1998). Hereafter referred to as *CG*; subsequent citations to book and chapter are given parenthetically in the text.

3. There are some extremely helpful comments on the way Augustine sees conversion as a "beginning, not an end, an entry into a perilous and confused world" in Rowan Williams, *The Wound of Knowledge,* 2nd ed. (London: Darton, Longman and Todd, 2002), see 73 and ch. 4, passim; similarly, Wetzel, *Augustine,* chs. 4–5, a very fine study to which I am deeply indebted.

4. See too I, Preface; I.31; II.20j; XIX.15. Books I–V pursue this topic. See too the nice illustration through Christ's parable of those who excused themselves from the great feast (Luke 14.18–20); see Sermon 112.2 in Augustine, *Sermons,* vol. 4.

5. See, with this, *CG* V.12, V.17–19.

6. See Milbank, *Theology and Social Theory,* 392–93, with Dodaro, "Augustine's Secular City"; Williams, "Politics and the Soul"; O'Donovan, "Political Thought."

7. See Milbank, *Theology and Social Theory,* 393, citing II.22, III.13, V.12, IX.6–23, to which one should add IV.30–32, VIII.5, 9, 12–13, 17, 22.

8. See, e.g., IX.15, X.6, X.20, X.22, X.24, X.32. For helpful introductions to Augustine's Trinitarian theology, see Lewis Ayres, "The Fundamental Grammar of Augustine's Trinitarian Theology," ch. 5 in Dodaro and Lawless, *Augustine and His Critics,* and *Nicaea and Its Legacy: An Approach to Fourth-Century Trinitarian Theology* (Oxford: Oxford University Press, 2004), ch. 15.

9. See John C. Cavadini, "'Feeling Right': Augustine on the Passions and Sexual Desire," *Augustinian Studies* 26 (2005): 195–217.

10. See, e.g., *CG* XX.9, XX.11, XIII.6, XVI.2, XVII.1.

11. A church of the predestinate: on Wyclif's ecclesiology, see David Aers, *Faith, Ethics and Church: Writing in England, 1360–1409* (Cambridge: Brewer, 2000), ch. 6; and on one of his disciples, William Thorpe, see Aers, *Sanctifying Signs,* 83–98. For a reading of Augustine's true Church in analogous terms, see Miika Ruokanen, *Theology of Social Life in Augustine's De Civitate Dei* (Göttingen: Vandenhoeck and Ruprecht, 1993), 87 n. 26, 88.

12. John Milton, *The Complete Poems,* ed. John Leonard (London: Penguin, 1998).

13. Charles Taylor, *Sources of the Self: The Making of the Modern Identity* (Cambridge: Cambridge University Press, 1989). On Augustine, see his ch. 7; page citations are given parenthetically in the text.

14. Ibid., 129, see too 133; on Descartes, see ch. 8. For a sustained attempt to develop such an argument, see Stephen Menn, *Descartes and Augustine*

(Cambridge: Cambridge University Press, 1998), with Hanby's critique of Menn's thesis, *Augustine and Modernity,* ch. 5.

15. Augustine, *On True Religion,* 39.72 (written in 391), quoted in Taylor, *Sources of the Self,* 129. Taylor also draws heavily on *The Free Choice of the Will (De Libero Arbitrio),* especially book II. This work was written between 388 and 395. He does refer, very briefly, to the *City of God, Confessions,* and *On the Trinity.* There is no doubt that Augustine constantly called Christians to turn their attention from exterior things toward interior things, but this conversion becomes Christologically formed, following Col. 3.3–4: see, e.g., Epistle 55.2–3 and 9 in Augustine, *Letters,* trans. Roland J. Teske, WSA, pt. 2, vols. 1–4 (Hyde Park, NY: New City Press, 2001–5), vol. 1.

16. We meet remarkably similar views in scholars working out of very different disciplines: e.g., Paula Fredriksen, "Paul and Augustine: Conversion Narratives, Orthodox Traditions, and the Retrospective Self," *Journal of Theological Studies* 37 (1986): 3–34; Phillip Cary, *Augustine's Invention of the Inner Self: The Legacy of a Christian Platonist* (Oxford: Oxford University Press, 2000), a hyper-Plotinian version. For brief but pertinent comment on Cary's book, see Hanby, *Augustine and Modernity,* 181–82 n. 4.

17. Stanley Hauerwas and David Matzko, "The Sources of Charles Taylor," *Religious Studies Review* 18 (1992): 289. See too Hanby, *Augustine and Modernity,* 8–11.

18. Augustine, *Confessions,* trans. Henry Chadwick (Oxford: Oxford University Press, 1991); for the Latin text and commentary I use *Confessions,* ed. James J. O'Donnell, 3 vols. (Oxford: Clarendon Press, 1992). Subsequent citations are given parenthetically in the text.

19. I return to Augustine's treatment of the Fall in chapter 5. For the Fall as privatization, see *CG* XI.13, XII.1, XII.6. See R. A. Markus, "*De Ciuitate Dei*: Pride and the Common Good," reprinted in his *Sacred and Secular: Studies on Augustine and Latin Christianity* (Aldershot: Variorum, 1994), and his *Conversion and Disenchantment in Augustine's Spiritual Career* (Villanova: Villanova University Press, 1989), 31. See too Paul J. Griffiths, *Lying: An Augustinian Theory of Duplicity* (Grand Rapids, MI: Brazos, 2004), 62–71; and Cary, *Augustine's Invention.* Cary also notes that "inner privacy" is a consequence of the Fall (117), but he assimilates this insight to his hyper-Plotinian thesis. This maintains that Augustine developed a distinctively "Plotinian" version of the Fall: "His mature brand of inwardness" combines "Plotinus's inward turn, with a Plotinian Fall" and "an orthodox Christian distinction between creature and Creator" (115). For a more precise study of Augustine's critical use of Plotinus, one that takes account of his ecclesiology and Christology, see Kenney, *Mysticism*

of Saint Augustine, together with the fine chapter on Augustine in Bernard McGinn, *The Foundations of Mysticism: Origins to the Fifth Century* (New York: Crossroads, 1995), ch. 7. Also relevant here are John Freccero's reflections on Augustine, Dante, and Platonism in *Dante: The Poetics of Conversion* (Cambridge, MA: Harvard University Press, 1986), 6–11, 18–24.

20. The quotations here are from Taylor, *Sources of the Self,* 129, 131.

21. On the overcoming of the antique "antinomy of *polis* and *oikos*" in Augustine's work, see Milbank, *Theology and Social Theory,* 407–10; see too 366–77.

22. On this, see Dodaro, *Christ and the Just Society,* 107–10.

23. For an excellent discussion of *CG* X, see Dodaro, *Christ and the Just Society,* 97–104; invaluable here is Henri de Lubac, *Corpus Mysticum: The Eucharist and the Church in the Middle Ages,* trans. Gemma Simmonds with Richard Price (London: SCM Press, 2006) (translating the second edition of *Corpus Mysticum,* 1949). See particularly, in the present context, 65–67, 176–86, 252–62. Also helpful on Augustine's eucharistic teaching is Gerald Bonner's "The Church and the Eucharist in the Theology of St. Augustine," *Sobornost* 6 (1978): 448–61.

24. "Quod autem socialem vitam volunt esse sapientis, nos multo amplius adprobamus" (XIX.5); here I accept Oliver O'Donovan's correction of both Bettenson's and Dyson's translation of "nos multo amplius adprobamus." See O'Donovan, "Political Thought," 51–52.

25. O'Donovan, "Political Thought," 51–52; the whole essay is relevant here, as is Milbank, *Theology and Social Theory,* 406, 290–91.

26. Milbank, *Theology and Social Theory,* 407. One of Milbank's most distinguished opponents here was Markus, *Saeculum.* In his recent book, *Christianity and the Secular* (Notre Dame: University of Notre Dame Press, 2006), Markus responds to Milbank by acknowledging "the justice of criticisms of my minimizing unduly in my *Saeculum* the social character of the church," though he adds, "I would have reservations about John Milbank's view that the Church is, for Augustine, a 'political' reality" (42 n. 27). For a brief but clear account of the argument between Milbank and Markus, see Michael J. Hollerich, "John Milbank, Augustine, and the 'Secular,'" in *History, Apocalypse, and the Secular Imagination: New Essays on Augustine's City of God,* ed. Mark Vessey, Karla Pollman, and Allan D. Fitzgerald (Bowling Green, OH: Philosophy Documentation Center, 1999), 311–26.

27. Sermon 251, in Augustine, *Sermons,* vol. 7. On the date, see 126, 131 n. 1.

28. Sermon 251.3. See similarly *CG* XVIII.48–49 (using the same parable in XVIII.49) and XX.9. Gerald Bonner puts the position clearly: "Although perfection is possible only in the future in the Church Triumphant, in a certain fashion this future hope is already realized in the Church Militant which, in an

eschatological sense, is even now the Kingdom of God on earth." "Augustine's Understanding of the Church as a Eucharistic Community," in *Saint Augustine the Bishop: A Book of Essays,* ed. Fannie Le Moine and Christopher Kleinhenz (New York: Garland, 1994), 39–63; see too 39, 44–46, 45, 50, 54. Also on "the mixed church," consult Tariscius J. van Bavel's entry by that name in *Augustine through the Ages: An Encyclopedia,* ed. Allan D. Fitzgerald (Grand Rapids, MI: Eerdmans, 1999), 172–73. There are interesting comparisons with Karl Barth's complex ecclesiology here; see *Church Dogmatics,* trans. Geoffrey W. Bromiley (Edinburgh: T and T Clark, 1956–75), IV/1 [vol. 4, pt. 1], 668–69; IV/2, 655–60; and IV/4 (*The Christian Life: Lecture Fragments*), 244. Hereafter referred to as *CD*; subsequent citations to volume, part, and page are given parenthetically in the text. "The concept of the body of Christ necessarily comprehends the perception of the being of the community [Church] as visible in faith, while "the *ecclesia militans* and the *ecclesia triumphans* are not two Churches but one Church" (IV/1, 668, 669).

29. For a survey of Augustine's statement on this relationship in the *City of God,* see J. van Oort, *Jerusalem and Babylon: A Study into Augustine's City of God and the Sources of His Doctrine of the Two Cities* (Leiden: Brill, 1991), 127–29.

30. See, e.g., *On Baptism, against the Donatists,* in *St. Augustine: The Writings against the Manichaeans and against the Donatists,* trans. Richard Stothert, Albert H. Newman, and J. R. King, Select Library of the Nicene and Post-Nicene Fathers of the Christian Church, 1st ser., vol. 4 (1989; repr., Grand Rapids, MI: Eerdmans, 1996), III.18.23; IV.10.17; V.27.38; VI.3.5; VII.51.99; and *The Correction of Donatists,* 9.38 (this is also Epistle 185 written to Boniface in 417; see Augustine, *Letters,* vol. 3). For a classic example of the claim that ecclesiology is only "peripheral" in the *City of God* and that this city is solely eschatological, the Wycliffite church of the predestinate (quoting, e.g., *CG* XX.8), see Ruokanen, *Theology of Social Life,* 87–88.

31. For an eloquent exposition of this, see Karl Barth, *Church Dogmatics,* IV/4 (*The Christian Life: Lecture Fragments*), 205–71.

32. As for discerning who are wheat and who are tares, no human being can ever know her or his own identity here. We can pray for the gifts of persevering grace in hope and faith, in the practices of the Church. On this, see, e.g., from Augustine, the following works in *Answer to the Pelagians IV,* WSA, pt. 1, vol. 26 (Hyde Park, NY: New City Press, 1999): *Rebuke and Grace,* 13.40–42, 15.46, 49; *The Predestination of the Saints,* 6.11, 8.16; and *The Gift of Perseverance,* 22.58, 22.62: "You ought to ask for it [the gift of final perseverance] by daily prayers and, in doing this, you ought to be confident that you are not strangers to the predestination of his people, because he himself also grants that you say these prayers and have this confidence. But heaven forbid that

you despair about yourselves because you are commanded to place your hope in him, not in yourselves."

33. See *Confessions,* VII.7.11–10.6; for "externals," VII.7.11. The best treatment of Augustinian contemplation and its forms of inwardness that I have encountered is Kenney, *Mysticism of Saint Augustine.*

34. See Williams, *Wound of Knowledge,* ch. 4, and Wetzel, *Augustine,* ch. 4.

35. Sermon 71.28, and see similarly 71.33, in Augustine, *Sermons,* vol. 3; on the date, see the invaluable work by Pierre-Marie Hombert, *Nouvelles recherches de chronologie augustinienne* (Paris: Institut d'études augustiniennes, 2000), 370 n. 17. Further citations of Augustine's sermons are given in the text.

36. Taylor, *Sources of the Self,* 131. For arguments congruent with the Augustinian texts being considered here, see Eugene TeSelle, *Augustine the Theologian* (New York: Herder and Herder, 1970), 175–76; however, TeSelle's account of the later writings would seem closer to Taylor's (332–33). For a powerful corrective to claims of a rupture in Augustine's theology of grace in the second decade of the fifth century, see Hombert, *Gloria Gratiae.*

37. The Latin title is *De Peccatorum Meritis et Remissione et de Baptismo Parvulorum.* The English translation by Roland J. Teske is in *Answer to the Pelagians I,* WSA, pt. 1, vol. 23 (Hyde Park, NY: New City Press, 1997): on the date, see pp. 21–22; the quotation above is from III.4.7. Hereafter, citations to this work are given parenthetically in the text.

38. Sermon 213.9 in Augustine, *Sermons,* vol. 6.

39. See Sermons 272 and 227–29 in Augustine, *Sermons,* vols. 7 and 6. Here Henri de Lubac's work is invaluable: see *Corpus Mysticum,* passim, *Catholicism: Christ and the Common Destiny of Man* (San Francisco: Ignatius Press, 1988), chs. 3 and 7, and *The Christian Faith* (San Francisco: Ignatius Press, 1986), chs. 6 and 7.

40. Kenney, *Mysticism of Saint Augustine,* quoting from 107, but the whole book is relevant to the argument I summarize here. It is a decisive supersession of R. J. O'Connell's influential Platonizing of Augustine's theology in *St. Augustine's Confessions* (Cambridge, MA: Harvard University Press, 1969), *Images of Conversion in St. Augustine's Confessions* (New York: Fordham University Press, 1996), and *The Origins of the Soul in St. Augustine's Later Writings* (New York: Fordham University Press, 1987). See too McGinn, *Foundations of Mysticism,* ch. 7.

41. Barth, *CD* IV/2, 545; see too 539–42 on this theme.

42. See the excellent remarks of Wetzel, *Augustine,* 124–25.

43. See Barth, *CD* IV/4, 3, with Augustine, *Confessions,* X.

44. Exposition of Ps. 136, especially 136.2.11–15, in the sixth volume of the English translation by Maria Boulding, *Expositions of the Psalms,* 6 vols.,

WSA, pt. 3, vol. 20 (Hyde Park, NY: New City Press, 2001–5). For Rome as the second Babylon, see *CG* XVIII.2 and 22.

45. See Wetzel, *Augustine,* 197–206 (excellent reflections on "irresistible grace") and ch. 4 ("Grace and Conversion").

46. *CD* IV/3, 528; see too the argument about freedom at IV/3, 447.

47. *De Doctrina Christiana [On Christian Teaching]* is quoted from *Teaching Christianity,* trans. Edmund Hill, WSA, pt. 1, vol. 11 (Hyde Park, NY: New City Press, 1996), Prologue, 5. There is also a good translation with Latin text by R. P. H. Green, *De Doctrina Christiana* (Oxford: Clarendon Press, 1995), Preface, 5.11.

48. Hill's translation in *Teaching Christianity,* Prologue, oddly deletes Augustine's description of Peter's instruction.

49. Here I quote from Green's translation.

50. *On Baptism,* I.8.10. For a reading of Cornelius's conversion directed against the Pelagians, see *The Predestination of the Saints,* 7.12.

51. See *CG* XX.9, XIII.6, XVI.3, XI.2. See too the expositions of Psalm 138.2, Psalm 147.18, and Psalm 122.5 (all in *Expositions of the Psalms,* vol. 2); Sermon 179 A.7 (*Sermons,* vol. 5); Sermon 227.1 (*Sermons,* vol. 6). For a related commentary, see McGinn, *Foundations of Mysticism,* 238–40, 251.

52. As Barth seems to suspect: *CD* IV/4 (*The Christian Life: Lecture Fragments*), 244. On this issue, see especially Hombert, *Gloria Gratiae.*

53. For a fairly typical example, see Leszek Kolakowski, *God Owes Us Nothing: A Brief Remark on Pascal's Religion and on the Spirit of Jansenism* (Chicago: University of Chicago Press, 1995), 15, affirming the irresistibility of grace as teaching shared by Jansen and Augustine; contrast the arguments of Wetzel, *Augustine,* 197–235.

54. E. Ann Matter, "Conversion(s) in the *Confessiones,*" in *Collectanea Augustiniana,* ed. Joseph C. Schnaubelt and Frederick Van Fleteren (Leuven: Leuven University Press, 1990), 25. Matter's criticism focuses on Fredriksen, "Paul and Augustine." I shall return to this essay below; also relevant here is Leo C. Ferrari, "Paul at the Conversion of Augustine," *Augustinian Studies* 11 (1980): 5–20, and "Saint Augustine and the Road to Damascus," *Augustinian Studies* 13 (1982): 151–70.

55. See *De Diversis Quaestionibus ad Simplicianum,* ed. A. Mutzenbecher (Turnhout: Brepols, 1970); there is a translation of book 1 in *Augustine: Earlier Writings,* ed. John H. S. Burleigh (London: SCM Press, 1953). See Hombert, *Gloria Gratiae,* 91–112.

56. *Confessions,* XIII.1.1; here I use my own translation. O'Donnell's commentary on this passage is brief but pertinent: *Confessions,* 3:346. For a

fine and relevant meditation on Augustine's theology of speech, see Griffiths, *Lying,* ch. 4.

57. See O'Donnell's note to "audirem de longinquo," 3:346, and to "in regione dissimilitudinis," 2:443–44; see too the discussion of *Confessions* in Hombert, *Gloria Gratiae,* 112–29, especially 119–21.

58. Chadwick's edition of Augustine's *Confessions,* 123 n. 18, refers this to Plotinus, *Enneads,* V.1.1; O'Donnell's commentary on VII.10.16 includes a substantial excursus on "discussions of Augustine's Platonic indebtednesses" and particularly on his relation to Plotinian contemplation (2:434–37); see too the notes on "redire" and "duce te" on 438. For important comments on O'Donnell's assessment of the relations, see Kenney, *Mysticism of Saint Augustine,* 5–6; Kenney's entire book is relevant to these discussions.

59. See too the "region of destitution" [region egestatis] in II.10.18.

60. For a fascinating meditation on the theology of "invocation," see Barth, *CD* IV/4 (*The Christian Life: Lecture Fragments*), 84–109, 234. For further reflections on invoking God by Augustine, see especially the expositions of Psalm 30.4, Psalm 41.1, and Psalm 74.2 and 4 (in *Expositions of the Psalms,* vols. 1, 2, and 4 respectively). For a related account of agency, see David C. Schindler, "Freedom beyond Our Choosing: Augustine on the Will and Its Objects," ch. 4 in *Augustine and Politics,* ed. John Doody, Kevin L. Hughes, and Kim Paffenroth (Lanham, MD: Lexington Books, 2005), especially 80–84.

61. See George Hunsinger, *How to Read Karl Barth: The Shape of His Theology* (New York: Oxford University Press, 1991), ch. 7, "Double Agency as a Test Case."

62. See too *Confessions* VIII.7.18, where he still defers conversion and, as in VI.11.20, cites Ecclus. 5.8: "Delay not to be converted [converti] to the Lord, and defer it not from day to day." For a congruent study of St. Thomas Aquinas and Augustine, see Reinhard Hütter, "St. Thomas on Grace and Free Will in the *Initium Fidei*: The Surpassing Augustinian Synthesis," *Nova et Vetera: The English Edition of the International Theological Journal* 5/3 (Summer 2007): 521–54.

63. James O'Donnell's preoccupation with trying to write a biography of Augustine that adheres jauntily to what he takes to be the canons of postmodernism presents a very different picture. For example, the *Confessions* simply "portrayed his god as the actor and himself as the object" and consistently "undervalued the role of the human, fallible experiential person." James O'Donnell, *Augustine: A New Biography* (New York: Perennial, 2005), 297, 295. For a contrasting and sensitive account of Augustine's "psychology of grace" in a classic study, see John Burnaby, *Amor Dei: A Study of the Religion of St. Augustine* (London: Hodder and Stoughton, 1938), 221–28, 239; more recently, Wetzel, "Grace and Conversion" ch. 4 of his book *Augustine.*

64. The translation of *De Gratia Christi et Peccato Originali, The Grace of Christ and Original Sin,* is in *Answer to the Pelagians I*; for the Latin text I use *Select Anti-Pelagian Treatises,* ed. William Bright (Oxford: Clarendon Press, 1880), 202–71; citations given parenthetically in the text.

65. Matt. 7.18; *Grace of Christ,* I.18.19. On the good and bad trees, see too *Enchiridion,* IV.15 (Matt. 7.18 and 12.33), translated by Bruce Harbert as *The Augustine Catechism: The Enchiridion on Faith, Hope, and Love,* ed. John E. Rotelle (Hyde Park, NY: New City Press, 1999).

66. The conflict between an Augustinian understanding of the "intrinsic" form of grace, complexly mediated in the Church, and one that composes an "extrinsic" model will be addressed in chapter 2.

67. *Grace of Christ,* I.45.49.

68. See too the related meditation on memory, Peter, and the opacity of the self in another late work (419–21): *The Nature and Origin of the Soul,* IV.7.9–IV.8.12 (in *Answer to the Pelagians I*; on the date, see p. 467). Also, *Enchiridion,* 22.82 (translated into English as *The Augustine Catechism*).

69. *Grace of Christ,* I.45.49. I have slightly revised the translation to bring out Augustine's language of invocation and calling discussed above (*Confessions,* XIII.1.1) and returned to below.

70. Here I draw on Barth, *CD* IV/3, 528.

71. Translated by Roland J. Teske in *Answer to the Pelagians IV.*

72. Barth, *CD* IV (I, 688; see also 650–725).

73. Sermon 169.13 (in *Sermons,* vol. 5); for the date, see Hombert, *Nouvelles recherches,* 370 n. 18, 641. References to this sermon given below in the text. See similarly Sermon 156.11 (*Sermons,* vol. 5), which will be discussed in chapter 4 below.

74. I will show the contrast in "modern" theology of the fourteenth century as well as its supposedly Augustinian opponent, Bradwardine, in chapters 2 and 3. Sermon 169 does reflect on a different kind of conversion, that of the apostle Paul as related by Luke (Acts 9 and 22). I address this different model immediately below. In Sermon 169 Augustine does not offer Paul's conversion as a countermodel but instead uses it to explore Paul's mistaken attempts to found justice on himself and his own will rather than searching for God's justice. This is a picture of a temptation facing Christians: to weave into their attempted self-construction a self that occludes Christ. In such a building program the Christian builds a ruin (169.5–11). Here Augustine is not attending to questions about the mediations of the Church and the processes of conversion, as he does elsewhere in passages exemplified above. See the commentary below on his uses of Paul's conversion against the Donatists.

75. I refer here to the discussion above of the preface to *On Christian Teaching.*

76. Cf. the delicate treatment of agency in the conversion of Cornelius in the same work, *Predestination of Saints,* 7.12.

77. This may be particularly true of Reformation and Counter-Reformation dispositions; see Brian Cummings, *The Literary Culture of the Reformation: Grammar and Grace* (Oxford: Oxford University Press, 2002), 366–71, 389.

78. In *Sermons,* vol. 8; for the date of delivery as 413, see Hombert, *Nouvelles recherches,* 386–98. See similarly Sermon 87.15 (in *Sermons,* vol. 3), in which it is stated that Christ "slew the persecutor" and so "gave life to the preacher," and Letter 93 (407 or 408) in *Letters,* vol. 1, in which the statement that Paul was forced to the truth "by the great violence of Christ who compelled him" (93.2.5) links this compelling with Luke 14.23 and coercion of Donatists to become Catholics. For a recent discussion of Augustine and the Donatists, see Peter I. Kaufman, *Incorrectly Political: Augustine and More* (Notre Dame: University of Notre Dame Press, 2007), ch. 3.

79. Fredriksen, "Paul and Augustine," 26–27 n. 93; F. H. Russell, "Persuading the Donatists: Augustine's Coercion by Words," in *The Limits of Ancient Christianity,* ed. E. Klingshire and Mark Vessey (Ann Arbor: University of Michigan Press, 1999), 115–30, here 125–26, 128–29; also relevant, John von Heyking, *Augustine and Politics as Longing in the World* (Columbia: University of Missouri Press, 2001), ch. 7; Robert Dodaro and Margaret Atkins, *Augustine: Political Writings* (Cambridge: Cambridge University Press, 2001), xxi–xxv; Leo C. Ferrari, *The Conversions of Saint Augustine* (Villanova: Villanova University Press, 1984), "Paul at the Conversion," and "Saint Augustine." For an example of those who claim that Paul's conversion is "Augustine's favorite example of the working of grace," see John M. Rist, *Augustine: Ancient though Baptised* (Cambridge: Cambridge University Press, 1994), 181, following Fredriksen.

80. Here I quote from Augustine, *Letters,* 3:156–210; for Augustine on this letter, see *The Retractions,* trans. Mary I. Bogan (1968; repr., Washington, DC: Catholic University of America Press, 1999), book II, ch. 48, numbered here ch. 74. For an introduction to Donatism and Augustine, see Robert A. Markus's entry in *Augustine through the Ages,* ed. Fitzgerald, 284–86, and Maureen Tilley's entry, 34–39; Michael Cameron, *Augustine's Construction of Figurative Exegesis against the Donatists in the Enarrationes in Psalmos* (Ann Arbor: UMI Dissertation Services, 1997), chs. 7–8; also Peter Brown, *Augustine of Hippo: A Biography,* 2nd ed. (Berkeley: University of California Press, 2000), chs. 19, 21, and "New Evidence," 460–61.

81. Letter 185.6.22 (*Letters,* vol. 3, 192); subsequent citations are given parenthetically in the text. It should be read with Letter 93 (*Letters,* vol. 1) of

407 or 408, since this is his first application of Luke 14.21–23 to coercing Donatist Christians to become Catholics.

82. See the discussion above of *On Christian Doctrine,* Preface, 6.12.

83. Frederiksen, "Paul and Augustine," 27; *Ad Simplicianum,* I.22. For an English translation of I.1–22, see *Augustine: Earlier Writings.*

84. Rowan Williams, *Why Study the Past? The Quest for the Historical Church* (Grand Rapids, MI: Eerdmans, 2005), 16; similarly, Williams, *Wound of Knowledge,* ch. 4.

85. On the implications of the difference between the Vulgate's word, translated as "compel" (*compelle*), and the Old Latin text, using the verb *cogo,* see Russell, "Persuading the Donatists," 121–23.

86. See Robert Dodaro, "Between the Two Cities: Political Action in Augustine of Hippo," ch. 5 in Doody, Hughes, and Paffenroth, *Augustine and Politics,* 102. See too Russell, "Persuading the Donatists," 122–23, 126; also von Heyking, *Augustine,* ch. 7, and Williams, *Why Study the Past?* 44–50.

87. "Select quotations from Augustine's anti-Donatist writings enabled some medieval canonists to make him look as if he were justifying the stern measure against heretics adopted in the later Middle Ages. Augustine would have been horrified by the burning of heretics, by the belief, found not only among sixteenth-century Protestants and medieval Catholics but even in the medieval world of Byzantine Orthodoxy, that heretical ideas are of so insidious and diabolical a nature that the only way of stopping them is to exterminate the propagators." Medieval uses of Augustine to justify medieval practices of killing heretics picked texts out of contexts and "ignored the numerous places where he wholly opposed torture and capital punishment or any discipline that went beyond what a truly loving father might administer to an erring son." See Henry Chadwick, *Augustine: A Very Short Introduction* (Oxford: Oxford University Press, 2001), 85–86. See similarly many years earlier, John N. Figgis, *The Political Aspects of S. Augustine's "City of God"* (London: Longmans, 1921), 77–79, 91. In discussing Luke 14.23 in the *Summa Theologiae,* Aquinas quotes from Augustine's letter to Boniface and argues that Christian wars against unbelievers can never be to compel them to faith because belief depends on freedom of the will. The justification of war is to stop unbelievers hindering or blaspheming the faith of Christians. Only heretics and apostates can be compelled, and this is to make them fulfill broken promises. But St. Thomas does defend the practice of burning heretics to death; see *Summa Theologiae* (London: Blackfriars, 1964–81), II-II 10.8 and II-II.11.3–4. Thomas More is following the medieval Catholic tradition rationalized by St. Thomas when he defends burning heretics, but he is simply wrong to claim that the Church is doing "no more" than Augustine in these practices: *The*

Complete Works of St. Thomas More, vol. 6 (two parts), ed. Thomas M. C. Lawler, G. Marc'hadour, and R. C. Marius (New Haven: Yale University Press, 1981), pt. 1, p. 428.

88. For a different approach but congruent outcome, see Milbank, *Theology and Social Theory,* 423–29. See too the discussion in Rist, *Augustine,* 239–45.

89. I quote from Phil. 2.7–8 and *CG* XI.2.

Chapter 2.   ILLUSTRATING "MODERN THEOLOGY"

In the epigraph, the Latin text for the *Confessions* is taken from the three-volume edition of James O'Donnell (Oxford: Clarendon Press, 1992), and the English translation is Henry Chadwick's (Oxford: Oxford University Press, 1991).

1. William of Ockham, *Opera Philosophica et Theologica,* 17 vols. (St. Bonaventure, NY: St. Bonaventure University, 1967–88); citations of volume and page of this edition are given parenthetically in the text. The discussion here refers to the first book, d. 17, q. 1 (III.440–66).

2. For informative accounts of this history, see the following: Heiko A. Oberman, *The Harvest of Medieval Theology* (Cambridge, MA: Harvard University Press, 1963), 39–45, 160–84, 353–56; Francis Oakley, *Omnipotence, Covenant, and Order: An Excursion in the History of Ideas from Abelard to Leibniz* (Ithaca: Cornell University Press, 1984); Cross, *Duns Scotus,* ch. 8; Rega Wood, "Ockham's Repudiation of Pelagianism," ch. 10 in *The Cambridge Companion to Ockham,* ed. Paul V. Spade (Cambridge: Cambridge University Press, 1999), especially 354, 356–57; Marilyn McCord Adams, *William Ockham,* 2 vols. (Notre Dame: University of Notre Dame Press, 1987), vol. 2, ch. 30; Courtenay, *Schools and Scholars,* 186, 213; Hester G. Gelber, *It Could Have Been Otherwise: Contingency and Necessity in Dominican Theology at Oxford, 1300–1350* (Leiden: Brill, 2004), ch. 8; Eugenio Randi, "A Scotist Way of Distinguishing between God's Absolute and Ordained Powers," in *From Ockham to Wyclif,* ed. Anne Hudson and Michael Wilks (Oxford: Blackwell, 1987), 43–50; Leonard A. Kennedy, "Thomism and Divine Absolute Power," *Thomistic Papers* 5 (1990): 49–62; Olivier Boulnois, ed., *La puissance et son ombre de Pierre Lombard à Luther: Textes traduits et commentés* (Paris: Aubier, 1994), especially 53–65; see too the brilliant study by Muralt, *L'unité.* In his account of Ockham's politics and his allegedly Republican ecclesiology, Takashi Shogimen touches on these concepts in passing; *Ockham and Political Discourse in the Late Middle Ages* (Cambridge: Cambridge Uni-

versity Press, 2007), 19–20, 203–4; for Ockham's ecclesiastical Republicanism, see 256–61. On the consequences of sinful habits for "liberty" and the virtues, Shogimen has nothing to say. Perhaps this is because he shares the following view with Ockham: "Ockham is fundamentally optimistic regarding each individual's right reason" (250). Although Shogimen is not particularly interested in the matters of Christian theology addressed in this chapter, his book is an extremely helpful contribution to Ockham's treatment of fraternal correction, dominion, and liberty.

3. See Wood, "Ockham's Repudiation," and Adams, *William Ockham,* 2:1295.

4. Wood, "Ockham's Repudiation," 352, 361, 364.

5. Ibid., 365 and 367.

6. See reference to Aquinas, III.468 n. 1. The Augustinian theologian Gregory of Rimini uses Ockham's response to this question as an example of modern Pelagianism; *Lectura super Primum et Secundum Sententiarum,* ed. A. Damasus Trapp and Venicio Marcolino, vol. 6 (Berlin: de Gruyter, 1980), in II *Sent.* d. 26–28, q. 1.3 (p. 65).

7. This reply (III.469) was cited in 1326 by the Avignon masters, who were investigating suspicions about the Pelagian implications of Ockham's theology; see III.469 n. 1. For the master's views, see Augustus Pelzer, "Les 51 articles de Guillaume Occam," *Revue d'histoire ecclésiastique* 18 (1922): 240–70. The text is on 249–70. For the commentaries on Ockham's theology of grace, see especially art. 1–4, 7–8, 40.

8. See "Les 51 articles," art. 1 (251–52), and III.470–71 nn. 1–2.

9. William of Ockham, *Ockham on the Virtues,* trans. Rega Wood, with commentary (West Lafayette: Purdue University Press, 1997), here pp. 31–32; subsequent citations to this work are given parenthetically in the text. In developing the master's objections to Ockham's thinking here it would be important to contrast with his views the arguments of the tradition in which charity is a participation in the divine life: e.g., Thomas Aquinas, *Summa Theologiae,* II-II.23.2; it is a matter of grace, II-II.24.2. Throughout this chapter I am using the Blackfriars parallel-text edition, Thomas Aquinas, *Summa Theologiae* (London: Blackfriars, 1964–81); subsequent citations (*ST*), to part, question, and article, are given parenthetically in the text.

10. Ockham, *Ockham on the Virtues,* art. 4, 162–65.

11. Compare, for example, "If you love me, keep my commandments. And I will ask the Father, and he shall find you another Paraclete, that he may abide with you forever" (John 14.15–16); "In this is charity: not as though we had loved God but because he hath first loved us, and sent his son to be a

propitiation for our sins" (1 John 4.10); "I am come that they may have life, and may have it more abundantly" (John 10.10); see too John 6.57–59.

12. Wood's commentary in Ockham, *Ockham on the Virtues,* 268–69.

13. On Ockham's *ex professo* treatment of the Incarnation, see Adams, *William Ockham,* 2:982–96.

14. See *ST* I-II.107.1.

15. Fergus Kerr, *After Aquinas: Versions of Thomism* (Oxford: Blackwell, 2002), 135. The whole of ch. 8 is relevant.

16. Characteristic of Scotist theology; see Cross, *Duns Scotus,* 95–96; also relevant is Scotus's approach to penance, 109–16.

17. This is an issue that seems quite ignored by those seeking to align Langland and Ockham (see the first section of chapter 4). In his study of Henri de Lubac's theology, John Milbank moves from Scotus to Ockham in observing a tendency to render grace "extrinsic" and identifies the "extrinsicism" of Ockham's model of grace and human agency. He relates this to Ockham's view of "the divine *potentia absoluta,*" a view that allows him "to say that God might have saved us without grace—by sheer decree." See John Milbank, *The Suspended Middle: Henri de Lubac and the Debate Concerning the Supernatural* (Grand Rapids, MI: Eerdmans, 2005), 80, 92, 95: the whole of ch. 8 is relevant. I will return to the issue of God's *potentia absoluta* below. For a rigorous criticism of Milbank's Lubacian reading of Aquinas, see Reinhard Hütter, "*Desiderium Naturale Visionis Dei—Est autem duplex hominis beatitudo sive felicitas*: Some Observations about Lawrence Feingold's and John Milbank's Recent Interventions in the Debate over the Natural Desire to See God," *Nova et Vetera: The English Edition of the International Theological Journal* 5 (2007): 81–132.

18. He also treated predestination in *De Praedestinatione et de Praescientia Dei Respectu Futurorum Contingentium,* II.507–39, trans. Marilyn McCord Adams and Norman Kretzmann as *Predestination, God's Foreknowledge, and Future Contingents* (New York: Meredith, 1969). From the substantial literature on the issues here I have been especially helped by the following: Paul Vignaux, *Justification et prédestination au XIVe siècle* (Paris: Leroux, 1934), 134–45; Oberman, *Harvest of Medieval Theology,* ch. 7; Wood, "Ockham's Repudiation," 361–66; James L. Halverson, *Peter Aureol on Predestination: A Challenge to Late Medieval Thought* (Leiden: Brill, 1998), 113–22.

19. Wood, "Ockham's Repudiation," 234; see also, in the same work, 359, 362, 363–64, and Halverson, *Peter Aureol,* 121.

20. For Ockham's definition of how he uses "cause" here, see Halverson, *Peter Aureol,* 115–16. Ockham attacks St. Thomas's treatment of predestination and divine foreknowledge of merits in *ST* I.23.5 (see IV.598–99).

21. "Unde secundum Sanctos et Doctores, quamis opera facta in peccato mortali nihil faciant ad vitam, nec remunerabuntur in vita aeterna, tamen remunerantur temporaliter, et sunt faciendum ut citius Deus det alicui gratiam qua mereatur vitam aeternam. Igitur aliquot modo, quamvis non sufficienter nec simpliciter meritorie, talia opera bona disponunt ad gratiam, et per consequens ad effectum praedestinationis" (IV.600).

22. Wood, "Ockham's Repudiation," 362: a concession to arguments against her own position?

23. This is not just a matter of genre. Augustine shows the attention I am discussing across a wide range of genres, and one could contrast Ockham's blandness with the approach by Gregory of Rimini also commenting on the *Sentences*: see, e.g., II d. 26–28, q. 1 (pp. 17–87) and q. 2 (pp. 87–114), in *Lectura*, vol. 6.

24. Also see *ST* I.23 with III.24 (Christ's predestination).

25. Brian Davies, *The Thought of Thomas Aquinas* (Oxford: Oxford University Press, 1993), 168; see 166–69, with 94–97, 321–32.

26. Here he uses Augustine, *Predestination of the Saints,* 15.

27. Wood, "Ockham's Repudiation," 363.

28. The history of this proposition has been outlined by Artur Landgraf in *Dogmengeschichte der Frühscholastik,* pt. 1, vol. 1 (Regensburg: Pustet, 1952), 249–64.

29. Courtenay, *Schools and Scholars,* 213.

30. Ibid., 297.

31. Heiko A. Oberman, "*Facientibus quod in se est Deus non denegat gratiam*: Robert Holcot, O.P., and the Beginnings of Luther's Theology," *Harvard Theological Review* 55 (1962): 317–42; see too on this topic Oberman's *Harvest of Medieval Theology,* 128–45, 240–41, 248.

32. "*Facientibus quod in se est,*" 327; see too 323.

33. Ibid., 328 n. 50.

34. Ibid., 335–36.

35. See Oberman, *Harvest of Medieval Theology,* 160–78, 210–11; Heiko A. Oberman, *Archbishop Thomas Bradwardine: A Fourteenth Century Augustinian* (Utrecht: Kemink and Zoon, 1957), especially ch. 6. I have found arguments by Gregory of Rimini relevant here: see his *Lectura* on the *Sentences,* II d. 24–44, especially d. 26–28 (pp. 17–114).

36. For the treatise on grace, see *ST* I-II.109–14, in vol. 30 of the Blackfriars edition. I have found the following extremely informative: Joseph P. Wawrykow, *God's Grace and Human Action: "Merit" in the Theology of Thomas Aquinas* (Notre Dame: University of Notre Dame Press, 1995).

37. This is a commonplace, but see its exemplification in the following: W. J. Courtenay, "Theology and Theologians from Ockham to Wyclif," ch. 1 in

The History of the University of Oxford, vol. 2, *Late Medieval Oxford,* ed. J. I. Catto and R. Evans (Oxford: Clarendon Press, 1992), 25–26, 17; Oberman, *Harvest of Medieval Theology,* 153–54, 161, 163–64, 175, 210–11.

38. For Courtenay's work, see *Schools and Scholars,* 209–13; *Covenant and Causality in Medieval Thought* (London: Variorum, 1984); *Capacity and Volition: A History of the Distinction of Absolute and Ordained Power* (Bergamo: Pierluigi Lubrina Editore, 1990); for Oberman, see *Harvest of Medieval Theology,* chs. 2 and 7. For Leff's early work, see Gordon Leff, *Bradwardine and the Pelagians: A Study of His "De Causa Dei" and Its Opponents* (Cambridge: Cambridge University Press, 1957); the treatment of Ockham in this work was critically transformed in his *William of Ockham: The Metamorphosis of Scholastic Discourse* (Manchester: Manchester University Press, 1975). For a lucid account of the current revisionist arguments, see Gelber, *It Could Have Been Otherwise,* ch. 8. It is worth noting, however, that Holcot's commentary on the *Sentences* apparently offers abundant speculation and argument that is congruent with Leff's early claims about Bradwardine's "opponents": see Leonard A. Kennedy, *The Philosophy of Robert Holcot: Fourteenth-Century Skeptic* (Lewiston, NY: Mellen Press, 1993). For illuminating comparison with Ockham (not made by Kennedy), see especially chs. 8–9, on grace and merit. See also Leonard A. Kennedy, "Osbert of Pickenham, O. Carm. (fl. 1360), on the Absolute Power of God," *Carmelus* 35 (1988): 178–225, and "Andrew of Novo Castro, O. F. M., and the Moral Law," *Franciscan Studies* 48 (1988): 28–39.

39. William of Ockham, *Quodlibetal Questions,* trans. Alfred J. Freddoso and Francis E. Kelley, 2 vols. (New Haven: Yale University Press, 1991); see too VI.2. There is another lucid discussion of the distinction in Ockham's detailed attack on John XXII's teaching on evangelical poverty in his *Opus Nonaginta Dierum,* ch. 95, translated by John Kilcullen and John Scott as *Work of Ninety Days,* 2 vols. (Lewiston, NY: Mellen Press, 2001), vol. 2. For an extremely helpful account of these and related texts, see Adams, *William Ockham,* 2:1198–1207. Her exposition brings out "vacillation" in his arguments (see especially 1207).

40. This abstraction is not entailed by the distinction in itself, as we can see by its use in the work of St. Thomas Aquinas: Adams, *William Ockham,* 2:1187–90.

41. William of Ockham, *Quaestiones in Librum Quartum Sententiarum (Reportatio),* ed. Rega Wood and Gedeon Gal, in *Opera,* vol. 7. Here I refer to q. 2–5 (pp. 20–61); citations to volume and page are again given parenthetically in the text.

42. On this, see Adams, *William Ockham,* 2:1264–65.

43. See Wood's commentary in Ockham, *Ockham on the Virtues,* 270, citing I.503–6 and IX.256 (*Quodlibetal Questions* III.14.3).

44. See Marilyn McCord Adams, "The Structure of Ockham's Moral Theory," *Franciscan Studies* 46 (1986): 1–35; here 29–30 addresses III *Sent.* q. 15 (v. 352). Adams goes on to discuss the famous passage in IV *Sent.* q. 16, where Ockham claims that God could command us to hate him and that we, in our own freedom, can do so (VII.352, discussed above); see too pp. 30–33.

45. Adams, "Structure," 30.

46. Ibid.; see Ockham's *Opera,* 5:352. On the language of law and its politics in such models of divine agency, see Oakley, *Omnipotence, Covenant, and Order,* review of *Capacity and Volition,* by W. J. Courtenay, *Speculum* 68 (1993): 739–42, and "Jacobean Political Theology: The Absolute and Ordinary Powers of the King," *Journal of the History of Ideas* 29 (1968): 323–46; Eugenio Randi, "Ockham, John XXII and the Absolute Power of God," *Franciscan Studies* 46 (1986): 205–16; J. Marrone, "The Absolute and the Ordained Powers of the Pope: An Unedited Text by Henry of Ghent," *Medieval Studies* 36 (1974): 7–27; see too Randi, "Scotist Way," and Muralt, *L'unité.*

47. Adams, "Structure," 30.

48. See the discussions by Mark Jordan, *The Alleged Aristotelianism of Thomas Aquinas* (Toronto: Pontifical Institute of Mediaeval Studies, 1992), and Kerr, *After Aquinas,* ch. 7.

49. For example, see Ockham, I *Sent.* d. 17, q. 1 (III.462). For an illuminating treatment of the issues within a grand narrative, see Servais Pinckaers, *The Sources of Christian Ethics,* trans. Mary Noble (Washington, DC: Catholic University of America Press, 1995), especially chs. 9–11, 16. Although Pinckaers's book was first published in 1985, the commentary on Ockham lacks any engagement with recent scholarship; nevertheless it poses some key questions about Ockham's version of freedom and the cultural story to which it belongs.

50. Hans Urs von Balthasar, *The Theology of Karl Barth: Exposition and Interpretation,* trans. Edward T. Oakes (San Francisco: Ignatius Press, 1992), 129 (von Balthasar's italics).

51. Ibid., 124, 131 (von Balthasar's italics).

52. Barth, *Church Dogmatics,* II/1 (vol. 2, pt. 1), 257–321; I use the English translation by Geoffrey W. Bromiley (Edinburgh: T and T Clark, 1956–75). Subsequent citations to page are given parenthetically in the text.

53. Adams, *William Ockham,* vol. 2, ch. 28, especially 1186–1231.

54. For examples of St. Paul on Christ's reconciliation of the world to God, see 2 Cor. 5.17–19, Col. 1.20–23; for Langland's representation of such dinner parties, see *Piers Plowman: The C Version; Will's Vision of Piers Plowman, Do-Well, Do-Better, and Do-Best,* ed. George Russell and George Kane (London: Athlone Press, 1997), XI.33–42.

55. Adams, *William Ockham,* 2:1278; for Scotus's similar account of sacramental efficacy, see Cross, *Duns Scotus,* 135–38.

56. See Adams, *William Ockham,* 2:1266–71, 1273–77, 1291–97. I discussed this earlier in the present chapter. See too Courtenay, *Schools and Scholars,* 213.

57. See Marilyn McCord Adams, "Ockham on Will, Nature, and Morality," in Spade, *Cambridge Companion to Ockham,* ch. 11, here quoting from 250.

58. See ibid., 262 (Adams's exclamation mark).

59. *ST,* vol. 56, p. 20.

60. This also builds on St. Thomas's account of human nature; see *ST* I.75–89.

61. The editor identifies these people as Richard Fishacre, Robert Kilwardby, and Bonaventure. On Fishacre, see William J. Courtenay, "The King and the Leaden Coin: The Economic Background of *sine qua non* Causality," *Traditio* 28 (1972): 185–209, 191–93, and, on Bonaventure, 201–2.

62. As Courtenay shows, Aquinas had discussed this example in his earlier commentary on the *Sentences.* He quotes the relevant text in "King and the Leaden Coin," 185 n. 1. His own attention is largely devoted to "the immediate economic background of the example," to the history of contractualism, to commercial activity and "the theory of monetary value" (187; see too 193–201, "The Medieval Economic Uses of Ascribed Value," and 202–9, "Thomas and Intrinsic Value for Money and the Sacraments"). He aims to show that Aquinas ascribed an "intrinsic value" to money (206) and that this impeded his thinking. Courtenay claims that St. Thomas's social model is taken from "a glorified village" and that his analysis is distorted by his social origins among "the lesser aristocracy" and an "anti-urban" disposition (206). So he (unlike the theologian Richard Fishacre) apparently found it difficult "to understand a causality based on ascribed value and covenant." Therefore his "less sophisticated theory of sacrament causality," which I address below. Courtenay's characterization of St. Thomas's social experience is quite inadequate: it simply deletes his years in Cologne and Paris. See Jean-Pierre Torrell, *Saint Thomas Aquinas,* vol. 1, *The Person and His Work* (Washington, DC: Catholic University of America Press, 1996), chs. 1–3. His characterization of Aquinas's thought on markets, trade, and money is also inadequate, and I doubt that Courtenay would offer such an account today in the light of work by, for example, Joel Kaye: *Economy and Nature in the Late Fourteenth Century: Money, Market Exchange, and the Emergence of Scientific Thought* (Cambridge: Cambridge University Press, 1998), especially 85–101; Odd Langholm, "The Medieval Schoolmen (1200–1400)," in *Ancient and Medieval Economic Ideas and Concepts of Social Justice,* ed. S. Todd Lowry and Barry Gordon (Leiden: Brill, 1998),

439–501, and *Economics in the Medieval Schools: Wealth Exchange, Value, Money and Usury* (Leiden: Brill, 1992) chs. 8 and 9; John Finnis, *Aquinas: Moral, Political, and Legal Theory* (Oxford: Oxford University Press, 1998), ch. 6. Courtenay does not mention Ockham's use of the image in question or John Lutterell's reply.

63. Donne's "Ecstasie" belongs to his *Songs and Sonnets*. It is quoted here from *The Poems of John Donne,* ed. Herbert J.C. Grierson (London: Oxford University Press, 1966), 1:51–52, lines 71–72. The quotation at the end of this paragraph is from Davies, *Thought of Thomas Aquinas,* 352.

64. See Ockham on IV *Sent.* q. 1 in *Opera,* 7:3–19.

65. The passages he refers to are cited in VIII.5, n. 3, and VII.7, n. 1: *Scriptum super libros sententiarum,* iv, d. 1, q. 1, a. 4, qa. 1, resp., and qa. 2, resp.

66. Girard J. Etzkorn, "Ockham at a Provincial Chapter: 1323; A Prelude to Avignon," *Archivum Franciscanum Historicum* 83 (1990): 557–67.

67. See Pelzer, "Les 51 articles," 240–70; J. Koch, "Neue Aktenstücke zu dem gegen Wilhelm Ockham in Avignon geführten Prozess," *Recherches de théologie ancienne et médiévale* 7 (1935): 353–80 and 8 (1936): 79–93, 158–97; William J. Courtenay, "The Academic and Intellectual Worlds of Ockham," ch. 1 in Spade, *Cambridge Companion to Ockham,* 24–26.

68. Courtenay, "Academic and Intellectual Worlds," 26 and 25.

69. See text in Fritz Hoffman, *Die Schriften des Oxforder Kanslers Johannes Lutterell* (Leipzig: St. Benno-Verlag, 1959), and full discussion in Adams, *William Ockham,* 2:1280–96.

70. Adams, *William Ockham,* 2:1280–81.

71. Translation by Adams, *William Ockham,* 2:1284; Latin text in Hoffman, *Die Schriften,* 47–48, art. 14.

72. Translated by Adams, *William Ockham,* 2:1285; Hoffman, *Die Schriften,* 48, art. 14.

73. Adams, *William Ockham,* 2:1285; Hoffman, *Die Schriften,* 49, art. 14.

74. Adams, *William Ockham,* 2:1285.

75. Ibid., 2:1287, addressing the leaden coin.

76. See text of Chatton's lecture on I *Sent.* d. 17, q. 1, published with introduction by Girard J. Etzkorn, "Walter Chatton and the Controversy on the Absolute Necessity of Grace," *Franciscan Studies* 37 (1977): 32–65, with further citations given in the text; see Adams's discussion in *William Ockham,* 2:1286, 1289–95.

77. Etzkorn, "Walter Chatton," 44–48; for his use of Augustine, see, e.g., 39, 45, 46, 47. Page references to Chatton's text are subsequently given parenthetically in the text.

78. See ibid., 45, 48, 49, 53.

79. Adams, *William Ockham,* 2:1295. For Okham's Christology, such as it is, see Marilyn McCord Adams, "Relations, Inherence and Subsistence: or, Was Ockham a Nestorian in Christology?" *Noûs* 16 (1982): 62–75.

80. See Langland, *Piers Plowman,* XI.33–41 (C version, Russell/Kane). Also see a passage in the earlier version of the poem that explicitly associates learned friars with such theologizing: *Piers Plowman: The B Version,* ed. George Kane and E. Talbot Donaldson, rev. ed. (London: Athlone Press, 1988), X.65–78.

Chapter 3.   THOMAS BRADWARDINE

The translation in the first epigraph is taken from *The City of God against the Pelagians,* trans. R. W. Dyson (Cambridge: Cambridge University Press, 1998). The Latin text I use for this source is *De Civitate Dei,* ed. B. Dombart and A. Kalb, 5th ed., 2 vols. (Stuttgart: Teübner, 1993), hereafter referred to as *CG,* with citation of book and chapter. See too *CG* XII.7–8, and contrast Augustine's denial that God is efficient cause of all with Bradwardine's treatment of divine causality. For Karl Barth's *Church Dogmatics,* I cite (by volume, part, and page) the second edition, ed. G. W. Bromiley and T. F. Torrance (Edinburgh: T and T Clark, 1956–75).

1. Such commentators include most of those who subsume Langland's theology to "modern" semi-Pelagianism; see the first section of chapter 4, below.

2. See Courtenay, *Schools and Scholars,* chs. 7 and 10; William J. Courtenay, "The Reception of Ockham's Thought in Fourteenth-Century England," in *From Ockham to Wyclif,* ed. Anne Hudson and Michael Wilks (Oxford: Blackwell, 1987), 89–108, especially 106–7.

3. A nice example of this is given by Halverson's study of predestination in the fourteenth century and the dissolution of a thirteenth-century consensus, *Peter Aureol;* see the outlines of this history, 3–10, 172–73.

4. On the contrary: see Courtenay, "Reception of Ockham's Thought," 106–7.

5. The text of Bradwardine's *De Causa Dei contra Pelagium et de Virtute Causarum* used in this study is the edition published in London, 1618 (Cambridge University Library, copies G*.8.26 [B] and E.3.2); I have also used a facsimile edition (Frankfurt am Main: Minerva, 1964). All citations to book, chapter, and/or pages are given parenthetically in the text. I have modernized uses of *u* and *v.* The scholarly works on Bradwardine that have most engaged my own reading are the following: Oberman, *Archbishop Thomas Bradwardine;* Leff, *Brad-*

wardine and the Pelagians; Courtenay, *Capacity and Volition,* 155–58; Jean-François Genest, *Prédétermination et liberté créée à Oxford au XIV siecle: Buckingham contre Bradwardine* (Paris: Vrin, 1992); Edith W. Dolinkowski, *Thomas Bradwardine: A View of Time and a Vision of Eternity in Fourteenth-Century Thought* (Leiden: Brill, 1995); Bartholomew R. de la Torre, *Thomas Bradwardine and the Contingency of Futures: The Possibility of Human Freedom* (Notre Dame: University of Notre Dame Press, 1987), 91–101. It is also worth recalling the early attempt on Pelagianizing modern theology by Karl Werner, *Der Augustinismus in der Scholastik des spätern Mittelalters,* vol. 3 of *Die Scholastik des späteren Mittelalters* (1883; repr., New York: B. Franklin, 1960), 233–306. My own reading of Bradwardine in the contexts of this book's concerns tends toward Leff's rather than Oberman's. The latter seeks to show that Bradwardine is "on the line from Paul to Augustine" (*Archbishop Thomas Bradwardine,* 25), "a pupil of Augustine" (84), "relying particularly on Paul and Augustine" (119), and showing the same understanding of "God's sovereignty" as Augustine (120–21); in his treatment of predestination (121) and grace (148–49) his theology is "a rediscovery of the Augustinian heritage" (119). Oberman celebrates Bradwardine's "evangelical battle" (233), seeing Bradwardine as a "beam of light in medieval theology" that shows us "that the Spirit of God had not forsaken the Church" (185). The only weak point Oberman detects in Bradwardine's theology is that it emphasizes "too little the seriousness of sin," a mistake with consequences for his doctrine of grace (134; see ch. 6). On Bradwardine's un-Augustinian treatment of sin both Leff and Oberman agree. But Leff argues that Bradwardine has selected certain strands of Augustine's teaching and elaborated them into a theology and anthropology that deliver positions and modes of reflection quite alien to Augustine. Despite his sharp differences with Leff, Oberman does concede that Bradwardine reduces human freedom of the will "to the minimum" and that "a determinist tendency cannot be denied" (90); cf. the criticism of Leff's "misinterpretation" of Bradwardine's teaching on the will at 83 n. 1. I should also observe that I find Dolinkowski's claim that Leff is simply mistaken to treat Bradwardine as a theologian unwarranted, as it would have surprised Bradwardine (*Thomas Bradwardine,* 190, 213; for her observations on Leff and Oberman, see 166–67, 188–95). The contexts in which Bradwardine thought about contingency are illuminated by Gelber, *It Could Have Been Otherwise.*

6. As cited in the previous note, Oberman's book includes the description "Fourteenth Century Augustinian" in the title; in that note I gave examples of this claim. For more recent and uncritical examples of the application of the unqualified term *Augustinian* to Bradwardine's theology, see Dolinkowski, *Thomas Bradwardine,* 165–66 (on 183 she asserts that both Bradwardine and Ockham "echoed Augustine" by "emphasizing free will from the human

perspective"); Kathryn Kerby-Fulton, *Books under Suspicion: Censorship and Tolerance of Revelatory Writing in Late Medieval England* (Notre Dame: University of Notre Dame Press, 2006), 327; D. Vance Smith, *The Book of the Incipit: Beginnings in the Fourteenth Century* (Minneapolis: University of Minnesota Press, 2001), 174; Ian C. Levy, *John Wyclif: Scriptural Logic, Real Presence, and the Parameters of Orthodoxy* (Milwaukee: Marquette University Press, 2003), 41, 42.

7. Both Leff and Oberman cover this texture of allusion. For an example of the copious use of Augustine in Bradwardine's arguments that Pelagians propose a model of cheap grace, see Bradwardine, *De Causa Dei,* I.38 (320–21).

8. See, e.g., D. Smith, *Book of the Incipit,* 171; for characteristic use of *conservative* and *liberal* in the study of fourteenth-century theological discourse, see Frank Grady, *Representing Religious Heathens in Late Medieval England* (New York: Palgrave Macmillan, 2005), 20 ("more liberal side—to the left of Dante"), 34 ("more liberal," "much more conservative"), 35 ("conservative," "reactionary," "probably not so conservative," "conservative reading," "in one sense indeed a conservative"), 36 ("liberal understanding"); Kerby-Fulton, *Books under Suspicion,* 382 ("a conservative qualifying clause"), 383 ("a daringly liberal salvational message"), where *conservative* seems to mean "Augustine's hardline anti-Pelagianism" (383).

9. On Augustine, see chapter 1; on justice and politics in Augustinian theology, see especially Dodaro, *Christ and the Just Society*; Ruokanen, *Theology of Social Life*; Williams, "Politics and the Soul."

10. See Heiko A. Oberman and J. A. Weisheipl, "The *sermo epinicius* Ascribed to Thomas Bradwardine (1346)," *Archives d'histoire doctrinale et littéraire du moyen âge* 33 (1958): 295–329, briefly discussed in Janet Coleman, *English Literature in History, 1350–1400: Medieval Readers and Writers* (London: Hutchinson, 1981), 266–67.

11. For Augustine's reflections on lust for dominion, violence, and war in the *City of God* see, e.g., *CG* I.1, I.31, III.10, III.14, IV.3, V.13, XIV.28.

12. See chapter 1.

13. I use the English translation of the *Confessions* by Henry Chadwick (Oxford: Oxford University Press, 1991); the Latin text I use is from James J. O'Donnell, *Confessions,* 3 vols. (Oxford: Clarendon Press, 1992).

14. Here Chadwick's translation is slightly revised.

15. I return to this below, but even Luke's account includes an important role for the disciple Ananias. On Augustine's narration of conversion, see chapter 1. Also relevant to the issues here is Cummings, *Literary Culture,* chs. 2 and 9.

16. While Bradwardine conveys the kind of assurance about his eternal election that obsessed so many seventeenth-century English Protestants, he often states the traditional Catholic teaching that nobody can discern predes-

tination or reprobation during this life with certainty (see, e.g., 250, 338). This was affirmed by the Council of Trent in a chapter "Against the Vain Confidence of Heretics" [Contra Inanem Haereticorum Fiduciam], session 6, ch. 9 in *Decrees of the Ecumenical Councils,* ed. Norman P. Tanner, 2 vols. (London: Sheed and Ward, 1990), 2:674.

17. See, e.g., *De Causa Dei,* I.4–10, 14, 26, 33–34, 40–41. The argument continues in the treatment of necessity and contingency in III.12–52. On this complex topic the following are helpful: Oberman, *Archbishop Thomas Bradwardine,* ch. 3; Leff, *Bradwardine and the Pelagians,* chs. 1–3, 6; Genest, *Prédétermination,* 23–26, 52–76, 82–86; Dolinkowski, *Thomas Bradwardine,* 182, 184, 200–210. In general, see exemplification of much that Bradwardine opposed in Gelber, *It Could Have Been Otherwise.*

18. Bradwardine writes: "existimo quod Divina voluntas est causa efficiens cuiuslibet rei factae, movens seu motrix cuiuslibet motionis, ac universaliter omnium amantissima genetrix & vivifica conservatrix" (I.9, 190).

19. On Bradwardine's concentration on ontology here, rather than the consequences of the Fall and sin, see Leff, *Bradwardine and the Pelagians,* 57–66, especially 58, together with Oberman, *Archbishop Thomas Bradwardine,* ch. 6, especially 126, 128–30; also Genest, *Prédétermination,* 22–23. In my view, Jean Gerson's attack on Bradwardine's treatment of divine agency and sinful human agency is well directed against "doctor ille anglicanus quam profundum cognominant" [that English doctor whom they call profound]. See tractate VIII of his *Collectorium super Magnificat,* in *Oeuvres complètes,* ed. P. Glorieux, vol. 8 (Paris: Desclée and Cie, 1971), 163–534, tr. VIII at 322–76, and the discussion of the doctor who is Bradwardine at 356–58. Gerson focuses on Bradwardine's way of resolving the relations between divine agency and human agency in a sinful act. In Gerson's view Bradwardine's arguments make God the cause of sin ("causa peccati") and thus ascribe to God the will that humans sin against divine precepts (356–57). In Gerson's view, a lack of necessary distinctions leads to insane blasphemy. Bradwardine forgot that all reason that undermines Christian piety is sophistical.

20. On the convergence that I suggest here, see the discussion of freedom in chapter 3. On Bradwardine's own use of the distinction between God's absolute and ordained power, see the revisions to Leff and Oberman in Genest, *Prédétermination,* 76–86; see too Courtenay, *Capacity and Volition,* 155–58, focusing on Bradwardine's earlier *De Futuris Contingentibus,* ed. J.-F. Genest, in *Recherches augustiniennes* 14 (1979): 249–336 (text, 281–336). However, Courtenay argues that while the distinction "runs like a leitmotif throughout the second half" of *De Futuris Contingentibus* it "is all but absent" from *De Causa Dei* (157). Like Leff and Oberman, and unlike Genest, he does not discuss *De Causa Dei,* III.52. Genest's discussion includes a helpful account of different readings of

necessity and contingency in *De Causa Dei*. Nevertheless, it should be acknowledged that Bradwardine is critical of the way in which the customary dialectic between God's "absolute" and "ordained" power is deployed in fourteenth-century theology. He notes its generation of hypothetical outcomes that are incompatible with Christian tradition, outcomes often propounded with a blandness that has all the signs of minds that were simply idling: see, e.g., Bradwardine's acute observations in III.42, 785–87. Here he addresses contemporary speculations that God could have deceived Christ, "summa veritas." Certain modern theologians, he notes, thus imagine Christ as a pseudoprophet or even Antichrist and their un-Catholic speculations could mean that the sacraments instituted by Christians were falsely instituted delusions. For a recent exemplification of the kind of speculation Bradwardine had in mind, see the cornucopia of examples given by Kennedy, *Philosophy of Robert Holcot*. These examples display the consequences of the Christologically unformed theology touched on in chapter 2 of the present study. Kennedy's evidence tends to reinforce some of the most unfashionable lines in Gordon Leff's early work on early fourteenth-century theology, lines he tended to recant later; see Leff, *William of Ockham*. For a very different perspective on Holcot's theology and resources, see Gelber, *It Could Have Been Otherwise*, especially chs. 3–5.

21. William Blake, *Jerusalem*, 66.35–36, in *The Complete Poetry and Prose of William Blake*, rev. ed., ed. David V. Erdman (New York: Anchor, 1982). I have modernized punctuation. See similarly *Jerusalem*, 65.72–76.

22. See the account of current scholarship in chapter 4, section I. On Bradwardine here, see Leff, *Bradwardine and the Pelagians*, ch. 4, and Oberman, *Archbishop Thomas Bradwardine*, ch. 6.

23. On Richard of Bury, Bradwardine, and Holcot, see W. A. Pantin, *The English Church in the Fourteenth Century* (Cambridge: Cambridge University Press, 1955), 138–40, 144–45. On Holcot, see Oberman, *"Facientibus quod in se est"*; Heiko A. Oberman, *Forerunners of the Reformation: The Shape of Late Medieval Thought* (London: Lutterworth, 1967), 142–50; Leff, *Bradwardine and the Pelagians*, 216–27; Beryl Smalley, *English Friars and Antiquity in the Early Fourteenth Century* (Oxford: Blackwell, 1965), ch. 7 (see especially 137–48, 183–202); Courtenay, "Reception of Ockham's Thought," 98–101; Kennedy, *Philosophy of Robert Holcot*; Gelber, *It Could Have Been Otherwise*, 92–98, 171–222, 332–39.

24. Robert Holcot, *In Librum Sapientiae Regis Salomonis Praelectiones 213* (Basle, 1586) (I use the Cambridge University Library copy B*.1.9 [B]), lec. 36 (on Sap. 3.9), p. 126; subsequent citations to pages in this edition are given parenthetically in the text.

25. On this topic, see the essay and bibliographical materials by Nicholas Watson, "Visions of Inclusion: Universal Salvation and Vernacular Theology

in Pre-Reformation England," *Journal of Medieval and Early Modern Studies* 27 (1997): 145–87; Grady, *Representing Righteous Heathens.*

26. Bradwardine's vocabulary shows how the term *praescitus* cannot be taken as a distinctly Wycliffite term of art in fourteenth-century theology. I make this observation in response to some formidably erudite scholars who assume that Langland's talk of predestination and of "prescient inparfit, pult out of grace" must be distinctly Wycliffite; see *Piers Plowman, by William Langland: An Edition of the C-Text,* ed. Derek Pearsall, 2nd ed. (Exeter: Exeter University Press, 1994), XI.208–10, 204–8 nn. See similarly, Ralph Hanna, *London Literature, 1300–1380* (Cambridge: Cambridge University Press, 2005), 304 n. 50. For the text in *Piers Plowman,* see William Langland, *Piers Plowman: The C Version; Will's Vision of Piers Plowman, Do-Well, Do-Better, and Do-Best,* ed. George Russell and George Kane (London: Athlone, 1997), XI.205–7, hereafter cited as *Piers Plowman* (Russell/Kane). Pearsall asserted that Langland "alludes here" to specifically "Wycliffite doctrine," while Hanna asserts that the term *prescit* is "Lollard cant." Perhaps this judgment is symptomatic of a tendency among medieval literary historians to find Lollardy and its influence everywhere; see Eamon Duffy, *The Stripping of the Altars: Traditional Religion in England, 1400–1580,* 2nd ed. (New Haven: Yale University Press, 2005), xiii–xxxvii, especially xx–xxv.

27. I use the Blackfriars parallel-text edition of the *Summa Theologiae* (London: Blackfriars, 1964–81). Hereafter cited as *ST,* with citations to part, question, and article; subsequent citations to this work are given parenthetically in the text.

28. See *ST* III.61.1; III.62.2; III.62.3–6; III.64.1.

29. See *ST* III. 65.3; III.73.3, resp.; III.73.1, sed contra; III.73.4. A good introduction to St. Thomas on the sacraments is offered by Davies, *Thought of Thomas Aquinas,* ch. 17.

30. See *ST* III.85.3; III.86.4. On *Piers Plowman* in this context, see Aers, *Faith, Ethics and Church,* ch. 3. For a rich display of the social quality of medieval treatment of confession, see Michael Haren, *Sin and Society in Fourteenth-Century England: A Study of the Memoriale Presbiterorum* (Oxford: Clarendon Press, 2000), and Jacques Le Goff, "Trades and Professions as Represented in Medieval Confessors' Manuals," in his *Time, Work, and Culture in the Middle Ages,* trans. A. Goldhammer (Chicago: University of Chicago Press, 1980), 107–21.

31. See the edition by Heiko A. Oberman, "*De Praedestinatione et Praescientia*: An Anonymous 14th-Century Treatise on Predestination and Justification," *Nederlandsch Archief voor Kerkgeschiedenis* 43 (1960): 195–220; subsequent citations are given parenthetically in the text.

32. The most important influence on his theory of penance is Peter Lombard, *Sententiae in IV Libris Distinctae,* ed. Ignatius Brady, 3rd ed., 2 vols. (Grottaferrata: Editiones Collegii S. Bonaventurae ad Claras Aquas, 1971 and 1981), IV d. 14–22; see the commentaries by Marcia Colish, *Peter Lombard,* 2 vols. (Leiden: Brill, 1994), 2:583–609, and Philipp W. Rosemann, *Peter Lombard* (Oxford: Oxford University Press, 2004), 159–68 (important correction to Colish at 163–65).

33. Here I follow the interlinear gloss with the marginal gloss on the woman as "humana natura" published in Nicholas of Lyra, *Biblia Sacra cum Glossa Ordinaria* (Antwerp, 1634), vol. 5. On "incurvata," see Augustine on the penitential psalm that uses this term: *Exposition of the Psalms,* 2:153.

34. See Thomas Aquinas, *Catena Aurea,* ed. and trans. Cardinal John Henry Newman (1841; repr., London: Saint Austin Press, 1999), 3:484, 487.

35. Denis the Carthusian, *In Quatuor Evangelistas* (Paris, 1552), see fols. 196v–97r.

36. See chapter 4, where this exegetical tradition is discussed with Langland's deployment of it.

37. I use the C version of *Piers Plowman* (Russell/Kane).

38. "Iste autem habitus oppositus immediate peccato est gratia, per gratiamve suppletur, vel gratia necessario ipsum immediate restituit peccatori; aliter enim posset quis simul esse in gratia & in peccato mortali, quod praeostensis repugnant. Gratia ergo infusa immediate deletur peccatum, sicut per lucem tenebrae immediate tolluntur; vel statim gratia immediate restituit habitum oppositum immediate peccato, qui immediate per se tollit peccatum." The difference from St. Thomas is nuanced here because Aquinas himself argues that "justification occurs in an instant," which is not a period of time. But it does so, according to Aquinas, as a formal cause and not as an efficient cause; St. Thomas's intention is to show, in the language of Aristotelian physics and metaphysics, how God's grace changes the will without coercion. See the discussion by Eleonore Stump, *Aquinas* (London: Routledge, 2003), 391–401. Here I refer to her discussion of *De veritate* 28.9, resp., on 393. In his treatment of the sacrament of penance, Aquinas emphasizes the movement of free choice ("motus liberi arbitrii") in the justification of the wicked, a movement enabled by and simultaneous with the infusion of grace (*ST* III.89.2, resp.). Indeed, the intensity of grace is proportionate to the movement of free choice (III.89.2, resp.). One should relate this discussion to his earlier treatment of grace, *ST,* I-II.109–13, especially I-II.113.3.

39. On this consult Augustine, *The Deeds of Pelagius,* in *Answer to the Pelagians I,* especially I.7.20–10.22 and 20.44, together with the introduction to the historical context by Roland Teske, pp. 319–26.

40. Augustine, *Grace of Christ,* I.45.49–47.52, in *Answer to the Pelagians I.*

41. See chapter 1 above and Dodaro, *Christ and the Just Society.*

42. See I.39 (discussed above), with Leff, *Bradwardine and the Pelagians,* 74–79, and Oberman, *Archbishop Thomas Bradwardine,* 150–55.

43. "Sicque superflueret poenitentia quae in Ecclesia poenitentibus solet imponi in vita praesenti, & etiam ignis purgatoris post hanc vitam" (380).

44. See the constitutions of the Fourth Lateran Council (1215), const. 21, in Tanner, *Decrees of the Ecumenical Councils,* 1:245. On the issues here, see Oberman, *Archbishop Thomas Bradwardine,* 159–73, and Leff, *Bradwardine and the Pelagians,* 82–84, 121.

45. See Oberman, *Archbishop Thomas Bradwardine,* 175–76; Leff, *Bradwardine and the Pelagians,* 121.

46. The Church had of course made room for valid confession when no priest was available, but the contrite sinner had to have the intention of completing the sacrament by confessing to a priest, receiving absolution, and performing due satisfaction. It seems to me that Bradwardine also finds it very hard to give an account of why Christians pray: see, e.g., I.25, 249–50; I.23, 240–41.

47. See too *ST* III.62.4; III.64.1, ad 2. For teachings of Scotus on the sacrament of penance, see Cross, *Duns Scotus,* 109, 135–38; for Ockham on sacramental grace, see Adams, *William Ockham,* 2:1278.

48. Oberman, *Archbishop Thomas Bradwardine,* 172.

49. See the discussion of Augustine in chapter 1. Here consult his *Homilies on the Gospels of John* in *Homilies on the Gospel of John; Homilies on the First Epistle of John; Soliloquies,* ed. Philip Schaff, trans. John Gibb and James Innes, Select Library of the Nicene and Post-Nicene Fathers of the Christian Church, 1st ser., vol. 7 (Grand Rapids, MI: Eerdmans, 1986), tr. 49, 270–78. Cf. Nicholas Love's use of John 11 with Augustine's reading in Love's battle against Wycliffite attacks on the sacrament of penance: *Mirror of the Blessed Life of Jesus Christ,* ed. Michael G. Sargent (New York: Garland, 1992), ch. 34. It is intriguing to wonder how Archbishop Bradwardine would have responded to Wyclif's treatment of the sacrament of penance.

50. The hesitation is striking and reminds us that such reservations need have absolutely nothing to do with Wycliffism. Yet the Church's responses to Wycliffite arguments and polemic transformed the ecclesial meaning of such reservations. Beryl Smalley offers a shrewd observation: "Bradwardine himself never developed the practical consequences that his doctrine would have for the Sacramental system of the Church. Holcot did so for him, as a method of refutation" (*English Friars,* 191).

51. On this consult Oberman, *Archbishop Thomas Bradwardine,* 170–73.

52. *ST* III.84.5, resp.: "Sicut enim dicit Augustinus super *Jo., qui creavit te sine te, non justificabit te sine te*" (citing Augustine, *Sermones,* 169.11 in *PL* 38:923).

53. Oberman rightly observes that Bradwardine's theology of grace "does not proceed from soteriology" but "results from his theocentric sense of the distance between Creator and creature" (*Archbishop Thomas Bradwardine,* 135). In fact Trinity and the Incarnation get only passing references in this massive work. For commentary on Bradwardine's soteriology, see too Leff, *Bradwardine and the Pelagians,* 82–85.

54. See David Aers and Lynn Staley, *The Powers of the Holy: Religion, Politics, and Gender in Late Medieval English Culture* (University Park: Pennsylvania State University Press, 1996), ch. 1; Aers, *Sanctifying Signs,* ch. 1.

55. William Blake, *The Four Zoas,* IV.53, 20–24, in *Complete Poetry and Prose.*

56. Geoffrey Chaucer, "The Nun's Priest's Tale," *Canterbury Tales,* VII.3215–66, in *The Riverside Chaucer,* ed. Larry D. Benson, 3rd ed. (Boston: Houghton Mifflin, 1987).

57. Halverson, *Peter Aureol.*

58. See *ST* I.22–23 on providence and predestination. For Gregory of Rimini, see Gordon Leff, *Gregory of Rimini: Tradition and Innovation in Fourteenth Century Thought* (Cambridge: Cambridge University Press, 1961); Manfred Schulze, "'Via Gregorii' in Forschung und Quellen," in *Gregor von Rimini: Werk und Wirkung bis zur Reformation* (Berlin: de Gruyter, 1981), 1–126; Halverson, *Peter Aureol,* 143–57. On Bradwardine in this context, see Halverson, *Peter Aureol,* 128–33; Oberman, *Archbishop Thomas Bradwardine,* ch. 5; Leff, *Bradwardine and the Pelagians,* ch. 6.

59. Halverson, *Peter Aureol,* 131 and 8; contrast Oberman, *Archbishop Thomas Bradwardine,* 220.

60. Halverson, *Peter Aureol,* 132.

Chapter 4.   Remembering the Samaritan, Remembering Semyuief

The first epigraph is from *The Holy Bible, New Revised Standard Version* (Cambridge: Cambridge University Press, 1997). In the remainder of this chapter I will be quoting from the revised Douay Rheims translation of the Vulgate by Richard Chandler, *The Holy Bible* (Rockford: Tan Books, 1989), and, for the Latin, from *Biblia Sacra iuxta Vulgatam Clementinam,* 4th ed., ed. Alberto Colunga and Laurentio Turrado (Matriti: Biblioteca de Autores Cristianos, 1965). The second epigraph is from Karl Barth's *Church Dogmatics,* vol. 4, *The Doctrine of Reconciliation,* trans. G. W. Bromiley (Edinburgh: T and T Clark, 1957), pt. 2, p. 494. Hereafter cited as *CD*; subsequent citations to this work are given parenthetically by volume/part, page.

1. I concentrate on the final version: *Piers Plowman: The C Version; Will's Vision of Piers Plowman, Do-Well, Do-Better, and Do-Best,* ed. George Russell and George Kane (London: Athlone Press, 1997), subsequently cited as *Piers Plowman* (Russell/Kane). I have also made use of Derek Pearsall's fine edition of the C version, soon to be revised, *Piers Plowman, by William Langland: An Edition of the C-Text,* 2nd ed. (London: Arnold, 1994), subsequently cited as *Piers Plowman* (Pearsall); and I have continued to consult the great edition of W. W. Skeat, *The Vision of William Concerning Piers the Plowman, in Three Parallel Texts: Together with Richard the Redeless,* 2 vols. (1886; repr., Oxford: Oxford University Press, 1968), subsequently cited as *Piers Plowman* (Skeat). For the B version, I refer to *Piers Plowman: The B Version,* rev. ed., ed. George Kane and E. Talbot Donaldson (London: Athlone, 1988), subsequently cited as *Piers Plowman* (Kane/Donaldson). For an account of the history and problems of editing the poem, see Charlotte Brewer, *Editing Piers Plowman: The Evolution of the Text* (Cambridge: Cambridge University Press, 2006).

2. For my own understanding of dialectical procedures in *Piers Plowman,* see Aers, *Sanctifying Signs,* ch. 5. Cf. M. W. Bloomfield, "*Piers Plowman* Is a Dialogic and Dialectical Poem," in *Piers Plowman as a Fourteenth-Century Apocalypse* (New Brunswick: Rutgers University Press, 1961), 149; unfortunately Bloomfield believed that this dialectic had a Joachite form and ideology (e.g., 148–49, but passim) while the poem was "apocalyptic." On such views, see David Aers, "Visionary Eschatology: *Piers Plowman,*" *Modern Theology* 15 (2000): 3–17. On the poem's form, see Elizabeth Salter, "*Piers Plowman*: An Introduction," ch. 5 in her *English and International: Studies in the Literature, Art, and Patronage of Medieval England,* ed. Derek Pearsall and Nicolette Zeeman (Cambridge: Cambridge University Press, 1988); also Elizabeth Kirk, *The Dream Thought of Piers Plowman* (New Haven: Yale University Press, 1972), 11–13, and Anne Middleton, "Narration and the Invention of Experience: Episodic Form in *Piers Plowman,*" in *The Wisdom of Poetry: Essays in Early English Literature in Honor of Morton W. Bloomfield,* ed. Larry D. Benson and Siegfried Wenzel (Kalamazoo: Medieval Institute Publications, Western Michigan University, 1982), 91–122. David Lawton's essay on Langland and the form of the subject in *Piers Plowman* is also relevant: "The Subject of *Piers Plowman,*" *Yearbook of Langland Studies* 1 (1987): 1–30.

3. See, e.g., Denise N. Baker, "From Plowing to Penitence: *Piers Plowman* and Fourteenth-Century Theology," *Speculum* 55 (1980): 718. For her second essay in support of her putatively "Augustinian" reading, see "The Pardons of *Piers Plowman,*" *Neuphilologische Mitteilungen* 85 (1984): 462–72. For an approach sympathetic to Baker's but stressing "uncertainties felt by Langland himself," see Hugh White, *Nature and Salvation in Piers Plowman* (Cambridge: Brewer

1988); here I refer to 34 n. 73. The most important forerunner to this kind of reading was Rosemary Woolf, "The Tearing of the Pardon," in *Piers Plowman: Critical Approaches,* ed. S. S. Hussey (London: Methuen, 1969), 50–75; see too D. W. Robertson and B. F. Huppé, on the tearing of the pardon, in *Piers Plowman and Scriptural Tradition* (Princeton: Princeton University Press, 1951), 93–94, 165. The most sustained attempt to show how Langland rejected "semi-Pelagian" theology and proposed a doctrine of justification by faith alone is Britton Harwood's *Piers Plowman and the Problem of Belief* (Toronto: University of Toronto Press, 1992). But it often seems that his account of conversions in the poem from "semi-Pelagian" ethics and legalism to evangelical faith is more Lutheran than Augustinian. Indeed, he sees "the conversion of the narrator" as foreshadowing "the most revolutionary aspect of Luther's theology." Similarly, in Piers's "conversion" before he destroys the pardon (in the B version of the poem) "he moves from knowledge of God the enemy to God the companion" (see 218 n. 66 and 155–56). Such language seems alien to Langland's writing about salvation. While I think the significantly anachronistic term *semi-Pelagian* is at best an unhelpful evasion of many issues that most preoccupied Augustine in his arguments against Pelagius, a matter to which I turn at the end of this section, it is the favored term of those conducting the debate I am addressing. For its meaning to the participants, see especially Baker, "From Plowing," and Robert Adams, "Piers's Pardon and Langland's Semi-Pelagianism," *Traditio* 39 (1983): 367–418. The debate has unfortunately also continued the jumbling of the quite disparate categories "Nominalism" and "semi-Pelagianism." On this unwarranted jumbling, see Alastair J. Minnis, "Looking for a Sign: The Quest for Nominalism in Chaucer and Langland," ch. 7 in *Essays in Ricardian Literature,* edited by A. J. Minnis, Charlotte Morse, and Thorlac Turville-Petre (Oxford: Clarendon Press, 1997), 144–45. And see the observations by Harry J. McSorley in *Luther: Right or Wrong? An Ecumenical-Theological Study of Luther's Major Work, The Bondage of the Will* (New York: Newman Press, 1969), 184.

　　4. R. Adams, "Piers's Pardon," 369; subsequent page citations to this essay are given parenthetically in the text.

　　5. Ibid., 377 (see 371–77, 392, 402–3); Janet Coleman, *Piers Plowman and the Moderni* (Rome: Edizioni di storia e litteratura, 1981), 39, 97. On this cliché, see Oberman, *"Facientibus quod in se est."* A history of the phrase has been written by Landgraf, in *Dogmengeschichte der Frühscholastik,* pt. 1, vol. 1, 239–68; also relevant is his section on *meritum de congruo,* 262–80. The phrase ("facere . . .") entered into discussions in chapters 2 and 3 above.

　　6. See, e.g., James Simpson, *Piers Plowman: An Introduction to the B-Text* (London: Longman, 1990), 126, 124–26, and, most movingly, Nicolette Zee-

man, *Piers Plowman and the Medieval Discourse of Desire* (Cambridge: Cambridge University Press, 2006), 257 and 229; see too 77–78, 170.

7. Here I quote from two recent works: D. Smith, *Book of the Incipit,* 172 and 174; James Simpson, *The Oxford English Literary History,* vol. 2, *1350–1547: Reform and Cultural Revolution* (Oxford: Oxford University Press, 2002), 353, 354. Smith describes some wavering in Langland's theology but declares, unambiguously, that "Langland's theology is essentially semi-Pelagian," a fact that "Adams has demonstrated" (*Book,* 183). Simpson's dazzling book is a grand narrative about the relations between medieval culture and a disastrous "cultural revolution" made by sixteenth-century Protestants. Langland is a hero of this narrative because his poem allegedly anticipated the theology of grace and human agency propagated in the sixteenth-century Reformation but subjected it to a devastating, prophetic critique (*Oxford English Literary History,* 2:322, 328–29, 345, 347–49, 356). Although he does not consider Harwood's *Piers Plowman,* in some ways he inverts Harwood's thesis about relations between Langland and Luther.

8. Thomas Aquinas, *In Omnes Sancti Pauli Apostoli Epistolas Commentaria,* 2 vols. (Turin: Marietti, 1912), vol. 2, *Ad Ephesios Expositio,* II, lec. 1, p. 19. There is a beautiful account of St. Thomas's Christological thinking on salvation and sin in Stump, *Aquinas,* ch. 15.

9. Closely related, though not addressed in this chapter, is the sidelining of the sacraments in the "semi-Pelagian" paradigm. Thus Robert Adams maintains that Langland's "semi-Pelagian" theology is "ethical and social rather than sacramental," indeed, that it is "vaguely anti-sacramental" ("Langland's Theology," in *A Companion to Piers Plowman,* ed. John A. Alford [Berkeley: University of California Press, 1988], 102, 110). Similarly, see Simpson, *Oxford English Literary History,* 2:362. Contrast the discussion of Langland's treatment of the sacrament of the altar by Aers in *Sanctifying Signs,* ch. 2.

10. Hanby, *Augustine and Modernity,* 74–75; I have been greatly helped by Hanby's work, especially ch. 3 ("Christology, Cosmology and the Mechanics of Grace"). But it was Pierre-Marie Hombert who first showed me how Augustine's rejection of Pelagianism was always profoundly Christological. See his wonderfully detailed study *Gloria Gratiae,* here especially ch. 3. For a much earlier identification of Christology as the heart of Augustine's sustained opposition to Pelagians, see Alfred Vanneste, *The Dogma of Original Sin,* trans. Edward P. Collins (Brussels: Vander Nouwelaerts, n.d.), ch. 3, especially 62. Also relevant here is Dodaro, *Christ and the Just Society.*

11. Augustine, *The Retractions,* trans. Mary I. Bogan (Washington, DC: Catholic University of America Press, 1999), 207.

12. Augustine, *Nature and Grace,* seriatim, 2.2, 7.7, 9.10, in *Answer to the Pelagians I,* 225–75.

13. St. Augustine, *Concerning the City of God against the Pagans,* trans. Henry Bettenson (London: Penguin, 1984), XI.2; all quotations of the *City of God* are from this translation unless otherwise indicated. For the Latin text I have used *De Civitate Dei,* ed. B. Dombart and A. Kalb, 5th ed., 2 vols. (Stuttgart: Teubner, 1993). Hereafter referred to as *CG*; subsequent citations to book and chapter are given parenthetically in the text.

14. Or even more strangely assimilated to claims that "Will's conversation with the Samaritan" shows no traces of any "bondage" of the will but confirms the "radical human freedom" affirmed in Langland's "semi-Pelagianism" (R. Adams, "Piers's Pardon," 394–95). For recent echoing of this judgment, see T. Lawler, "The Pardon Formula in *Piers Plowman,*" *Yearbook of Langland Studies* 14 (2000): 147, and Alexander Bruce, "Debating Justification: Faith, Deeds, and the Parables of *Pearl* and *Piers Plowman,*" in *Last Things: Apocalypse, Judgment, and Millennium in the Middle Ages,* ed. Susan J. Ridyard (Sewanee: University of the South Press, 2002), 5–26, on *Piers Plowman,* 18–24. For a recent celebration of the hegemonic semi-Pelagian paradigm as offering "superb guidelines" to both Langland's theology and fourteenth-century "covenantal theology," see Kerby-Fulton, *Books under Suspicion,* 338. This is part of her celebration of "a daringly liberal" Langland (383).

15. Cf. B XV.149–49a. The C revision changes the question about identity to figure the centrality of the Church and deletes the quotation of Matt. 18.3, the imperative to become as little children.

16. See *Summa Theologiae (ST,* cited by part, question, and article), II-II.23.4, resp. and ad 2; II-II.23.2, resp.; II-II.24.1, sed contra, resp., and ad 2; II-II.24.2–3. I use the Blackfriars parallel-text edition (London: Blackfriars, 1964–81); subsequent citations are given parenthetically in the text. The paradox here is at the heart of the theology of Henri de Lubac; see especially *Surnaturel: Études historiques,* rev. ed. (Paris: Desclée de Brouwer, 1991), and *Augustinianism and Modern Theology,* trans. L. Sheppard (New York: Herder, 1969). For a brief but stimulating meditation on de Lubac's work, see Milbank, *Suspended Middle.* Holy Church's hint of deification (I.86) was most fully developed in Edward Vasta's Bernardine reading of *Piers Plowman, Piers Plowman: The Spiritual Basis of Piers Plowman* (The Hague: Mouton, 1965). This disconcerted Derek Pearsall (see note to I.86 in *Piers Plowman* [Pearsall]), but hints of "deification" are hardly extrinsic to Christian tradition, and Langland's own hint here may be no more, nor less, than Augustine's; see Gerald Bonner, "Augustine's Conception of Deification," *Journal of Theological Studies* 37 (1986): 369–86.

17. See XIX.48–82 with Luke 10.25–37 and analysis and references in *Piers Plowman* (Pearsall), note to XIX.47. Add to his citation Rosemary Woolf,

"The Theme of Christ the Lover-Knight in Middle English Literature," *Review of English Studies* 13 (1962): 1–16; R. A. Waldron, "Langland's Originality: The Christ-Knight and the Harrowing of Hell," in *Middle English Religious and Ethical Literature,* ed. G. Kratzmann and J. Simpson (Cambridge: Brewer, 1986), 68–81; Jill A. Keen, *The Charters of Christ and Piers Plowman* (New York: Lang, 2002), 86–90. I return to Christ's joust later.

18. For a characteristically illuminating treatment of the consequence of sin in which this parable is invoked, see *ST* I-II.85.1; I-II.85 explores the effects of sin.

19. The supreme work on such allegory in the Middle Ages remains Henri de Lubac's *Exégèse médiévale: Les quatres sens de l'écriture,* 2 parts in 4 vols. (Paris: Aubier, 1959–64). On Augustine's exegesis of the Samaritan, see Roland J. Teske, "The Good Samaritan (Lk 10:29–37) in Augustine's Exegesis," in *Augustine: Biblical Exegete,* ed. F. Van Fleteren and J. C. Schnaubelt (New York: Lang, 2001), 347–67. This has a different task from the still essential essay by D. Sanchis, "*Samaritanus ille:* L'exégèse augustinienne de la parabole du bon Samaritain," *Recherches de science religieuse* 40 (1961): 406–27. For a broader history of exegesis on the parable, see Werner Monselewski, *Der barmherzige Samariter: Eine auslegungsgeschichtliche Untersuchung zu Lukas 10, 25–37* (Tübingen: Mohr, 1967), especially 67–68, 79–84.

20. Robertson and Huppé, *Piers Plowman,* 197–98, 204–8, quoting from 205, 207–8. For the liturgical contexts, not addressed by Robertson and Huppé, see Raymond St.-Jacques, "The Liturgical Associations of Langland's Samaritan," *Traditio* 25 (1969): 217–30, and "Langland's Christ-Knight and the Liturgy," *Revue de l'Université d'Ottowa* 37 (1967): 144–58.

21. Ben Smith, *Traditional Imagery of Charity in Piers Plowman* (The Hague: Mouton, 1966), ch. 4. Here I quote from 75 and 78; the table is on 75–77; subsequent citations to this work are given parenthetically in the text. Over twenty years later Stephen L. Wailes published *Medieval Allegories of Jesus' Parables* (Berkeley: University of California Press, 1987); this includes a section on *Piers Plowman* (41–46) and addresses the parable of the Samaritan in part 2 (item 28). His bizarre assertion that Langland abandons traditional exegesis might have been strongly qualified had he known Ben Smith's work. For a comparison of the treatment of the parable in relation to a set of claims about the treatment of the Jews in *Piers Plowman,* see Elisa Narin van Court, "The Hermeneutics of Supersession: The Revision of the Jews from the B to the C Text of *Piers Plowman,*" *Yearbook of Langland Studies* 10 (1996): 64–70. This essay does not notice Langland's exploration of the powers of sin in both B XVIII and C XIX. Some of the iconographic traditions are illustrated by Colette Manhes and

Jean-Paul Deremble, *Le vitrail du Bon Samaritain: Chartres, Sens, Bourges* (Paris: Notre Histoire/Le Centurion, 1986). There is a fascinating study of Abraham's bosom (see XVIII.269–91) by Jérôme Baschet, *Le sein du père: Abraham et la paternité dan l'Occident médiéval* (Paris: Gallimard, 2000), especially ch. 6.

22. Aquinas, *Catena Aurea*, 3:369–77; see too *ST* I-II.85.1, sed contra.

23. Nicholas of Gorran, *Commentaria in Quattuor Evangelia* (Cologne, 1537), fols. 382v–83v. Such caustic comments on the Church are not rare in medieval exegesis; see, e.g., Hugh of St. Cher, *Opera Omnia* (Venice, 1600), vol. 6, fols. 194v–95v (evil theologians, avaricious clerics, and mean priests set against generous, good lay people represented by the Samaritan). Langland needed no help from Wycliffites to develop a critical language and iconography for exploring relations between prelates, laity, and sanctity. For Wyclif's treatment of the parable, see, e.g., *Sermones*, 4 vols., ed. John Loserth (London: Trübner, 1887–90), 1:298–304; cf. the vernacular revision, in Anne Hudson and Pamela Gradon, eds., *English Wycliffite Sermons*, 5 vols. (Oxford: Oxford University Press, 1983–1996), 1:271–74.

24. Nicholas of Lyra, *Biblia Sacra*, 5:834–35. Ben Smith's reasons for not including Nicholas of Lyra are very odd (*Traditional Imagery of Charity*, 15–16).

25. Denis the Carthusian, *In Quatuor Evangelistas Enarrationes*, fol. 180r; see fols. 180r–81r. On *semyuief*: "quilibet homo post innocentiam baptismalem atque iustitiam ad iniquitates prolapsus. Talis ergo descendit, id est, peccando spiritualiter deorsum collapsus est . . . a caelesti Hierusalem, seu regno caelorum, in quo per spem et meritum est omnis iustus viator, cum et Apostolus dicat, Nostra conversatio in caelis est: vel a tranquillitate interna, et contemplatione pacis mentalis."

26. Denis the Carthusian notes that in sinning the baptized Christian is once again stripped naked, spiritually, of the gifts of grace and the virtues: "hoc est, donis gratiae ac virtutum spiritualiter nudaverunt" (fol. 180r).

27. This is part of the poem's responses to some panic-driven responses and mistaken utterances about baptism by Wille much earlier (XII.59–69).

28. Robertson and Huppé, *Piers Plowman*, refer briefly to Augustine's *Quaestiones Evangeliorum ex Matthaeo et Luca*, II.19 (*PL* 35:1340). The same passage is used in St.-Jacques, "Liturgical Associations," 219 n. 5. In "The Swift Samaritan's Journey: *Piers Plowman* C XVIII–XIX," *Anglia* 120 (2002): 184–99, Thomas D. Hill makes use of Augustine in his argument that Langland's emphasis on the "urgency" of the Samaritan's journey is introduced to Jesus's parable by Augustine and by the exegetical tradition. Hill points out the tradition relating the Samaritan and the giant of Psalm 18.6, finding an unremarked "parallel for the role of Abraham and Moses in the exegesis of Gilbert of Hollandia" (184; see 196–97). However, Hill's interest in Augustine and, for that

matter, in *Piers Plowman,* does not include the concerns of this chapter. It should also be noted that Jerome in Epistle 64 is actually dealing with *baptized* Christians (193–94).

29. For Augustine's treatment of the good Samaritan, see Sanchis, "*Samaritanus ille,*" and Teske, "Good Samaritan." For Augustine's sermons, I quote from the translation by Edmund Hill in Augustine, *Sermons,* vols. 1–2. For the sermons on the Psalms, I use *Enarrationes in Psalmos,* 3 vols. (Turnholt: Brepols, 1956–90), and the English translation by Maria Boulding, *Expositions of the Psalms.* For Augustine's teacher Ambrose on the parable, see *Expositio Evangelii Secundum Lucam,* VII.70–84, in *PL* 15:1805–8.

30. Sermons 131 and 156 in Augustine, *Sermons,* vol. 5; for the Latin I use the editions in *PL* 38.

31. Part of Piers's muddle over the thoroughly obscure "pardon" in Passus IX may be a forgetfulness about this, about the Church, the sacraments, and this process, a forgetfulness remedied by Passus XIX–XXI. On the limits of the healing processes in the Church, see the eloquent comments by Nicholas of Gorran in his exegesis of the parable, emphasizing that *stabulum* (inn, shed) is not *domum* (home) (*Commentaria in Quattuor Evangelia,* fol. 383v).

32. See 131.2 and 5 and 6 (*PL* 38:732). Note again that the attacked traveler represents the *baptized* Christian (131.6); consult Rist, *Augustine,* 284–85. On faith as God's gift, a pervasive theme in Augustine's later writings, see, e.g., *Enchiridion,* 30–31 (in English translation, *Augustine Catechism*). In the story of Augustine's development *Ad Simplicianum* (396) is important, and on this see Hombert, *Gloria Gratiae,* 104–7. We must also note, especially in the face of the version of Augustinian theology so common in Langland scholarship, another fact: Augustine himself emphasizes that faith without works is dead and cannot save us (*Enchiridion,* 67; see too *The Predestination of Saints,* trans. Roland J. Teske in *Answer to the Pelagians IV:* 3.7–4.8; 16.32; 20.40–21.43). Also in *Answer to the Pelagians IV* see *The Gift of Perseverance,* 3.6; 16.39; 17.43; 21.54. On the wounds sin makes in our nature, see *CG* XIV. 3–4, 6, 11–12, and XV.1–5, 7–8, as well as *Enchiridion,* 25–32. See too chapter 1 of the present book.

33. Augustine, *The Trinity,* trans. Edmund Hill, WSA, pt. 1, vol. 5 (Hyde Park, NY: New City Press, 1991), XIV.17.23. All quotes are taken from this translation.

34. The point of including the Latin text here is to register a warning about the translator's rendering of "liberum arbitrium" as "free will." This is a common move but unwarranted. It is especially misleading when one is addressing later medieval writing. On *liberum arbitrium* in medieval discourse, see O. Lottin, *La théorie du libre arbitre depuis S. Anselme jusqu'à S. Thomas d'Aquin* (Saint-Maximin: École de théologie, 1929).

35. So we cannot assume we know what such language means a priori, as though we had a key to it that made the particulars of texts and contexts superfluous. This "cannot" obviously has bearings on our reading of *Piers Plowman*. A place to revisit in the light of these remarks would be the brief statement of Lawrence the Levite, II.132–36 (not in the B version), and the language of Conscience and Mede in Passus III of the C version.

36. See Sermon 152.2 (*PL* 38:850–51) and 156.4–5 (*PL* 38:851–53). Rowan Greer's discussion of "operative grace" on Augustine is helpful here: *Christian Hope and Christian Life: Raids on the Inarticulate* (New York: Crossroad, 2001), 125–26, 139–41. For an extremely influential attempt to define the details of shifts and rupture in Augustine's theology of grace, see J. Patout Burns, *The Development of Augustine's Doctrine of Operative Grace* (Paris: Institut des études augustiniennes, 1980); however, the central argument about the rupture in question and its date must now be set against Hombert, *Gloria Gratiae,* especially ch. 3. See too Nico W. Den Bok, "Freedom of the Will," *Augustiniana* 44 (1994): 237–70, and Wetzel, *Augustine,* 197–218.

37. Augustine, *Ten Homilies on the Epistle of John,* X.1, in *Homilies on the Gospel of John.*

38. See chapter 1 on models of double agency. I have found the following especially instructive: Hunsinger, *How to Read Karl Barth,* ch. 7; Davies, *Thought of Thomas Aquinas,* chs. 13–14; Kerr, *After Aquinas,* chs. 8–9.

39. Alongside this passage in Sermon 156 it is instructive to read the brief but beautiful Sermon 63 (in Augustine, *Sermons,* 3:173–74) on Matt. 8.23–27, the disciples and the sleeping Christ in the boat, in a terrifying storm. This too should be recalled when we meet Langland's Franciscan friars with their nautical exemplum in Passus X.

40. Sermon 156.14; for pertinent examples of the uses of Rom. 5.5 in Augustine's work see Hombert, *Gloria Gratiae,* 183, 188, 206, 213. The healed Semyuief receives the reward or payment ("merces," 156.2) which is the inheritance given by God, an inheritance that is God (156.17). The reward or payment will certainly be paid to the world's Marthas. Aquinas's teaching on grace in the *Summa Theologiae* is thoroughly Augustinian: *ST* I-II.109–14. On this, see the indispensable study by Wawrykow, *God's Grace and Human Action,* chs. 3–4. The cliché that "facientibus quod in se est deus non denegat gratiam" [to those doing what is in them God does not deny grace], which we have already mentioned, is analyzed and rejected in *ST* I-II.109.6–7.

41. T. S. Eliot, *The Dry Salvages,* 5, from *The Four Quartets* (New York: Harcourt Brace, 1971).

42. On the urgency here, see B. Smith, *Traditional Imagery of Charity,* 79–80, and Hill, "Swift Samaritan's Journey."

43. See Aers, *Sanctifying Signs,* ch. 2.

44. Augustine, *The Trinity,* XIV.16.22; see too XIV.17.23, which includes an exquisite example of double agency in the process of conversion.

45. *Piers Plowman* (Pearsall) notes at XVII.72 that the "metaphor of the coin is traditional," referring to Barbara Raw, "Piers and the Image of God in Man," in Hussey, *Piers Plowman,* 143–79, especially 157. To Pearsall's citations should be added G. Ladner, "St. Augustine's Reform of Man to the Image of God," in *Augustinus Magister,* 3 vols. (Paris: Institut des études augustiniennes, 1954), 2:863–78.

46. Coleman, *Piers Plowman,* 39. See too James Simpson's brisk denial, on Langland's behalf, that "everything is God's gift," since this would be too "belittling" to the power of "human initiative," in *Oxford English Literary History,* 2:350, 356.

47. His landscape together with his representation of the subject and agency is fascinatingly different from that of Guillaume de Deguileville's *Le pèlerinage de la vie humaine,* ed. J. J. Stürzinger (London: Roxburghe Club, 1893); this has been translated by Eugene Clasby as *The Pilgrimage of Human Life* (New York: Garland, 1992). On Deguileville and Langland, see Dorothy Owen, *Piers Plowman: A Comparison with Some Earlier and Contemporary French Allegories* (1912; repr., Folcroft, PA: Folcroft Library, 1971); John Burrow, *Langland's Fictions* (Oxford: Clarendon Press, 1993), 54–55, 113–18.

48. XVIII.181–82; see note on XVIII.183 in *Piers Plowman* (Pearsall).

49. Russell and Kane change the text of their chosen manuscript (Huntington Library, MS Hm 143) but I see no good reason for this, so I follow Pearsall's edition here, retaining "wilde" instead of their conjecture, "wide."

50. "Many people know many things and do not know themselves." I follow Russell and Kane with "nessiunt." On the source, see *Piers Plowman* (Pearsall), note to XI.166.

51. "And hit are my blody bretherne for god bouhte vs all" (VIII.216). On "þe statuyt" and "lawes" catalyzing rebellion (VIII.324–40), see Aers, *Community, Gender, and Individual Identity: English Writing, 1360–1430* (London: Routledge, 1988), ch. 1, together with Anne Middleton, "Acts of Vagrancy: The C Version 'Autobiography' and the Statute of 1388," in *Written Work: Langland, Labor, and Authorship,* ed. Stephen Justice and Kathryn Kerby-Fulton (Philadelphia: University of Pennsylvania Press, 1997), 208–317.

52. On the history and theology of the Athanasian Creed, especially its relations with Augustine's theology, see J. N. D. Kelly, *The Athanasian Creed* (London: Blackwell, 1964), especially 119–23. I return to the pardon later.

53. See *ST* I-II.82.3, resp.; *ST* I-II.82.4, resp. and ad 1 and 3; *ST* I-II, 85.1; *ST* I-II.9.6, from a different perspective. This discussion, illustrated by the texts

I cite, should alert Langland scholars to the inadequacy of classifying Aquinas as "intellectualist" (most recently, see Zeeman, *Piers Plowman,* 70). In fact his understanding of relations between "wil" and "wit" is thoroughly dialectical. Consult, e.g., Peter Candler, *Theology, Rhetoric, Manuduction, or Reading Scripture Together in the Path of God* (Grand Rapids, MI: Eerdmans, 2006), 100–106.

54. *Confessions,* VIII.5.10; I quote from the translation by Henry Chadwick (Oxford: Oxford University Press, 1991). Augustine continues: "The consequence of a distorted will is passion. By servitude to passion, habit is formed."

55. See, e.g., Nicholas of Lyra, *Biblia Sacra,* 5:834; see too Ben Smith's table under "latrones," *Traditional Imagery of Charity,* 75–76.

56. Contrast the friars' model of the way sin does not impede those rowing with the figuration in Augustine's Sermon 156.12, discussed above; also cf. Sermon 63.2, as I suggested in note 55: "So as the wind blows and the waves break, the boat is a peril, your *heart* is in peril, your *heart* is tossed about"; my italics point to a strange lacuna in the friars' thinking (Augustine, *Sermons,* 3:173–74).

57. For an example of an enthusiastic reading of the friars' teaching, see Lawrence Clopper, *"Songes of Rechelesnesse": Langland and the Franciscans* (Ann Arbor: University of Michigan Press, 1997), 85–87.

58. The link was made by B. Smith, *Traditional Imagery of Charity,* 79, and Pearsall, *Piers Plowman,* note to XIX.71.

59. See Elizabeth Salter, "*Piers Plowman* and the Pilgrimage to Truth," *Essays and Studies* 11 (1958): 1–16; J. A. W. Bennett, ed., *Piers Plowman: The Prologue and Passus I–VII of the B Text* (Oxford: Clarendon Press, 1972), notes to Passus V.567–715; *Piers Plowman* (Pearsall), 139–43 nn.

60. As Denise Baker observed in "From Plowing," 721. D. Smith, in his explication of beginnings, *Book of the Incipit,* does not analyze this sequence. Harwood, however, does; see *Piers Plowman,* 148–50, 224 nn. 33–34.

61. I am indebted to conversation with Kate Crassons on this figure. On sloth in medieval discourses, see Siegfried Wenzel, *The Sin of Sloth: "Acedia" in Medieval Thought and Literature* (Chapel Hill: University of North Carolina Press, 1960).

62. For a typical example, see Denis the Carthusian, *In Quatuor Evangelistas Enarrationes,* fol. 180r: "Rursus, quamvis peccata dona naturae inficiant, non tamen totaliter destruunt ea: unde & vita gratiae deficiente, manet vita naturae." The contrast with a famous and extraordinarily influential English Protestant divine of the late sixteenth century is striking: William Perkins, in *A Reformed Catholike* (reprinted in *The Works of That Famous and Worthy Minister of Christ in the Universitie of Cambridge, Mr. William Perkins,* 3 vols. [Cambridge: John Legatt, 1616–18]), insists that Semyuief is "starke dead" (I.559). He needs not healing but "a new soule" (see I.558–61). See too Calvin on this parable in *Institutes of the*

Christian Religion, ed. John T. McNeill, trans. Ford L. Battles, 2 vols. (Louisville: Westminster John Knox Press, 1960), II.5.19: he rejects the traditional allegorization of *semivivus* and claims that the Word of God teaches us that we are utterly dead to salvation, not half-dead. However, fallen man undoubtedly has a mind capable of understanding, some judgment of honesty, some awareness of divinity although no true knowledge of God. Yet in this context the qualities of fallen man do not add up to much, and Calvin emphasizes, "The mind of man has been so completely estranged from God's righteousness that it conceives, desires, and undertakes only that which is impious, perverted, foul, impure, and infamous. The heart is so steeped in the poison of sin, that it can breathe out nothing but a loathsome stench." All appearances of the good are hypocritical. Barth's caveat quoted in the epigraph to this chapter is directed at Luther but should be considered also in relation to Calvin.

63. Passus XIX replaces plaster of penance with the plaster of patience (XIX.91; B XVII.98); nevertheless, the sacrament of penance is affirmed by the risen Christ in his gift to Piers and the Church (XXI.182–90).

64. I recently discussed this issue in *Sanctifying Signs,* 36–39.

65. See *CG* XIX.5; on the Church and the kingdom, see, e.g., *CG* XX.9; XIX.17; XVI.2; XVII.4.

66. All quotations are from C VIII.112–342. See Aers, *Community, Gender,* and Middleton, "Acts of Vagrancy."

67. See VIII.56–65, 1–4. I allude here to the widespread acceptance of the substitutionary thesis propounded by John Burrow, "The Action of Langland's Second Vision," *Essays in Criticism* 15 (1965): 247–68.

68. I see no reason for Russell's and Kane's deletion of "And" to open Pr. 58 (see their apparatus on this line) hence "glossede." The following passages are referred to here, seriatim: Pr. 62–64; II.38–67 (sacrament of penance); Pr. 66–80 (Pardons); II.184–96 with II.23–24 (Simony).

69. Many works cited in part one of the chapter are relevant here. See especially Baker, "From Plowing" and "Pardons of *Piers Plowman*"; Woolf, "Tearing of the Pardon"; R. Adams, "Piers's Pardon"; Coleman, *Piers Plowman,* 102–7; Simpson, *Piers Plowman,* 71–75; Harwood, *Piers Plowman,* 124–32; D. Smith, *Book of the Incipit,* 187–94. Not cited there but including substantial readings of the pardon are N. Coghill, "The Pardon of Piers Plowman," *Proceedings of the British Academy* 30 (1944): 303–57; Emily Steiner, *Documentary Culture and the Making of Medieval English Literature* (Cambridge: Cambridge University Press, 2003), 109–15, 126–42; Madeline Kasten, *Piers Plowman and the Origin of Allegorical Dynamics* (Amsterdam: ASCA Press, 2001), 93–106; Ruth M. Ames, *The Fulfillment of the Scriptures: Abraham, Moses, and Piers* (Evanston: Northwestern University Press, 1970), 166–69; Alastair J. Minnis, "Piers' Protean Pardon:

The Letter and Spirit of Langland's Theology of Indulgences," ch. 14 in *Studies in Late Medieval and Early Renaissance Texts,* ed. Anne M. D'Arcy and Alan J. Fletcher (Dublin: Four Courts, 2005).

70. Aers, *Sanctifying Signs,* 107–14 on Passus IX.

71. I refer to XIX. 65–95 and imply *ST* III.86.2.

72. See chapter 2, where I discussed the systematic extrinsicizing of grace and the effects of divine action in Ockham. Drawing similar conclusions from different concerns, see Milbank, *Suspended Middle,* 94: "Ockham's extrincisism, linked to the priority of the divine *potentia absoluta,* even went so far as to say that God might have saved us without grace—by sheer decree or else as a reward for deemed merit." This is a different universe of theological discourse to Langland's. To show this is, of course, one of the roles of chapter 2 in the present book.

73. Once again consult Kelly, *Athanasian Creed,* especially his demonstration of this Creed's "dependence on the theology of Augustine" (123).

74. Such writing is a major component of Passus VIII–IX. On the language of "lollares" in *Piers Plowman* and Langland's culture there is a substantial literature; the most illuminating discussion, with full documentation of earlier scholarship, is by Andrew Cole, *England after Heresy, 1377–1420: Middle English Literature in the Age of Wyclifism* (Cambridge: Cambridge University Press, forthcoming), chs. 2–3.

75. Note the sed contra in *ST* II-II.17.7: "*Abraham genuit Isaac,* id est, fides spem, sicut dicit Glos" (*Abraham begot Issac,* that is, faith begets hope). The whole discussion of Hope in *ST* II-II.17–18 is relevant here, as is the comment on Hope in the discussion of Faith at *ST* II-II.4.7. On the relations between Hope, Faith, and Charity, see Appendix 6 by W. J. Hill to vol. 33 of the Blackfriars *ST* (II-II.17–22).

76. Russell and Kane select "wyrdes" over their base manuscript's "wordes" bringing out a pun that would also have been hearable with "wordes." The pun brings out the fusion of word, Word, and the Christocentric providence elaborated within Christian tradition.

77. On the kingdom of heaven, see V.98a–b (Matt. 13.44; Luke 15.10). Pearsall's note to V.98a in his edition of *Piers Plowman* rightly observes that both "gospel texts have a poignant relevance to Langland's profession of faith (94–101)." So does conventional exegesis of these texts: see Aquinas, *Catena Aurea,* 1:512–13 (on Matt. 13.44) and 3:527–29 (on Luke 15.8–10).

78. See XI.164–201a (Wille turning into Rechelesnesse) and XV.188 (the land of the minstral, *actiua vita;* Langland seems to invoke Augustine, *Confessions,* I.18.28 and II.10.18. On the B version parallel to C X.128–XIV.217, see

J. S. Wittig, *"Piers Plowman* B IX–XII: Elements in the Design of the Inward Journey," *Traditio* 28 (1972): 211–80.

79. *ST* I-II.85.1, sed contra and resp.

80. With this memory, see XXI.182–90 and XIX.65–95; on Langland's theology of the Eucharist, Aers, *Sanctifying Signs,* ch. 2.

81. See *ST* II-II.23.1 and 3; II-II.25.1, sed contra, resp., and ad 1 and 2.

82. I quote from *ST* III.73.2, sed contra. On the sacrament of unity, *ST* III.7.2–4 and III.79.1.

83. This is essential for that part of the City of God "on pilgrimage in the world" but embodying the peace of God through faith and in obedience to the Lord's Prayer, "Forgive us our debts, as we forgive our debtors," a text to which Conscience appeals, as we shall see; *CG* XIX.27.

84. We should note that the Holy Spirit recognizes the possibility of a form of buying and selling within the Christian community sanctified by his grace; XXI.234–35. Conscience's demands are congruent with this: he is not now seeking to expropriate those with material assets and destroy all markets.

85. Quoted more fully earlier in this chapter.

86. XIX.48–61: on the reading of "wilde" here, see note 49 above.

87. Contrast Julian of Norwich, chapter 5 below.

88. On the blind knight Longius and the relevant sources, see Pearsall's note to XX.82 in his edition of *Piers Plowman.* For the treatment of Longius in *The Golden Legend* by Jacobus de Voragine, see the translation by William G. Ryan, 2 vols. (Princeton: Princeton University Press, 1993), 1:184. Allen J. Frantzen offers an important discussion of Longius in the thirteenth-century poem *Ordene de chevalerie* in his *Bloody Good: Chivalry, Sacrifice, and the Great War* (Chicago: University of Chicago Press, 2004), 82–83. Whereas Frantzen shows the ambiguity of Longius's act in this text, in my view Langland (not discussed by Frantzen here) is careful to develop the "antisacrificial" nature of the event. Frantzen's term *antisacrificial* belongs to his extremely productive reading of René Girard (see especially 44–45 but also 39–48 and passim).

89. See Simpson, *Piers Plowman,* 214–16; more fully, paying attention to the sources with which and against which Langland works, C. W. Marx, *The Devil's Rights and the Redemption in the Literature of Medieval England* (Cambridge: Brewer, 1995), ch. 6. Still useful is Jean Rivière, *Le dogme de la Rédemption au début du moyen âge* (Paris: Vrin, 1934).

90. On this imagery, see Jill Mann, "Eating and Drinking in *Piers Plowman,*" *English Studies* 32 (1979): 26–43; Salter, "*Piers Plowman,*" 113–14.

91. Ps. 142.2; XX.442a: "Non intres in iudicium cum servo tuo." The verse continues: "Quia non iustificabitur in conspectu tuo omnis vivens."

92. See, e.g., R. W. Chambers, "Long Will, Dante, and the Righteous Heathen," *English Studies* 9 (1924): 50–69; G. H. Russell, "The Salvation of the Heathen: The Exploration of a Theme in *Piers Plowman*," *Journal of the Warburg and Courtauld Institute* 29 (1966): 101–16; George Kane, "The Perplexities of *Piers Plowman*," in his *Chaucer and Langland: Historical and Textual Approaches* (London: Athlone, 1989), 120–21; Mary C. Davlin, *The Place of God in Piers Plowman and Medieval Art* (Aldershot: Ashgate, 2001), 131–38, 143–46, 149–51; Watson, "Visions of Inclusion," especially 154–57; Grady, *Representing Righteous Heathens*, 20–40. Also relevant is Ames, *Fulfillment of the Scriptures*, ch. 7. Langland's Christ clearly leaves some behind in hell: cf. Augustine, *De Genesi ad Litteram*, XII.33.63 (*PL* 34:481) and the opacity of divine judgment to us, at the moment (English translation, *The Literal Meaning of Genesis*, by Edmund Hill, in Augustine, *On Genesis*, WSA, pt. 1, vol. 13 [Hyde Park, NY: New City Press, 2002]).

93. See George Hunsinger, *Disruptive Grace: Studies in the Theology of Karl Barth* (Grand Rapids, MI: Eerdmans, 2000), ch. 10, quoting here from 243.

94. For the puns on *kynde* in this passage, see Mary C. Davlin, *A Game of Heuene: Word Play and the Meaning of Piers Plowman* (Cambridge: Brewer, 1989), 105–6.

95. For Augustine on this, see Sermon 130.2 (*Sermons*, vol. 4) and *CG* XX.7. For traditional exegesis of this text, see Aquinas, *Catena Aurea*, 1:452–53, and on parallel texts, 2:66 (Mark 3.27) and 3:404–9 (Luke 11.21–22); Nicholas of Gorran, *Commentaria in Quatuor Evangelia*, fol. 62r–v (Matt. 12.29), fol. 176r–v (Mark 3.27), fols. 388v–89r (Luke 11.21); Denis the Carthusian, *In Quatuor Evangelistas Enarrationes*, fol. 44v (Matt. 12.29), fol. 183v (Luke 11.21).

96. I will return to Wille's reference to this "mangerye" below. The wedding garment of Matt. 22.12 is commonly read as charity or the grace of the Holy Spirit or the precepts of the Lord that constitute the new humanity of God's kingdom. See, e.g., Aquinas, *Catena Aurea*, 1:747; Nicholas of Lyra, *Biblia Sacra*, 5:367; Hugh of St. Cher, *Opera Omnia*, vol. 6, fol. 70r; Denis the Carthusian, *In Quatuor Evangelistas Enarrationes*, fol. 70v. See too note 104 below on Matt. 22 and its exegesis.

97. Here I paraphrase and quote from Barth, *CD* IV/3, 477–78; once again, consult Hunsinger, *Disruptive Grace*, ch. 10.

98. See XIX.219a–227a; at XIX.219a he quotes Matt. 25.12, from the parable of the bridegroom and bridesmaids (25.1–13). Medieval readers habitually saw the lamps that went out for lack of oil as figuring the absence of charity and works of virtue. See, e.g., Aquinas, *Catena Aurea*, 1:846: "The *oil* denotes charity, alms." See too Robertson and Huppé, *Piers Plowman*, 209–10.

99. On Langland's systematic use of the liturgy in B XVI–XIX (C XVIII–XXI), see M. F. Vaughan, "The Liturgical Perspectives of *Piers Plow-*

man B, XVI–XIX," *Studies in Medieval and Renaissance History* 3 (1980): 87–155. I am unpersuaded by his unmitigatedly critical account of Wille here, an argument he elaborated later in "'Til I gan Awake': The Conversion of the Dreamer into Narrator in *Piers Plowman* B," *Yearbook of Langland Studies* 5 (1991): 175–92. On the liturgical allusions at the end of Passus XX (the joyful Easter morning after the harrowing of hell) there is an excellent essay by Raymond St.-Jacques, "Langland's Bells of the Resurrection and the Easter Liturgy," *English Studies in Canada* 3 (1977): 129–35.

100. Following Pearsall's text, I do not capitalize "a" in XX.472. On the Good Friday creeping to the cross, see Duffy, *Stripping of the Altars,* 29. However, St.-Jacques demonstrates an Easter ceremony involving creeping to the cross, and this is obviously the one to which Langland alludes ("Langland's Bells," 131). See too Bruce Harbert, "Langland's Easter," in *Langland, the Mystics, and the Medieval English Religious Tradition,* ed. Helen Phillips (Cambridge: Brewer, 1990), 68.

101. *De Trinitate* XV.28.51 (quoting from the translation by Edmund Hill, *The Trinity*).

102. Characteristic of the scholarship on Trajan and his place in Langland's theology is Robert Adams: "No episode in the poem marks Langland more clearly as a semi-Pelagian than this one" (R. Adams, "Piers's Pardon," 390). See too Coleman, *Piers Plowman,* 108–9, 131–34 (continuities between B and C, 133–34); Cindy L. Vitto, *The Virtuous Pagan in Middle English Literature* (Philadelphia: American Philosophical Society, 1989), section 5; Pamela Gradon, "*Trajan Redivivus*: Another Look at Trajan in *Piers Plowman,*" in *Middle English Studies,* ed. Douglas Gray and E. G. Stanley (Oxford: Oxford University Press, 1983), 113–14. Gradon argues that in Trajan "a clearly Pelagian position" is affirmed (101; reiterated at 102 and again at 103). Gradually the agent of such an affirmation becomes not just Trajan but Langland: "Langland was concerned to point out that Trajan was saved by his own merits" (104), that he was "saved *ex puris naturalibus*" (110). She also identifies Langland's theology with Ymagenatyf's discussion of the saved robber (106), an issue that I address later. See also on this much-discussed episode Simpson, *Piers Plowman,* 126–28; Wittig, "*Piers Plowman* B IX–XII," 249–63; Harwood, *Piers Plowman,* 77–82 (one of the few scholars who sees that Langland is not to be identified with Trajan); Frank Grady, "*Piers Plowman, St. Erkenwald,* and the Rule of Exceptional Salvations," *Yearbook of Langland Studies* 6 (1992): 61–86, revised in *Representing Righteous Heathens,* see especially 20–40; Zeeman, *Piers Plowman,* 228–34. For a learned argument on the irrelevance of arguments about the "semi-Pelagian" nature of the episode, see Minnis, "Looking for a Sign," 142–78, especially 150–69. In both the B version (B XI) and the C version (C XII) of this episode

there has been disagreement about where Trajan stops speaking. On this dispute I am fully persuaded by the agreement between five great editors of the C version: *Piers Plowman* (Skeat), 1:341, 2:169 n. 88; *Piers Plowman* (Pearsall), XII, note to 87 (p. 215); *Piers Plowman* (Russell/Kane), XII.88; and on the B version, *Piers Plowman* (Skeat), 1:340; *Piers Plowman* (Kane/Donaldson), XI.153. Contrast A.V. C. Schmidt's decision to continue Trajan to XI.318, which is XI.319 in *Piers Plowman* (Kane/Donaldson); *Piers Plowman: A Parallel-Text Edition of the A, B, C and Z Versions,* ed. A.V. C. Schmidt (London: Longman, 1995). The passage that most concerns those advocating a semi-Pelagian reading of both the episode and the poem is unambiguously ascribed to Trajan: C XII.75–88; B XI.140–53. Although I attend to the C version, I note that B XI includes an extremely reckless misrepresentation of Trajan's own, already confused account of his salvation and that this is deleted in the C revision: B XI.154–70 (see the textual apparatus to XI.160–70 in *Piers Plowman* (Kane/Donaldson), 446, together with their description of manuscripts R and F, pp. 12–13, 8). It is striking that in both B and C Langland moves *from* a speaker who refers to himself in the first person ("I troianes . . . y was ded . . . me . . . my lawes . . . my soule . . . my werkes . . . y were saued . . . y saued . . . saued me" (XII.76–88; see similarly B XI.141–13) *to* one who refers to Trajan in the third person (XII.91; B XI.154–55, 157, 159). Furthermore, in both B XI and C XII, at the break identified by Skeat, Pearsall, Donaldson, and Kane and Russell, the preoccupation becomes distinctly Christian, including focus on poverty and the poor, together with much invocation of those "bokes" that Trajan had just dismissed, the books of Scripture. Still useful is Louis Capéran, *Le problème du salut des infidèles,* 2nd ed., 2 vols. (Toulouse: Grand Séminaire, 1934), on Aquinas and Dante, 1:186–98, 206–11.

103. *Piers Plowman* (Pearsall), note to XII.45–47.

104. Here I refer to Nicholas of Lyra, *Biblia Sacra,* 5:365, for Nicholas of Lyra and *Glossa Ordinaria,* 365–68. Neither of these read predestination here. See too Nicholas of Gorran, *Commentaria in Quatuor Evangelia,* fols. 110v–12r; Hugh of St. Cher, *Opera Omnia,* fol. 70r–v (no discussion of predestination); Denis the Carthusian, *In Quatuor Evangelistas Enarrationes,* fol. 70r–v (here *multi* and *pauci* are glossed as relative terms concerning the many called to the nuptials of the Church militant and the relatively few called to the nuptial of the Church triumphant; see the gloss earlier on the same terms in Matt. 20.15 at fol. 65r; here he also stresses that nobody knows who is elect); Aquinas, *Catena Aurea,* 1:739–48. St. Thomas compiles a commentary paying considerable attention to the Church, Christology, and pneumatology in a contemplation of salvation history. He does not assimilate *multi* and *pauci* to talk about predestination (748). Robertson and Huppé, discussing B XI in *Piers Plowman,* 134–35, set Augustine's emphasis on charity and faith against Will's "lapse into

predestinarianism." They do not wonder what a theology of predestination without "lapse" might be, and it is simply not clear what they mean by "predestinarianism"; after all, did St. Paul "lapse into predestinarianism" at Rom. 8.29–30 and Eph. 1.5, 11? Certainly not according to the orthodox Christian tradition that Robertson and Huppé claim to be mediating. For an early fifteenth-century sermon on the wedding feast, see *Middle English Sermons,* ed. Woodburn O. Ross, EETS 209 (London: Oxford University Press, 1940), 17–19; this preacher makes no mention of predestination issues, and instead of glossing "Many ben called, butt fewe ben chosen" (17) concentrates on "clennes" and the fourteen works of mercy (18–19). Driven by panic, Wille's attention and exegesis are, in terms of the tradition to which he belongs, thoroughly inadequate.

105. As Augustine writes in the *Enchiridion,* his survey of Christian doctrine for Laurentius, "The sure and proper foundation of the Catholic faith is Christ, as the apostle says, *for no one can lay any foundation other than the one that has been laid; that foundation is Jesus Christ* (1 Corinthians 3:11)." *Augustine Catechism,* 1.5. Despite his panic, Wille glimpses something of this.

106. Russell and Kane's "quod y" in XII.58 resolves any ambiguity as to whether this is still Wille talking or his surrogate Rechelesnesse. See *Piers Plowman* (Pearsall), note to XII.56, where Pearsall acknowledges the mention of "rechlesnes" in XII.67 (= XII.69 in *Piers Plowman* [Russell/Kane]). Against Wille's seriously misguided position set Christ's careful instructions for Christians at XXI.191–98; see similarly *CG* XXI.19–21, 25–26. Also pertinent here is Harwood, *Piers Plowman,* 77.

107. See Rom. 5–6 with Augustine, *Enchiridion,* 14.48–53.

108. Col. 3.9, Gal. 3.26 (as joined in Augustine, *De Trinitate,* XII.12); on Christ as the image of God, see, e.g., 2 Cor. 4.4, Heb. 1.3.

109. Note the echo between "teneful tyxst" in Conscience's exegetical lesson to Mede and Wille's "tene" and the "tyxst" of the part of Christ's parable he hears: III.497, XII.50.

110. *ST* I.1.10, resp.; see too I.1.8, ad 2 on the inextricable unity of revelation, sacred doctrine, and Scripture; and citing Gal. 1.9 in *Lectura super Johannem,* ch. 21, lec. 6, n. 2 (*Opera Omnia,* 25 vols. [New York: Musurgia Press, 1948–49], 10:645): "sola canonica Scriptura est regula fidei." This is, of course, Augustine's view: see, e.g., *CG* IX.19, X.7, XI.1 and especially XI.3 on Scripture in God's law (e.g., in *De Doctrina Christiana,* translated by Edmund Hill as *Teaching Christianity,* II.7.9).

111. Of course, and significantly, this text offers more than one version of the story, as did the theologians who discussed it: *The Golden Legend,* chs. 36 and 46, respectively Saint Ignatius and Saint Gregory (vol. 1), note that in the

former Trajan tortures a Christian martyr (141–42). Indispensable is Gordon Whatley's history of the story, "The Uses of Hagiography: The Legend of Pope Gregory and the Emperor Trajan in the Middle Ages," *Viator* 15 (1984): 25–63. Whatley also comments on the treatment of Trajan in B XII: "*Piers Plowman* B 12.277–94: Notes on Language, Text, and Theology," *Modern Philology* 82 (1984): 1–12.

112. Russell and Kane substitute "pyne" for "helle." In this case I see no warrant for going against the reading of all known manuscripts (see their apparatus to XII.77).

113. St. Thomas links the quotations I have just made from Gal. 3 and Rom. 3 in his commentary on Rom. 3.20: *In Omnes Sancti Pauli Apostoli Epistolas Commentaria*, 2 vols. (Turin: Marietti, 1912), vol. 1, *Ad Romanos*, ch. 3, lec. 2, p. 51. On justification, see ch. 3, lec. 3, and ch. 5, lec. 5.

114. Langland's Trinitarian theology is central to his poem, but see VII.120–54 and XVII–XXI passim; see too Ames, *Fulfillment of the Scriptures*, ch. 5, "The Triune God of *Piers Plowman*." On Christ as the one mediator, with uncompromising rejection of other claims to mediatorship, see XVII.150–62, 252–61.

115. Minnis is among the minority of critics who have fully acknowledged the centrality of St. Gregory's intervention; Minnis, "Looking for a Sign," 163–65. Wittig also rightly emphasizes the role of St. Gregory, "*Piers Plowman* B IX–XII," 253–54, but later asserts that Trajan's own practice "won him, in the end, both grace and salvation" (258). Whatley notes that Ymagenatyf "ignores Gregory's role completely" in "Uses of Hagiography," 54. This is not the only lack in Ymagenatyf's thinking, as I show later.

116. On sacrifice, see *CG* X.6. Such a version of sacrifice sets aside the version of sacrificial violence and scapegoating argued by René Girard in *Things Hidden since the Foundation of the World*, trans. Stephen Bann and Michael Metteer (Stanford: Stanford University Press, 1987). With *CG* XIX.24 quoted in my text here, see XIX.25 together with the account of Roman culture and religion in books I–V.

117. Liberum Arbitrium urgently advocates a nonviolent Christian mission of evangelism to Moslems and Jews. Minnis rightly emphasizes the relevance of Liberum Arbitrium's teaching to the episode of Trajan in "Looking for a Sign," 159–62. On the poem's treatment of the Jews, see Narin van Court, "Hermeneutics of Supersession."

118. On Langland's striking reflections on Phil. 2.5–11, see David Aers, *Piers Plowman and Christian Allegory* (London: Arnold, 1975), 107–9.

119. For examples of Augustine's emphasis here, see *CG* IX.15, IX.17, X.6, X.22, X.24, XI.2.

120. On this figure see *ST* I.78.4 and I.84.6–7; also see the note to XIV.1 in *Piers Plowman* (Pearsall), together with Wittig, "*Piers Plowman* B IX–XII," 264–74; Alastair J. Minnis, "Langland's Ymagenatyf and Late-Medieval Theories of Imagination," *Comparative Criticism* 3 (1981): 71–103; Zeeman, *Piers Plowman,* 78–84, 246–57. An extremely speculative work on this figure is Ernest Kaulbach's *Imaginative Prophecy in the B-Text of "Piers Plowman"* (Cambridge: Brewer, 1993).

121. This discomfort may be related to his discomfort at Jesus being born in a manger (Luke 2.7, 16), a discomfort he deals with by bringing us the good news that Jesus was actually born in "a burgeises hous, the beste of þe toune" (XIV.88a–91). He does not like the company Jesus kept, in birth or in death.

122. On the poem's writing in these areas, see especially Geoffrey Shepherd, "Poverty in *Piers Plowman,*" in *Social Relations and Ideas,* ed. T. H. Aston, P. R. Coss, and C. Dyer (Cambridge: Cambridge University Press, 1983), 169–89; Derek Pearsall, "Poverty and Poor People in *Piers Plowman,*" in *Medieval English Studies,* ed. E. D. Kennedy, R. Waldron, and J. S. Wittig (Cambridge: Brewer, 1981), 167–85.

123. See Thomas Aquinas, *The Sermon-Conference of St. Thomas Aquinas on the Apostles' Creed,* trans. Nicholas Ayo (Notre Dame: University of Notre Dame Press, 1988), 134–35, 140–41. See too, for a very different but related emphasis, Duffy, *Stripping of the Altars,* ch. 4 ("Corporate Christians"). Aquinas and Duffy are thinking of the City of God on pilgrimage in history, yet Ymagenatyf claims to be imagining, grasping eschatology.

124. Pearsall glosses *losliche* as "uneasily." *The Middle English Dictionary,* ed. Hans Kurath and Sherman M. Kuhn (Ann Arbor: University of Michigan Press, 1952–2001), gives the opposite meaning for this passage, "at ease," but seems to do so without supporting contemporary evidence. The dictionary's own examples seem to suggest a word that meant "not rigidly, not tightly, slackly." B XII.213 has "loosely," which E. T. Donaldson translated as "loosely" in *Piers Plowman: An Alliterative Verse Translation,* ed. Elizabeth Kirk and Judith Anderson, trans. E. T. Donaldson (New York: Norton, 1990). George Kane gives the gloss "insecurely, precariously" for *losliche* in C.XIV.152 and "loosely" in B XII.213; see his *Piers Plowman: Glossary* (London: Continuum, 2005).

125. In Passus IX we learned that in "þe engelisch of oure elders" one who "lolleth" is maimed and that counterfeit hermits, those maimed members of the Church and polity, "Lollen aȝen þe bylueue and lawe of holy churche" (IX.214–19); there is an echo of the last line (IX.219) at XIV.152. One should also consider a later use of the language of lolling in *Piers Plowman* that might puzzle Ymagenatyf. This occurs where we meet "a lazar" who is "Lollynge" in

Abraham's lap, awaiting emancipation by Christ (XVIII.270–86). The best treatment of this disputed terminology is by Cole, *England after Heresy,* chs. 2–3.

126. Were Ymagenatyf thinking with any kind of theological cogency, this part of his teaching could be ascribed to the "semi-Pelagian" position projected onto Langland by so many scholars: "Langland believed fervently in man's obligation to do his very best (*facere quod in se est*) and its guaranteed complement, divine acceptation" (R. Adams, "Piers's Pardon," 377; see the first section of the present chapter). But Ymagenatyf is a lower power of the soul whose theology, as I have shown, includes teaching that is idiosyncratic, incoherent, and un-Catholic. I suppose that if Ymagenatyf could think beyond these limitations he would become Liberum Arbitrium or the Conscience of Passus XXI–XXII. For an account of "imagination" in medieval Christian culture very different from Langland's, see Barbara Newman, *God and the Goddesses: Vision, Poetry, and Belief in the Middle Ages* (Philadelphia: University of Pennsylvania Press, 2003).

127. For Aquinas's early speculations on the case of Trajan, see Whatley, "Uses of Hagiography," 36–37, 39–40. Unfortunately Whatley ignores the chronology of St. Thomas's work and seems not to understand the status of the Supplement to part 3 of the *Summa Theologiae* or its relation to the early commentary on the *Sentences.* Here I consider not the latter, which does include formulations that converge with what is now called, however inadequately, "semi-Pelagianism," but his later, thoroughly Augustinian *Summa Theologiae.* On the contrasts and self-critical developments, see the excellent study by Wawrykow, *God's Grace and Human Action.*

128. On the version of this in B XVI, see Aers, *Piers Plowman,* 88–108; on the Tree of Charity in the C version, see E. T. Donaldson, *Piers Plowman: The C-Text and Its Poet* (New Haven: Yale University Press, 1949), 187–92. G. Russell, "Salvation of the Heathen," 110–11, refuses to read Liberum Arbitrium in XVII and Anima in B XV as offering a critical and corrective perspective on the claims of Trajan. Minnis rightly refuses this refusal in "Looking for a Sign," 159–62.

129. *CG* XI.2. For an example of Augustine's comments on Gal. 3.1 in these contexts, see his *De Natura et Gratia,* II.2–5, 9–10 passim.

Chapter 5.   Sin, Reconciliation, and Redemption

In the first epigraph and elsewhere in the chapter, my translation of Augustine's *Concerning the City of God against the Pagans* is that of Henry Bettenson (London: Penguin, 1984). For the Latin text I quote from *De Civitate Dei,* ed. B. Dombart and A. Kalb, 5th ed., 2 vols. (Stüttgart: Teubner, 1993). Hereafter referred to as *CG*; subsequent citations to book and chapter are given parenthetically in the text. In the second epigraph and elsewhere in the chapter, the translation of the Bible that I am using is *The Holy Bible: Douay Rheims Version,* rev. Richard Challoner (Rockford: Tan Books, 1971).

1. I refer to *The Writings of Julian of Norwich,* ed. Nicholas Watson and Jacqueline Jenkins (University Park: Pennsylvania State University Press, 2006), 21; for the modern reception of Julian's work, see 17–24, 473–74. Watson and Jenkins provide a text based on "a synthetic approach," providing their own composition from the available manuscripts, a composition based on the editors' "detailed experience of the aesthetic and intellectual principles" on which Julian's writing is "based" (30; see 27–43). I have chosen to stay with the edition of the Paris manuscript (Bibliothèque nationale, Fonds anglais 40) by Edward Colledge and James Walsh, *A Book of Showings to the Anchoress Julian of Norwich,* 2 vols. (Toronto: Pontifical Institute of Mediaeval Studies, 1978), hereafter referred to as *Showings* (Colledge/Walsh); all quotations and references to Julian, unless otherwise specified, are to the later, much longer second version of Julian's *Showings,* vol. 2 of Colledge and Walsh, *A Book of Showings.* I give reference to chapter and page in this volume.

2. See the back cover of Julian of Norwich, *Writings,* and Williams, *Wound of Knowledge,* 142 and 143.

3. There is a good bibliography of this commentary in Julian of Norwich, *Writings,* 466–69. I have found helpful a work not mentioned there, Julian of Norwich, *The Showings of Julian of Norwich,* ed. Denise N. Baker (New York: Norton, 2005), hereafter referred to as *Showings* (Baker). Published since *Writings* is Caroline Bynum, *Wonderful Blood: Theology and Practice in Late Medieval Northern Germany and Beyond* (Philadelphia: University of Pennsylvania Press, 2007), which contains a brief and admiring section on Julian's theology (204–8).

4. Denise N. Baker, *Julian of Norwich's Showings: From Vision to Book* (Princeton: Princeton University Press, 1994), 106. For an earlier brisk dismissal of Julian's teaching here, see Clifton Wolters's introduction to his translation of Julian of Norwich's *Revelations of Divine Love* (Harmondsworth: Penguin, 1966), 37.

5. Baker, *Julian of Norwich's Showings,* seriatim: 86, 67, 84, 63; see chs. 3–4 passim. Nevertheless, as I discuss later in this chapter, Baker also states that these anti-Augustinian commitments are *combined* with "a thoroughly Augustinian understanding of human peccability and predestination" and a rejection of both "Pelagian" and "semi-Pelagian" notions about human powers of virtuous works and their divine reward (74). She even associates Julian's "views

on human peccability and predestination" with Bradwardine and Gregory of Rimini (74). She does not pursue these strange assertions of affinity. On Bradwardine, see chapter 3 above. For introduction to Gregory of Rimini and scholarship on his work, see Pascale Bermon, "La *Lectura* sur les deux premiers livres des *Sentences* de Grégoire de Rimini," in *Medieval Commentaries on the Sentences of Peter Lombard: Current Research,* ed. G. R. Evans (Leiden: Brill, 2002), 268–85; still useful is Leff, *Gregory of Rimini.*

6. Baker, *Julian of Norwich's Showings,* 67, 64.

7. All references to *Piers Plowman* unless otherwise specified are to *Piers Plowman: The C Version,* ed. George Russell and George Kane (London: Athlone, 1997). For another recent attempt to read Julian's theology contextually, see Frederick C. Bauerschmidt, *Julian of Norwich and the Mystical Body Politic of Christ* (Notre Dame: University of Notre Dame Press, 1999).

8. The treatment of creation and faith in *CG* XI–XIV is closely related to *The Literal Meaning of Genesis,* especially book XI, and *The Confessions,* XI–XIII. For the former, see the translation by Edmund Hill in Augustine *On Genesis*; for the latter, *The Confessions,* trans. Henry Chadwick (Oxford: Oxford University Press, 1991). For dates, see Hombert, *Nouvelles recherches,* 9–23, 137–88.

9. See chapter 1 above.

10. Aspects of this were discussed in chapter 1, with references to relevant scholarship.

11. Augustine, *The Trinity,* trans. Stephen McKenna (Washington, DC: Catholic University of America Press, 1988).

12. Latin text of *De Natura et Gratia* from *Select Anti-Pelagian Treatises of St. Augustine,* ed. William Bright (Oxford: Clarendon Press, 1880); English translation, *Nature and Grace,* by Roland J. Teske in Augustine, *Answer to the Pelagians I.*

13. *The Spirit and the Letter,* trans. Roland J. Teske, in Augustine, *Answer to the Pelagians I*; Latin text in *Select Anti-Pelagian Treatises.*

14. Two books in particular helped my thinking here: Dodaro, *Christ and the Just Society,* and L. Gregory Jones, *Embodying Forgiveness: A Theological Analysis* (Grand Rapids, MI: Eerdmans, 1995).

15. On Augustine's reading of Scripture, see especially Lubac, *Exégèse médiévale,* 1:177–87; also Cameron, *Augustine's Construction*; and Carol Harrison, *Augustine: Christian Truth and Fractured Humanity* (Oxford: Oxford University Press, 2000), 48–76.

16. All citations and quotations of St. Thomas's *Summa Theologiae* (*ST,* cited by part, question, and article) are to the Blackfriars parallel-text edition (London: Blackfriars, 1964–81). Subsequent citations are given parenthetically in the text.

17. Robert W. Jenson, *Systematic Theology,* 2 vols. (New York: Oxford University Press, 1997 and 1999), 1:71–72.

18. I quote from ibid., 2:133, and then return to 1:72. There is a good discussion of Augustine's politics in 2:77–86.

19. On "propria," see *Oxford Latin Dictionary,* ed. P. G. W. Glare (Oxford: Clarendon Press, 2000), "propius," 3 and 4 and 6. Here I draw on Markus, *"De Ciuitate Dei."*

20. For a good example of this, see Haren, *Sin and Society.*

21. I quote from the English translation, *The Literal Meaning of Genesis,* in Augustine, *On Genesis.*

22. See the discussion of *Confessions* and of Peter's conversion (*The Grace of Christ,* I.45.49) in chapter 1.

23. As he observed later, "sin only happens by an act of will" (XIV.4). This is one of the strands in Augustine's teaching that Baker condemns most severely and celebrates Julian for opposing: *Julian of Norwich's Showings,* 67–69, 86–87.

24. See too XIII.1 and XIII.3, together with *The Literal Meaning of Genesis,* XI.18.24.

25. See *CG* XI.2–4, 19; XIII.21; XV.1–3; *Confessions,* XII–XIII.

26. See William S. Babcock, "The Human and the Angelic Fall: Will and Moral Agency in Augustine's *City of God,"* in *Augustine: From Rhetor to Theologian,* ed. Joanne M. Williams (Waterloo: Wilfrid Laurier University Press, 1992), 133–49.

27. Glare, *Oxford Latin Dictionary,* "proprius," 3.

28. Of particular relevance here is Dodaro, "Eloquent Lies, Just Wars."

29. Augustine's reading of John's text is emphatically pneumatological: "without the Holy Spirit, we can neither love Christ nor keep his commandments." *Homilies on the Gospel of John,* 74.2 (see 74.1–5 and 82.3).

30. Babcock, "Human and Angelic Fall," 133.

31. See *Confessions,* VI.3.4–5.7; V.14.24. The congruence between Augustine and St. Thomas's later work is very clear in this domain. Sin consists in an act of free choice ("liberum arbitrium") which is an ability of the will and reason (*ST* I-II.77.6, resp.). Evil can be done only by free creatures. In sinning, such creatures destroy the bonds of justice without which human communities cannot flourish (*ST* II-II.64.2; II-II.66.1–6, 8–9; II-II.108.1). As in Augustine, love and justice or injustice are bound together. This conjunction is at the heart of the doctrine of reconciliation and its Christology in part III of the *Summa Theologiae.*

32. See note 5 above.

33. The *Showings* precede these visions with Julian's account of the "thre gyftes" she had sought (2/285–3/293).

34. For the earlier discussion I refer to here, see Aers and Staley, *Powers of the Holy,* ch. 3.

35. This decision is further highlighted by the absence of the reproaches from the Cross, built around Lam. 1.12: "O all ye that pass by," part of the Good Friday liturgy. See, e.g., Carleton Brown, ed., *Religious Lyrics of the XIVth Century,* 2nd ed. (Oxford: Clarendon Press, 1952), item 72, and *Religious Lyrics of the XVth Century* (Oxford: Clarendon Press, 1939), item 105. See Rosemary Woolf, *The English Religious Lyric in the Middle Ages* (Oxford: Oxford University Press, 1968), 40–45.

36. See chapter 4, above, and Christ's oration as Samaritan in *Piers Plowman,* XIX.136–335.

37. See *CG* XIV.15; XV.5. On the lordless powers, see the fine discussion by Karl Barth in *Church Dogmatics,* IV/4 (*The Christian Life: Lecture Fragments*), 213–33; all references to this work are to the English translation by G. W. Bromiley (Edinburgh: T and T Clark, 1956–75), hereafter *CD,* cited by volume, part, and page.

38. In St. Thomas's collection of glosses on this text, "The Devil is head among the wicked; what wonder that He [Christ] suffered Himself to be led up a mountain by the wicked one himself, who suffered Himself to be crucified by his members." Aquinas, *Catena Aurea,* 1:123.

39. *The N-Town Play: Cotton MS Vespasian D.8,* ed. Stephen Spector, 2 vols. EETS, s.s., 11 and 12 (Oxford: Oxford University Press, 1991), Play 26, here see lines 165–84, 195, 309–10, 319–20, but passim; see too Play 29. On the fusion of heresy and treason, see the classic study by Margaret Aston, "Lollardy and Sedition, 1381–1431," *Past and Present* 17 (1960): 1–44; on the legal apparatus and detection of heresy, see Ian Forrest, *The Detection of Heresy in Late Medieval England* (Oxford: Oxford University Press, 2005).

40. Sarah Beckwith, *Signifying God: Social Relations and Symbolic Act in the York Corpus Christi Plays* (Chicago: University of Chicago Press, 2001), 65–117.

41. See Aers and Staley, *Powers of the Holy,* chs. 1 and 3.

42. The editions of Julian's text from British Library, MS Sloane 2499, by Marion Glasscoe, *A Revelation of Love,* rev. ed. (Exeter: University of Exeter Press, 1986), and Georgia R. Crampton, *The Shewings of Julian of Norwich* (Kalamazoo: Medieval Institute Publications, Western Michigan University, 1994), give "dede name" instead of "dede" in the Paris manuscript edited by Colledge and Walsh. The "synthetic" edition of Watson and Jenkins selects the Sloane reading here and glosses "hame" as "skin or membrane" (Julian of Norwich, *Writings,* 159 and 158 nn. 27–28).

43. On the Veronica and its cult, see *Showings* (Colledge/Walsh), 1:53–57, and Watson and Jenkins's commentary in Julian of Norwich, *Writings,* 158.

44. See Aers and Staley, *Powers of the Holy,* 85–87, 89–90.

45. Ibid., 87–92.

46. See 1 Pet. 2.24, with the following: Isa. 53.1–10; Gal. 1.4; 1 Cor. 15.3; Heb. 9.28. See too Aquinas, *ST* III.46.4, resp.; III.47.2; III.47.3 (including discussion of the cry of dereliction); III.48.2 and 4; III.49.1 and 4. Compare the B version of *Piers Plowman,* XVI.214–214a, in *Piers Plowman: The B Version,* ed. George Kane and E. Talbot Donaldson, 2nd ed. (London: Athlone, 1988). Here the cry of dereliction is ascribed to the Son of God as a widow. This is a powerful image replete with risks of misconstrual by literalizing readers; it is omitted from the C version revisions (XVIII). Yet the C version retains a strong sense of God's identification with sin as separation from God; see XX.217–26, 231–36, 141–46. God suffers to "see þe sorwe of deynge" (XX.223).

47. As addressed in Aers and Staley, *Powers of the Holy,* 85–90.

48. For a good account of Augustine's theology on this issue, see G. R. Evans, *Augustine on Evil* (Cambridge: Cambridge University Press, 1982).

49. On this, see Baker, *Julian of Norwich's Showings,* 63–67.

50. In Anselm of Canterbury, *The Major Works,* ed. Brian Davies and G. R. Evans (Oxford: Oxford University Press, 1998); I quote from section 7 (366). Further references are given in the text.

51. See Evans, *Augustine on Evil,* 98.

52. Despite the appearance of the fiend in her visions, she insists that she sees neither purgatory nor hell, although "one point of oure feyth is that many creatures shall be dampnyd" (32/425; cf. 33/427–29). See Baker, *Julian of Norwich's Showings,* 79–81, 86, and Watson, "Visions of Inclusion," on Julian, 160–66, 168–71.

53. In the words of Frederick Bauerschmidt, this "famous (or notorious)" doctrine. Bauerschmidt, *Julian of Norwich,* 134; Baker, *Julian of Norwich's Showings,* 64, 67–68, 75–76. On Julian's teaching in this domain as manifesting "the seeds of universalism" but not going "beyond the brink of universalism," see Richard Harries, "On the Brink of Universalism," in *Julian: Woman of Our Day,* ed. R. Llewelyn (London: Darton, Longman and Todd, 1985), 41–60 (here quoting from 54 and 57); see too Ellen T. Charry, *By the Renewing of Your Minds: The Pastoral Function of Christian Doctrine* (New York: Oxford University Press, 1997), ch. 8, on Julian and St. Thomas Aquinas, with comments on the "godly will" at 188–89.

54. Baker rightly observes that this doctrine "contrasts" with Augustine's teaching, *Julian of Norwich's Showings,* 75–76; see too on this Bauerschmidt, *Julian of Norwich,* 134–35, 155–56; and Joan Nuth, *Wisdom's Daughter: The Theology of Julian of Norwich* (New York: Crossroad, 1991), ch. 6. Perhaps Julian belongs to

a tradition that is displayed by Thomas Cole of Maidstone, who in 1553 recanted (in front of Archbishop Cranmer, himself soon to be burnt by the Roman Church in England) the view that "the inward man sinneth not, when the outer man sinneth." D. Andrew Penny associates this view with "continental" Anabaptism, especially Balthasar Hubmaier's "conviction that the spirit of man was not involved in the Adamic fall"; see Penny, *Free Will and Predestination: The Battle over Saving Grace In Mid-Tudor England* (Woodbridge: Boydell, 1990), 70–71.

55. Plotinus, *The Enneads,* trans. Stephen MacKenna, rev. B. S. Page (London: Faber, 1969), IV.8.8, with further references given in the text.

56. See John P. Kenney, *The Mysticism of Saint Augustine: Rereading the Confessions* (New York: Routledge, 2004), 82. I am indebted to this book's comparison of Plotinus and Augustine.

57. See ibid., 23–26, 42–46. For an early if generalized observation on Neoplatonic influence on Julian's theology, see William R. Inge, *Studies of English Mystics: St. Margaret Lectures, 1905* (London: Murray, 1907), 70–73; see too Hans Urs von Balthasar, *The Glory of the Lord: A Theological Aesthetics,* vol. 5, *The Realm of Metaphysics in the Modern Age* (Edinburgh: Clark, 1991), 86; and especially Baker, *Julian of Norwich's Showings,* 95–96, 114–24.

58. *Exposition of the Psalms,* trans. Maria Boulding, vol. 2. For a rather different but relevant reading of Augustine's homily on Ps. 50, see Dodaro, *Christ and the Just Society,* 174–79.

59. Her thoroughly Augustinian warnings against literalizing the language of divine "wrath" deployed in Scripture may have contributed to this confusion.

60. In ch. 58 our mother Christ reforms us by his passion, death, and resurrection; this reformation is again identified with uniting "vs" to "our substannce," which never turned from God (58/586–87).

61. See Evans, *Augustine on Evil,* 33–40, 74–76, 112–18, 137–49.

62. Some readers might want to assimilate this statement to Rom. 7.15–23. This is unwarranted because of the markedly different theological contexts established in Paul's letter to the Romans. There is no equivalent in Julian here to Rom. 5.10–21 or to Rom. 9–11. In Rom. 7.15–23 Paul dramatizes a divided will, conflicting laws, and the confessed enactment of evil ("malum") in a war in which he is enslaved by sin.

63. See the lucid illustration of such absence in Manichean ideology by Augustine in his homily on Ps. 140: "It is not I who have sinned . . ." (140.10, in *Exposition of the Psalms,* vol. 6). For relevant comments on a modern version of the absence of the sinner's will from sinful acts, see Karl Barth, *CD* IV/2, 394. And for recent reflections on such ideology and therapeutic strategies for disowning sin and its consequences, see Ephraim Radner and Philip Turner,

The Fate of Communion: The Agony and the Future of a Global Church (Grand Rapids, MI: Eerdmans, 2006), 244–49 and ch. 10, passim. Perhaps the most plausible sources for Julian's thinking on the two wills may be within the line of theologians trying to distinguish Christ's divine will and his human will, the latter containing a rational *affectus* congruent with divine will and one *secundum sensualitatem* potentially resistant to the divine will. See, for example, Peter Lombard, *Sententiae in IV Libris Distinctae,* ed. Ignatius Brady, 3rd ed., 2 vols. (Grottaferrata: Editiones Collegii S. Bonaventurae ad Claras Aquas, 1971 and 1981), III.17.1–2.

64. For examples of this commonplace, see Matt. 26.27–28; Mark 11.25; Eph. 4.32; Col. 1.12–14; Col. 2.13; 2 Cor. 5.19.

65. See, e.g., *Showings,* 32/424–26; 33/427–29; 26/402–3; 45/487–88; see Bauerschmidt, *Julian of Norwich,* 108–13.

66. See especially Baker, *Julian of Norwich's Showings,* ch. 4; Bauerschmidt, *Julian of Norwich,* ch. 4; Grace M. Jantzen, *Julian of Norwich: Mystic and Theologian* (New York: Paulist Press, 1987), 192–200.

67. Baker states that Julian "mitigates the malice assigned to Adam in the Augustinian interpretation," *Julian of Norwich's Showings,* 88; but "mitigates" is a strange understatement of what Julian has done. For a history of "felix culpa," see A. O. Lovejoy, "Milton and the Paradox of the Fortunate Fall," *English Literary History* 4 (1937): 161–79.

68. Ludwig Wittgenstein, *Philosophical Investigations,* trans. G. E. M. Anscombe (Oxford: Blackwell, 1963), #271.

69. Contrast Bauerschmidt's claims that Julian is as concerned with politics as Bauerschmidt is: *Julian of Norwich,* 174–90. The claim that Julian "does not retreat from the particulars of historical, embodied ecclesial existence" (180) is unwarranted.

70. See *Showings* (Baker), 76 n. 4. Here Baker emphasizes Neoplatonic elements in Julian's theology (xv–xvi, 76 n. 5), as she does in her book *Julian of Norwich's Showings,* 95–96, 111, 114–24. See note 57 above, together with my brief discussion earlier in this chapter of Plotinian dimensions to Julian's ontology of the human will.

71. For *Piers Plowman,* see XX.1–25, XXI.1–14, 161–98; on the figuration in the B version of the poem, see Aers, *Piers Plowman,* 85–109, 128–31.

72. As in *Showings* (Baker), I delete the punctuation Colledge and Walsh insert after "moder" and the second use of "person," as do Watson and Jenkins in Julian of Norwich, *Writings,* 307. On Christ as mother, see Aers, *Powers of the Holy,* 95–104, with references to relevant literature.

73. Compare *CG* XIX–XXII. See chapter 1 of this book and Milbank, *Theology and Social Theory,* 404–40.

74. See also *CD* IV/1, 59, passim.

BIBLIOGRAPHY

PRIMARY WORKS

Anselm of Canterbury. *The Major Works*. Edited by Brian Davies and G. R. Evans. Oxford: Oxford University Press, 1998.

Aquinas, Thomas. *Catena Aurea*. Edited and translated by Cardinal John Henry Newman. 4 vols. 1841. Reprint, London: Saint Austin Press, 1999.

———. *In Omnes Sancti Pauli Apostoli Epistolas Commentaria*. 2 vols. Turin: Marietti, 1912.

———. *Opera Omnia*. 25 vols. New York: Musurgia Press, 1948–49.

———. *Opuscula Theologica*. Edited by R. A. Verardo, R. M. Spiazzi, and M. Calcaterra. 2 vols. Rome: Marietti, 1954.

———. *The Sermon-Conference of St. Thomas Aquinas on the Apostles' Creed*. Translated by Nicholas Ayo. Notre Dame: University of Notre Dame Press, 1988.

———. *Summa Theologiae*. 61 vols. London: Blackfriars, 1964–81.

Augustine. *Answer to the Pelagians I*. Translated by Roland J. Teske. Edited by John E. Rotelle. WSA, pt. 1, vol. 23. Hyde Park, NY: New City Press, 1997.

———. *Answer to the Pelagians IV*. Translated by Roland J. Teske. Edited by John E. Rotelle. WSA, pt. 1, vol. 26. Hyde Park, NY: New City Press, 1999.

———. *The Augustine Catechism: The Enchiridion on Faith, Hope, and Love*. Translated by Bruce Harbert. Edited by John E. Rotelle. Hyde Park, NY: New City Press, 1999.

———. *Augustine: Earlier Writings*. Edited by John H. S. Burleigh. London: SCM, 1953.

———. *The City of God against the Pagans*. Translated by R. W. Dyson. Cambridge: Cambridge University Press, 1998.

———. *Concerning the City of God against the Pagans*. Translated by Henry Bettenson. London: Penguin, 1984.

———. *Confessions*. Translated by Henry Chadwick. Oxford: Oxford University Press, 1991.

———. *Confessions.* Edited by James J. O'Donnell. 3 vols. Oxford: Clarendon Press, 1992.

———. *De Civitate Dei.* Edited by B. Dombart and A. Kalb. 5th ed. 2 vols. Stuttgart: Teubner, 1993.

———. *De Doctrina Christiana.* Translated by R. P. H. Green. Oxford: Clarendon Press, 1995.

———. *De Gratia Christi et Peccato Originali.* In *Select Anti-Pelagian Treatises of St. Augustine,* edited by William Bright. Oxford: Clarendon Press, 1880.

———. *De Natura et Gratia.* In *Select Anti-Pelagian Treatises of St. Augustine,* edited by William Bright. Oxford: Clarendon Press, 1880.

———. *The Deeds of Pelagius.* Translated by Roland J. Teske. In *Answer to the Pelagians I.* WSA, pt. 1, vol. 23. Hyde Park, NY: New City Press, 1997.

———. *Enarrationes in Psalmos.* 2nd ed. 3 vols. Turnholt: Brepols, 1956–90.

———. *Enchiridion.* See *Augustine Catechism.*

———. *Expositions of the Psalms.* 6 vols. Translated by Maria Boulding. WSA, pt. 3, vols. 15–20. Hyde Park, NY: New City Press, 2001–5.

———. *The Gift of Perseverance.* Translated by Roland J. Teske. In *Answer to the Pelagians IV.* WSA, pt. 1, vol. 26. Hyde Park, NY: New City Press, 1999.

———. *Grace and Free Choice.* Translated by Roland J. Teske. In *Answer to the Pelagians IV.* WSA, pt. 1, vol. 26. Hyde Park, NY: New City Press, 1999.

———. *The Grace of Christ and Original Sin.* Translated by Roland J. Teske. In *Answer to the Pelagians I.* WSA, pt. 1, vol. 23. Hyde Park, NY: New City Press, 1997.

———. *Homilies on the Gospel of John; Homilies on the First Epistle of John; Soliloquies.* Edited by Philip Schaff. Translated by John Gibb and James Innes. Select Library of the Nicene and Post-Nicene Fathers of the Christian Church, 1st ser., vol. 7. Grand Rapids, MI: Eerdmans, 1986.

———. *Letters.* Translated by Roland J. Teske. 4 vols. WSA, pt. 2, vols. 1–4. Hyde Park, NY: New City Press, 2001–5.

———. *The Literal Meaning of Genesis.* Translated by Edmund Hill. In *On Genesis.* WSA, pt. 1, vol. 13. Hyde Park, NY: New City Press, 2002.

———. *Nature and Grace.* Translated by Roland J. Teske. In *Answer to the Pelagians I.* WSA, pt. 1, vol. 23. Hyde Park, NY: New City Press, 1997.

———. *The Nature and Origin of the Soul.* Translated by Roland J. Teske. In *Answer to the Pelagians I.* WSA, pt. 1, vol. 23. Hyde Park, NY: New City Press, 1997.

———. *On Baptism, against the Donatists.* In *St. Augustine: The Writings against the Manichaeans and against the Donatists.* Translated by Richard Stothert, Albert H. Newman, and J. R. King. Select Library of the Nicene and Post-Nicene Fathers of the Christian Church, 1st ser., vol. 4. 1989. Reprint, Grand Rapids, MI: Eerdmans, 1996.

————. *The Predestination of the Saints*. Translated by Roland J. Teske. In *Answer to the Pelagians IV*. WSA, pt. 1, vol. 26. Hyde Park, NY: New City Press, 1999.

————. *The Punishment and Forgiveness of Sins and the Baptism of Little Ones*. Translated by Roland J. Teske. In *Answer to the Pelagians I*. WSA, pt. 1, vol. 23. Hyde Park, NY: New City Press, 1997.

————. *The Retractions*. Translated by Mary I. Bogan. Washington, DC: Catholic University of America Press, 1999.

————. *Select Anti-Pelagian Treatises of St. Augustine*. Edited by William Bright. Oxford: Clarendon Press, 1880.

————. *Sermons*. Translated by Edmund Hill. 10 vols. WSA, pt. 3, vols. 1–10. Brooklyn: New City Press, 1990–95.

————. *The Spirit and the Letter*. Translated by Roland J. Teske. In *Answer to the Pelagians I*. WSA, pt. 1, vol. 23. Hyde Park, NY: New City Press, 1997.

————. *Teaching Christianity*. Translated by Edmund Hill. WSA, pt. 1, vol. 11. Hyde Park, NY: New City Press, 1996.

————. *The Trinity*. Translated by Stephen McKenna. Washington, DC: Catholic University of America Press, 1988.

————. *The Trinity*. Translated by Edmund Hill. WSA, pt. 1, vol. 5. Hyde Park, NY: New City Press, 1991.

Barth, Karl. *The Christian Life; Church Dogmatics IV, 4; Lecture Fragments*. Translated by Geoffrey W. Bromiley. Grand Rapids, MI: Eerdmans, 1981.

————. *Church Dogmatics*. Translated by Geoffrey W. Bromiley. 4 pts. in 12 vols. Edinburgh: T and T Clark, 1956–75.

Bible. *Biblia Sacra iuxta Vulgatem Clementinam*. 4th ed. Edited by Alberto Colunga and Laurentio Turrado. Matriti: Biblioteca de Autores Cristianos, 1965.

————. *The Holy Bible, New Revised Standard Version*. Cambridge: Cambridge University Press, 1997.

————. *The Holy Bible, Translated from the Latin Vulgate*. Revised by Richard Challoner. Rockford, IL: Tan Books, 1989.

Blake, William. *The Complete Poetry and Prose of William Blake*. Edited by David V. Erdman. New York: Anchor, 1982.

Boulnois, Olivier. *Être et representation: Une généalogie de la métaphysique moderne à l'époque de Duns Scot, XIIIe–XIVe siècle*. Paris: Presses universitaires, 1999.

————, ed. *La puissance et son ombre de Pierre Lombard à Luther: Textes traduits et commentés*. Paris: Aubier, 1994.

Bradwardine, Thomas. *De Causa Dei contra Pelagium et de Virtute Causarum*. Facsimile of 1618 edition. Frankfurt am Main: Minerva, 1964.

————. *De Futuris Contingentibus*. Edited by J.-F. Genest. *Recherches augustiniennes* 14 (1979): 249–336.

————. "*De Praedestinatione et Praescientia*: An Anonymous 14th-Century Treatise on Predestination and Justification." Edited by Heiko A. Oberman. *Nederlandsch Archief voor Kerkgeschiedenis* 43 (1960): 195–220.

————. "The *sermo epinicius* Ascribed to Thomas Bradwardine (1346)." Edited by Heiko A. Oberman and J. A. Weisheipl. *Archives d'histoire doctrinale et littéraire du moyen âge* 3 (1958): 295–329.

Brown, Carleton, ed. *Religious Lyrics of the XIVth Century.* 2nd ed. Oxford: Clarendon Press, 1952.

————, ed. *Religious Lyrics of the XVth Century.* Oxford: Clarendon Press, 1939.

Brown, Peter. *Augustine of Hippo: A Biography.* 2nd ed. Berkeley: University of California Press, 2000.

Calvin, John. *Institutes of the Christian Religion.* Edited by John T. McNeill. Translated by Ford L. Battles. 2 vols. Louisville: Westminster John Knox Press, 1960.

Chaucer, Geoffrey. *The Riverside Chaucer.* Edited by Larry D. Benson. 3rd ed. Boston: Houghton Mifflin, 1987.

Deguileville, Guillaume. *Le pèlerinage de la vie humaine.* Edited by J. J. Stürzinger. London: Roxburghe Club, 1893.

————. *The Pilgrimage of Human Life.* Translated by Eugene Clasby. New York: Garland, 1992.

Denis the Carthusian. *In Quatuor Evangelistas Enarrationes.* Paris, 1552.

Donne, John. *The Poems of John Donne.* Edited by Herbert J. C. Grierson. London: Oxford University Press, 1966.

Eliot, T. S. *The Four Quartets.* New York: Harcourt Brace, 1971.

Gerson, Jean. *Collectorium super Magnificat.* In *Oeuvres complètes,* edited by P. Glorieux, vol. 8. Paris: Desclée and Cie, 1971.

Gregory of Rimini. *Lectura super Primum et Secundum Sententiarum.* Edited by A. Damasus Trapp and Venicio Marcolino. Vol. 6. Berlin: de Gruyter, 1980.

Holcot, Robert. *In Librum Sapientiae Regis Salomonis Praelectiones 213.* Basle, 1586.

Hugh of St. Cher. *Opera Omnia.* Venice, 1600.

Julian of Norwich. *A Book of Showings to the Anchoress Julian of Norwich.* Edited by Edward Colledge and James Walsh. 2 vols. Toronto: Pontifical Institute of Mediaeval Studies, 1978.

————. *A Revelation of Love.* Edited by Marion Glasscoe. Exeter: University of Exeter Press, 1986.

————. *Revelations of Divine Love.* Translated by Clifton Wolters. Harmondsworth: Penguin, 1966.

————. *The Shewings of Julian of Norwich.* Edited by Georgia R. Crampton. Kalamazoo: Medieval Institute Publications, Western Michigan University, 1994.

————. *The Showings of Julian of Norwich.* Edited by Denise N. Baker. New York: W. W. Norton, 2005.

————. *The Writings of Julian of Norwich.* Edited by Nicholas Watson and Jacqueline Jenkins. University Park: Pennsylvania State University Press, 2006.

Langland, William. *Piers Plowman: A Parallel-Text Edition of the A, B, C and Z Versions.* Edited by A. V. C. Schmidt. London: Longmans, 1995.

————. *Piers Plowman: An Alliterative Verse Translation.* Edited by Elizabeth Kirk and Judith Anderson. Translated by E. T. Donaldson. New York: W. W. Norton, 1990.

————. *Piers Plowman: The Prologue and Passus I–VII of the B Text.* Edited by J. A. W. Bennett. Oxford: Clarendon Press, 1972.

————. *Piers Plowman, by William Langland: An Edition of the C-Text.* Edited by Derek Pearsall. 2nd ed. York Medieval Texts, 2nd ser. Exeter: University of Exeter Press, 1994.

————. *Piers Plowman: The A Version.* Edited by George Kane. London: Athlone, 1960.

————. *Piers Plowman: The B Version.* Edited by George Kane and E. Talbot Donaldson. Rev. ed. London: Athlone, 1988.

————. *Piers Plowman: The C Version; Will's Vision of Piers Plowman, Do-Well, Do-Better, and Do-Best.* Edited by George Russell and George Kane. London: Athlone, 1997.

————. *The Vision of William Concerning Piers the Plowman in Three Parallel Texts: Together with Richard de Redeless.* Edited by W. W. Skeat. 2 vols. 1886. Reprint, Oxford: Oxford University Press, 1968.

Lombard, Peter. *Sententiae in IV Libris Distinctae.* Edited by Ignatius Brady. 3rd ed. 2 vols. Grottaferrata: Editiones Collegii S. Bonaventurae ad Claras Aquas, 1971 and 1981.

Love, Nicholas. *Mirror of the Blessed Life of Jesus Christ.* Edited by Michael G. Sargent. New York: Garland, 1992.

Migne, J.-P., ed. *Patrologia Cursus Completus, Series Latina.* 221 vols. Paris, 1844–91.

Milton, John. *The Complete Poems.* Edited by John Leonard. London: Penguin, 1998.

More, Sir Thomas. *The Complete Works of St. Thomas More.* Edited by Thomas M. C. Lawler, G. Marc'hadour, and R. C. Marius. 21 vols. New Haven: Yale University Press, 1981.

Nicholas of Gorran. *Commentaria in Quattuor Evangelia.* Cologne, 1537.

Nicholas of Lyra. *Biblia Sacra cum Glossa Ordinaria.* Antwerp, 1634.

Perkins, William. *A Reformed Catholike.* Reprinted in *The Works of That Famous and Worthy Minister of Christ in the Universitie of Cambridge, Mr. William Perkins.* 3 vols. Cambridge: John Legatt, 1616–18.

Plotinus. *The Enneads*. Translated by Stephen MacKenna. Revised by B. S. Page. London: Faber, 1969.

Ross, Woodburn O., ed. *Middle English Sermons*. EETS, o.s., 209. London: Oxford University Press, 1940.

Shakespeare, William. *The Riverside Shakespeare*. Edited by G. Blakemore Evans. Boston: Houghton Mifflin, 1974.

Spector, Stephen, ed. *The N-Town Play: Cotton MS Vespasian D.8*. EETS, s.s., 11–12. Oxford: Oxford University Press, 1991.

Tanner, Norman, ed. *Decrees of the Ecumenical Councils*. 2 vols. London: Sheed and Ward, 1990.

Voragine, Jacobus de. *The Golden Legend*. 2 vols. Translated by William G. Ryan. Princeton: Princeton University Press, 1993.

William of Ockham. *Ockham on the Virtues*. Translated by Rega Wood. West Lafayette: Purdue University Press, 1997.

———. *Opera Philosophica et Theologica*. St. Bonaventure, NY: St. Bonaventure University, Franciscan Institute, 1967–88.

———. *Predestination, God's Foreknowledge and Future Contingents*. Translated by Marilyn McCord Adams and Norman Kretzmann. New York: Meredith, 1969.

———. *Quodlibetal Questions*. 2 vols. Translated by Alfred J. Freddoso and Francis E. Kelley. New Haven: Yale University Press, 1991.

———. *Work of Ninety Days*. 2 vols. Translated by John Kilcullen and John Scott. Lewiston, NY: Mellen Press, 2001.

Wyclif, John. *English Wycliffite Sermons*. 5 vols. Edited by Anne Hudson and Pamela Gradon. Oxford: Oxford University Press, 1983–96.

———. *Sermones*. 4 vols. Edited by John Loserth. London: Trübner, 1887–90.

SECONDARY SOURCES

Adams, Marilyn McCord. "Ockham on Will, Nature, and Morality." In *The Cambridge Companion to Ockham*, edited by Paul V. Spade, ch. 11. Cambridge: Cambridge University Press, 1999.

———. "Relations, Inherence and Subsistence: or, Was Ockham a Nestorian in Christology?" *Noûs* 16 (1982): 62–75.

———. "The Structure of Ockham's Moral Theory." *Franciscan Studies* 46 (1986): 1–35.

———. *William Ockham*. 2 vols. Notre Dame: University of Notre Dame Press, 1987.

Adams, Robert. "Langland's Theology." In *A Companion to Piers Plowman,* edited by John A. Alford, 87–114. Berkeley: University of California Press, 1988.

———. "Piers's Pardon and Langland's Semi-Pelagianism." *Traditio* 39 (1983): 367–418.

Aers, David. *Community, Gender, and Individual Identity: English Writing, 1360–1430.* London: Routledge, 1988.

———. *Faith, Ethics and Church: Writing in England, 1360–1409.* Cambridge: Brewer, 2000.

———. *Piers Plowman and Christian Allegory.* London: Arnold, 1975.

———. *Sanctifying Signs: Making Christian Tradition in Late Medieval England.* Notre Dame: University of Notre Dame Press, 2004.

———. "Visionary Eschatology: *Piers Plowman.*" *Modern Theology* 15 (2000): 3–17.

Aers, David, and Lynn Staley. *The Powers of the Holy: Religion, Politics, and Gender in Late Medieval English Culture.* University Park: Pennsylvania State University Press, 1996.

Ames, Ruth. *The Fulfillment of Scriptures: Abraham, Moses, and Piers.* Evanston: Northwestern University Press, 1970.

Aston, Margaret. "Lollardy and Sedition, 1381–1431." *Past and Present* 17 (1960): 1–44.

Ayres, Lewis. "The Fundamental Grammar of Augustine's Trinitarian Theology." In *Augustine and His Critics,* edited by Robert Dodaro and George Lawless, ch. 5. London: Routledge, 2000.

———. *Nicaea and Its Legacy: An Approach to Fourth-Century Trinitarian Theology.* Oxford: Oxford University Press, 2004.

Babcock, William S. "The Human and the Angelic Fall: Will and Moral Agency in Augustine's *City of God.*" In *Augustine: From Rhetor to Theologian,* edited by Joanne M. Williams, 133–49. Waterloo: Wilfrid Laurier University Press, 1992.

Baker, Denise N. "From Plowing to Penitence: *Piers Plowman* and Fourteenth-Century Theology." *Speculum* 55 (1980): 715–25.

———. *Julian of Norwich's Showings: From Vision to Book.* Princeton: Princeton University Press, 1994.

———. "The Pardons of *Piers Plowman.*" *Neuphilologische Mitteilungen* 85 (1984): 462–72.

Balthasar, Hans Urs von. *The Glory of the Lord: A Theological Aesthetics.* Vol. 5. *The Realm of Metaphysics in the Modern Age.* Edinburgh: Clark, 1991.

———. *The Theology of Karl Barth: Exposition and Interpretation.* Translated by Edward T. Oakes. San Francisco: Ignatius Press, 1992.

Baschet, Jérôme. *Le sein du père: Abraham et la paternité dans l'Occident médiéval.* Paris: Gallimard, 2000.

Bauerschmidt, Frederick C. *Julian of Norwich and the Mystical Body Politic of Christ.* Notre Dame: University of Notre Dame Press, 1999.

Beckwith, Sarah. *Signifying God: Social Relations and Symbolic Act in the York Corpus Christi Plays.* Chicago: University of Chicago Press, 2001.

Bermon, Pascale. "La *Lectura* sur lex deux premiers livres des *Sentences* de Grégoire de Rimini." In *Medieval Commentaries on the Sentences of Peter Lombard: Current Research,* edited by G. R. Evans, 268–85. Leiden: Brill, 2002.

Bloomfield, M. W. *Piers Plowman as a Fourteenth-Century Apocalypse.* New Brunswick: Rutgers University Press, 1961.

Bonansea, Bernardine M. "Duns Scotus' Voluntarism." In *John Duns Scotus, 1265–1965,* edited by John K. Ryan and Bernardine M. Bonansea, ch. 5. Washington, DC: Catholic University of America Press, 1965.

Bonner, Gerald. "Augustine's Conception of Deification." *Journal of Theological Studies* 37 (1986): 369–86.

———. "Augustine's Understanding of the Church as a Eucharistic Community." In *Saint Augustine the Bishop: A Book of Essays,* edited by Fannie Le Moine and Christopher Kleinhenz, 39–63. New York: Garland, 1994.

———. "The Church and the Eucharist in the Theology of St. Augustine." *Sobornost* 6 (1978): 448–61.

Boulnois, Olivier. *Être et representation: Une généalogie de la métaphysique moderne à l'époque de Duns Scot, XIIIe–XIVe siècle.* Paris: Presses universitaires, 1999.

Brewer, Charlotte. *Editing Piers Plowman: The Evolution of the Text.* Cambridge: Cambridge University Press, 2006.

Brown, Peter. *Augustine of Hippo: A Biography.* New ed. Berkeley: University of California Press, 2000.

Bruce, Alexander. "Debating Justification: Faith, Deeds, and the Parables of *Pearl* and *Piers Plowman.*" In *Last Things: Apocalypse, Judgment, and Millennium in the Middle Ages,* edited by Susan J. Ridyard, 5–26. Sewanee: University of the South Press, 2002.

Burnaby, John. *Amor Dei: A Study of the Religion of St. Augustine.* London: Hodder and Stoughton, 1938.

Burns, J. Patout. *The Development of Augustine's Doctrine of Operative Grace.* Paris: Institut des études augustiniennes, 1980.

Burrow, John. "The Action of Langland's Second Vision." *Essays in Criticism* 15 (1965): 247–68.

———. *Langland's Fictions.* Oxford: Clarendon Press, 1993.

Bynum, Caroline. *Wonderful Blood: Theology and Practice in Late Medieval Northern Germany and Beyond.* Philadelphia: University of Pennsylvania Press, 2007.

Cameron, Michael. *Augustine's Construction of Figurative Exegesis against the Donatists in the Enarrationes in Psalmos.* Ann Arbor: UMI Dissertation Services, 1997.

Candler, Peter. *Theology, Rhetoric, Manuduction, or Reading Scripture Together in the Path of God.* Grand Rapids, MI: Eerdmans, 2006.

Capéran, Louis. *Le problème du salut des infidèles.* 2 vols. 2nd ed. Toulouse: Grand Séminaire, 1934.

Cary, Phillip. *Augustine's Invention of the Inner Self: The Legacy of a Christian Platonist.* Oxford: Oxford University Press, 2000.

Cavadini, John C. "'Feeling Right': Augustine on the Passions and Sexual Desire." *Augustinian Studies* 26 (2005): 195–217.

Chadwick, Henry. *Augustine: A Very Short Introduction.* Oxford: Oxford University Press, 2001.

Chambers, R. W. "Long Will, Dante, and the Righteous Heathen." *English Studies* 9 (1924): 50–69.

Charry, Ellen T. *By the Renewing of Your Minds: The Pastoral Function of Christian Doctrine.* New York: Oxford University Press, 1997.

Clopper, Lawrence. *"Songs of Rechelesnesse": Langland and the Franciscans.* Ann Arbor: University of Michigan Press, 1997.

Coghill, N. "The Pardon of Piers Plowman." *Proceedings of the British Academy* 30 (1944): 303–57.

Cole, Andrew. *England after Heresy, 1377–1420: Middle English Literature in the Age of Wyclifism.* Cambridge: Cambridge University Press, forthcoming.

Coleman, Janet. *English Literature in History, 1350–1400: Medieval Readers and Writers.* London: Hutchinson, 1981.

———. *Piers Plowman and the Moderni.* Rome: Edizioni de storia e litteratura, 1981.

Colish, Marcia. *Peter Lombard.* 2 vols. Leiden: Brill, 1994.

Courtenay, William J. "The Academic and Intellectual Worlds of Ockham." In *The Cambridge Companion to Ockham,* edited by Paul V. Spade, 17–30. Cambridge: Cambridge University Press, 1999.

———. *Capacity and Volition: A History of the Distinction of Absolute and Ordained Power.* Bergamo: Perluigi Lubrina, 1990.

———. *Covenant and Causality in Medieval Thought.* London: Variorum, 1984.

———. "The King and the Leaden Coin: The Economic Background of *sine qua non* Causality." *Traditio* 28 (1972): 185–209.

———. "The Reception of Ockham's Thought in Fourteenth-Century England." In *From Ockham to Wyclif,* edited by Anne Hudson and Michael Wilks, 89–108. Oxford: Blackwell, 1987.

———. *Schools and Scholars in Fourteenth-Century England.* Princeton: Princeton University Press, 1987.

————. "Theology and Theologians from Ockham to Wyclif." In *The History of the University of Oxford,* vol. 2, *Late Medieval Oxford,* edited by J. I. Catto and R. Evans, ch. 1. Oxford: Clarendon Press, 1992.

Cross, Richard. *Duns Scotus.* Oxford: Oxford University Press, 1999.

Cummings, Brian. *The Literary Culture of the Reformation: Grammar and Grace.* Oxford: Oxford University Press, 2002.

Davies, Brian. *The Thought of Thomas Aquinas.* Oxford: Oxford University Press, 1993.

Davlin, Mary C. *A Game of Heuene: Word Play and the Meaning of Piers Plowman.* Cambridge: Brewer, 1989.

————. *The Place of God in Piers Plowman and Medieval Art.* Aldershot: Ashgate, 2001.

D'Costa, Gavin. *Theology in the Public Square: Church, Academy and Nation.* Oxford: Blackwell, 2005.

Den Bok, Nico W. "Freedom of the Will." *Augustiniana* 44 (1994): 237–70.

Dodaro, Robert. "Augustine's Secular City." In *Augustine and His Critics,* edited by Robert Dodaro and George Lawless, ch. 14. London: Routledge, 2000.

————. "Between the Two Cities: Political Action in Augustine of Hippo." In *Augustine and Politics,* edited by John Doody, Kevin L. Hughes, and Kim Paffenroth, ch. 5. Lanham, MD: Lexington Books, 2005.

————. *Christ and the Just Society in the Thought of Augustine.* Cambridge: Cambridge University Press, 2004.

————. "Eloquent Lies, Just Wars and the Politics of Persuasion: Reading Augustine's *City of God* in a 'Postmodern' World." *Augustinian Studies* 25 (1994): 77–138.

Dodaro, Robert, and Margaret Atkins. *Augustine: Political Writings.* Cambridge: Cambridge University Press, 2001.

Dolinkowski, Edith W. *Thomas Bradwardine: A View of Time and a Vision of Eternity in Fourteenth-Century Thought.* Leiden: Brill, 1995.

Donaldson, E. T. *Piers Plowman: The C-Text and Its Poet.* New Haven: Yale University Press, 1949.

Duffy, Eamon. *The Stripping of the Altars: Traditional Religion in England, 1400–1580.* 2nd ed. New Haven: Yale University Press, 2005.

Etzkorn, Girard J. "Ockham at a Provincial Chapter: 1323; A Prelude to Avignon." *Archivum Franciscanum Historicum* 83 (1990): 557–67.

————. "Walter Chatton and the Controversy on the Absolute Necessity of Grace." *Franciscan Studies* 37 (1977): 32–65.

Evans, G. R. *Augustine on Evil.* Cambridge: Cambridge University Press, 1982.

Ferrari, Leo C. *The Conversions of Saint Augustine.* Villanova: Villanova University Press, 1984.

———. "Paul at the Conversion of Augustine." *Augustinian Studies* 11 (1980): 5–20.

———. "Saint Augustine and the Road to Damascus." *Augustinian Studies* 13 (1982): 151–70.

Figgis, John N. *The Political Aspects of S. Augustine's "City of God."* London: Longmans, 1921.

Finnis, John. *Aquinas: Moral, Political, and Legal Theory.* Oxford: Oxford University Press, 1998.

Fitzgerald, Allan D., ed. *Augustine through the Ages: An Encyclopedia.* Grand Rapids, MI: Eerdmans, 1999.

Forrest, Ian. *The Detection of Heresy in Late Medieval England.* Oxford: Oxford University Press, 2005.

Frantzen, Allen J. *Bloody Good: Chivalry, Sacrifice, and the Great War.* Chicago: University of Chicago Press, 2004.

Freccero, John. *Dante: The Poetics of Conversion.* Cambridge, MA: Harvard University Press, 1986.

Fredriksen, Paula. "Paul and Augustine: Conversion Narratives, Orthodox Traditions, and the Retrospective Self." *Journal of Theological Studies* 37 (1986): 3–34.

Gelber, Hester G. *It Could Have Been Otherwise: Contingency and Necessity in Dominican Theology at Oxford, 1300–1350.* Leiden: Brill, 2004.

Genest, Jean-François. *Prédétermination et liberté créée à Oxford au XIV siecle: Buckingham contre Bradwardine.* Paris: Vrin, 1992.

Girard, René. *Things Hidden since the Foundation of the World.* Translated by Stephen Bann and Michael Metteer. Stanford: Stanford University Press, 1987.

Glare, P. G. W., ed. *Oxford Latin Dictionary.* Oxford: Clarendon Press, 2000.

Gradon, Pamela. "*Trajan Redivivus*: Another Look at Trajan in *Piers Plowman*." In *Middle English Studies,* edited by Douglas Gray and E. G. Stanley, 93–114. Oxford: Oxford University Press, 1983.

Grady, Frank. "*Piers Plowman, St. Erkenwald,* and the Rule of Exceptional Salvations." *Yearbook of Langland Studies* 6 (1992): 61–86.

———. *Representing Righteous Heathens in Late Medieval England.* New York: Palgrave Macmillan, 2005.

Greer, Rowan. *Christian Hope and Christian Life: Raids on the Inarticulate.* New York: Crossroad, 2001.

Griffiths, Paul J. *Lying: An Augustinian Theory of Duplicity.* Grand Rapids, MI: Brazos, 2004.

Halverson, James. *Peter Aureol on Predestination: A Challenge to Late Medieval Thought.* Leiden: Brill, 1998.

Hanby, Michael. *Augustine and Modernity*. London: Routledge, 2003.

Hanna, Ralph. *London Literature, 1300–1380*. Cambridge: Cambridge University Press, 2005.

Harbert, Bruce. "Langland's Easter." In *Langland, the Mystics and the Medieval English Religious Tradition*, edited by Helen Phillips, 57–70. Cambridge: Brewer, 1990.

Haren, Michael. *Sin and Society in Fourteenth-Century England: A Study of the Memoriale Presbiterorum*. Oxford: Clarendon Press, 2000.

Harries, Richard. "On the Brink of Universalism." In *Julian: Woman of Our Day*, edited by R. Llewelyn, 41–60. London: Darton, Longman and Todd, 1985.

Harrison, Carol. *Augustine: Christian Truth and Fractured Humanity*. Oxford: Oxford University Press, 2000.

Harwood, Britton. *Piers Plowman and the Problem of Belief*. Toronto: University of Toronto Press, 1992.

Hauerwas, Stanley, and David Matzko. "The Sources of Charles Taylor." *Religious Studies Review* 18 (1992): 286–89.

Heyking, John von. *Augustine and Politics as Longing in the World*. Columbia: University of Missouri Press, 2001.

Hill, Thomas D. "The Swift Samaritan's Journey: *Piers Plowman* C XVIII–XIX." *Anglia* 120 (2002): 184–99.

Hoffman, Fritz. *Die Schriften des Oxforder Kanslers Johannes Lutterell*. Leipzig: St. Benno-Verlag, 1959.

Hollerich, Michael J. "John Milbank, Augustine, and the 'Secular.'" In *History, Apocalypse, and the Secular Imagination: New Essays on Augustine's City of God*, edited by Mark Vessey, Karla Pollman, and Allan D. Fitzgerald, 311–26. Bowling Green, OH: Philosophy Documentation Center, 1999.

Hombert, Pierre-Marie. *Gloria Gratiae: Se glorifier en Dieu, principe et fin de la théologie augustinienne de la grace*. Paris: Institut d'études augustiniennes, 1996.

———. *Nouvelles recherches de chronologie augustinienne*. Paris: Institut d'études augustiniennes, 2000.

Hunsinger, George. *Disruptive Grace: Studies in the Theology of Karl Barth*. Grand Rapids, MI: Eerdmans, 2000.

———. *How to Read Karl Barth: The Shape of His Theology*. New York: Oxford University Press, 1991.

Hussey, S. S., ed. *Piers Plowman: Critical Approaches*. London: Methuen, 1969.

Hütter, Reinhard. "*Desiderium Naturale Visionis Dei—Est autem duplex hominis beatitudo sive felicitas*: Some Observations about Lawrence Feingold's and

John Milbank's Recent Interventions in the Debate over the Natural Desire to See God." *Nova et Vetera: The English Edition of the International Theological Journal* 5 (Summer 2007): 81–132.

———. "St. Thomas on Grace and Free Will in the *Initium Fidei*: The Surpassing Augustinian Synthesis." *Nova et Vetera: The English Edition of the International Theological Journal* 5 (Summer 2007): 521–54.

Inge, William R. *Studies of English Mystics: St. Margaret Lectures, 1905.* London: Murray, 1907.

Jantzen, Grace M. *Julian of Norwich: Mystic and Theologian.* New York: Paulist Press, 1987.

Jenson, Robert W. *Systematic Theology.* 2 vols. New York: Oxford University Press, 1997 and 1999.

Jones, L. Gregory. *Embodying Forgiveness: A Theological Analysis.* Grand Rapids, MI: Eerdmans, 1995.

Jordan, Mark. *The Alleged Aristotelianism of Thomas Aquinas.* Toronto: Pontifical Institute of Mediaeval Studies, 1992.

Kane, George. *Chaucer and Langland: Historical and Textual Approaches.* London: Athlone, 1989.

———. *Piers Plowman: Glossary.* London: Continuum, 2005.

Kasten, Madeleine. *Piers Plowman and the Origin of Allegorical Dynamics.* Amsterdam: ASCA Press, 2001.

Kaufman, Peter I. *Incorrectly Political: Augustine and More.* Notre Dame: University of Notre Dame Press, 2007.

Kaulbach, Ernest. *Imaginative Prophecy in the B-Text of "Piers Plowman."* Cambridge: Brewer, 1993.

Kaye, Joel. *Economy and Nature in the Late Fourteenth Century: Money, Market Exchange, and the Emergence of Scientific Thought.* Cambridge: Cambridge University Press, 1998.

Keen, Jill A. *The Charters of Christ and Piers Plowman.* New York: Lang, 2002.

Kelly, J. N. D. *The Athanasian Creed.* London: Blackwell, 1964.

Kennedy, Leonard A. "Andrew of Novo Castro, O. F. M., and the Moral Law." *Franciscan Studies* 48 (1988): 28–39.

———. "Osbert of Pickenham, O. Carm. (fl. 1360), on the Absolute Power of God." *Carmelus* 35 (1988): 178–225.

———. *The Philosophy of Robert Holcot: Fourteenth-Century Skeptic.* Lewiston, NY: Mellen Press, 1993.

———. "Thomism and Divine Absolute Power." *Thomistic Papers* (1990): 49–62.

Kenney, John P. *The Mysticism of Saint Augustine: Rereading the Confessions.* New York: Routledge, 2005.

Kerby-Fulton, Kathryn. *Books under Suspicion: Censorship and Tolerance of Revelatory Writing in Late Medieval England.* Notre Dame: University of Notre Dame Press, 2006.

Kerr, Fergus. *After Aquinas: Versions of Thomism.* Oxford: Blackwell, 2002.

Kirk, Elizabeth. *The Dream Thought of Piers Plowman.* New Haven: Yale University Press, 1972.

Koch, J. "Neue Aktenstücke zu dem gegen Wilhelm Ockham in Avignon geführten Prozess." *Recherches de théologie ancienne et médiévale* 7 (1935): 353–80; 8 (1936): 79–93, 158–97.

Kolakowski, Leszek. *God Owes Us Nothing: A Brief Remark on Pascal's Religion and on the Spirit of Jansenism.* Chicago: University of Chicago Press, 1995.

Kurath, Hans, and Sherman M. Kuhn, eds. *The Middle English Dictionary.* Ann Arbor: University of Michigan Press, 1952–2001.

Ladner, G. "St. Augustine's Reform of Man to the Image of God." In *Augustinus Magister,* 3 vols., 2:863–78. Paris: Institut des études augustiniennes, 1954.

Landgraf, Artur. *Dogmengeschichte der Frühscholastik.* 4 vols. Regensburg: Pustet, 1952–55.

Langholm, Odd. *Economics in the Medieval Schools: Wealth Exchange, Value, Money and Usury.* Leiden: Brill, 1992.

———. "The Medieval Schoolmen (1200–1400)." In *Ancient and Medieval Economic Ideas and Concepts of Social Justice,* edited by S. Todd Lowry and Barry Gordon, 439–501. Leiden: Brill, 1998.

Lawler, T. "The Pardon Formula in *Piers Plowman.*" *Yearbook of Langland Studies* 14 (2000): 117–52.

Lawton, David. "The Subject of *Piers Plowman.*" *Yearbook of Langland Studies* 1 (1987): 1–30.

Le Goff, Jacques. "Trades and Professions as Represented in Medieval Confessors' Manuals." In *Time, Work, and Culture in the Middle Ages,* translated by A. Goldhammer, 107–21. Chicago: University of Chicago Press, 1980.

Leff, Gordon. *Bradwardine and the Pelagians: A Study of His "De Causa Dei" and Its Opponents.* Cambridge: Cambridge University Press, 1957.

———. *Gregory of Rimini: Tradition and Innovation in Fourteenth Century Thought.* Manchester: Manchester University Press, 1961.

———. *William of Ockham: The Metamorphosis of Scholastic Discourse.* Manchester: Manchester University Press, 1975.

Levy, Ian C. *John Wyclif: Scriptural Logic, Real Presence, and the Parameters of Orthodoxy.* Milwaukee: Marquette University Press, 2003.

Lottin, O. *La théorie du libre arbitre depuis S. Anselme jusqu'à S. Thomas d'Aquin.* Saint-Maximin: École de théologie, 1929.

Lovejoy, A. O. "Milton and the Paradox of the Fortunate Fall." *English Literary History* 4 (1937): 161–79.

Lubac, Henri de. *Augustinianism and Modern Theology*. Translated by L. Sheppard. New York: Herder, 1969.

———. *Catholicism: Christ and the Common Destiny of Man*. Translated by Lancelot C. Sheppard and Elizabeth Englund. San Francisco: Ignatius Press, 1988.

———. *The Christian Faith*. Translated by Richard Arnandez. San Francisco: Ignatius Press, 1986.

———. *Corpus Mysticum: The Eucharist and the Church in the Middle Ages*. Translated by Gemma Simmonds with Richard Price. London: SCM Press, 2006.

———. *Exégèse médiévale: Les quatres sens de l'écriture*. 4 vols. Paris: Aubier, 1959–64.

———. *Surnaturel: Études historiques*. Rev. ed. Paris: Desclée de Brouwer, 1991.

MacIntyre, Alasdair. *Three Rival Versions of Moral Enquiry*. London: Duckworth, 1990.

———. *Whose Justice? Which Rationality?* London: Duckworth, 1988.

Manhes, Colette, and Jean-Paul Deremble. *Le vitrail du Bon Samaritain: Chartres, Sens, Bourges*. Paris: Notre Histoire/Le Centurion, 1986.

Mann, Jill. "Eating and Drinking in *Piers Plowman*." *English Studies* 32 (1979): 26–43.

Markus, R. A. *Christianity and the Secular*. Notre Dame: University of Notre Dame Press, 2006.

———. *Conversion and Disenchantment in Augustine's Spiritual Career*. Villanova: Villanova University Press, 1989.

———. "*De Ciuitate Dei*: Pride and the Common Good." In *Sacred and Secular: Studies on Augustine and Latin Christianity*. Aldershot: Variorum, 1994.

———. *Saeculum: History and Society in the Theology of St. Augustine*. Cambridge: Cambridge University Press, 1970.

Marrone, J. "The Absolute and the Ordained Powers of the Pope: An Unedited Text by Henry of Ghent." *Medieval Studies* 36 (1974): 7–27.

Marx, C. W. *The Devil's Rights and the Redemption in the Literature of Medieval England*. Cambridge: Brewer, 1995.

Matter, E. Ann. "Conversion(s) in the *Confessiones*." In *Collectanea augustiniana*, edited by Joseph C. Schnaubelt and Frederick Van Fleteren, 21–28. Leuven: Leuven University Press, 1990.

McGinn, Bernard. *The Foundations of Mysticism: Origins to the Fifth Century*. New York: Crossroad, 1995.

McSorley, Harry J. *Luther: Right or Wrong? An Ecumenical-Theological Study of Luther's Major Work, The Bondage of the Will*. New York: Newman Press, 1969.

Menn, Stephen. *Descartes and Augustine.* Cambridge: Cambridge University Press, 1998.

Middleton, Anne. "Acts of Vagrancy: The C Version 'Autobiography' and the Statute of 1388." In *Written Work: Langland, Labor, and Authorship,* edited by Stephen Justice and Kathryn Kerby-Fulton, 208–317. Philadelphia: University of Pennsylvania Press, 1997.

———. "Narration and the Invention of Experience: Episodic Form in *Piers Plowman.*" In *The Wisdom of Poetry: Essays in Early English Literature in Honor of Morton W. Bloomfield,* edited by Larry D. Benson and Siegfried Wenzel, 91–122. Kalamazoo: Medieval Institute Publications, Western Michigan University, 1982.

Milbank, John. *The Suspended Middle: Henri de Lubac and the Debate Concerning the Supernatural.* Grand Rapids, MI: Eerdmans, 2005.

———. *Theology and Social Theory: Beyond Secular Reason.* 2nd ed. Oxford: Blackwell, 2006.

———. *The Word Made Strange: Theology, Language, Culture.* Oxford: Blackwell, 1997.

Minnis, Alastair J. "Langland's Ymagenatyf and Late-Medieval Theories of Imagination." *Comparative Criticism* 3 (1981): 71–103.

———. "Looking for a Sign: The Quest for Nominalism in Chaucer and Langland." In *Essays in Ricardian Literature,* edited by A. J. Minnis, Charlotte Morse, and Thorlac Turville-Petre, ch. 7. Oxford: Clarendon Press, 1997.

———. "Piers' Protean Pardon: The Letter and Spirit of Langland's Theology of Indulgences." In *Studies in Late Medieval and Early Renaissance Texts,* edited by Anne M. D'Arcy and Alan J. Fletcher, ch. 14. Dublin: Four Courts, 2005.

Monselewski, Werner. *Der barmherzige Samariter: Eine auslegungsgeschichtliche; Untersuchung zu Lukas 10, 25–37.* Tübingen: Mohr, 1967.

Morrison, Karl. *Conversion and Text: The Cases of Augustine of Hippo, Herman-Judah, and Constantine Tsatsos.* Charlottesville: University Press of Virginia, 1992.

Muralt, André de. *L'unité de la philosophie politique de Scot, Occam et Suarez au libéralisme contemporain.* Paris: Vrin, 2002.

Narin van Court, Elisa. "The Hermeneutics of Supersession: The Revision of the Jews from the B to the C Text of *Piers Plowman.*" *Yearbook of Langland Studies* 10 (1996): 43–87.

Newman, Barbara. *God and the Goddesses: Vision, Poetry, and Belief in the Middle Ages.* Philadelphia: University of Pennsylvania Press, 2003.

Nuth, Joan. *Wisdom's Daughter: The Theology of Julian of Norwich.* New York: Crossroad, 1991.

Oakley, Francis. "Jacobean Political Theology: The Absolute and Ordinary Powers of the King." *Journal of the History of Ideas* 29 (1968): 323–46.

———. *Omnipotence, Covenant, and Order: An Excursion in the History of Ideas from Abelard to Leibniz.* Ithaca: Cornell University Press, 1984.

———. Review of *Capacity and Volition,* by W. J. Courtenay. *Speculum* 68 (1993): 739–42.

Oberman, Heiko A. *Archbishop Thomas Bradwardine: A Fourteenth Century Augustinian.* Utrecht: Kemink and Zoon, 1957.

———. "*De Praedestinatione et Praescientia*: An Anonymous 14th-Century Treatise on Predestination and Justification." *Nederlandsch Archief voor Kerkgeschiedenis* 43 (1960): 195–220.

———. "*Facientibus quod in se est Deus non denegat gratiam*: Robert Holcot, O.P., and the Beginnings of Luther's Theology." *Harvard Theological Review* 55 (1962): 317–42.

———. *Forerunners of the Reformation: The Shape of Late Medieval Thought.* London: Lutterworth, 1967.

———. *The Harvest of Medieval Theology.* Cambridge, MA: Harvard University Press, 1963.

Oberman, Heiko A., and Frank A. James, eds. *Via Augustini: Augustine in the Later Middle Ages, Renaissance and Reformation.* Leiden: Brill, 1991.

O'Connell, R. J. *Images of Conversion in St. Augustine's Confessions.* New York: Fordham University Press, 1996.

———. *The Origins of the Soul in St. Augustine's Later Writings.* New York: Fordham University Press, 1987.

———. *St. Augustine's Confessions.* Cambridge, MA: Harvard University Press, 1969.

O'Donnell, James. *Augustine: A New Biography.* New York: Perennial, 2005.

O'Donovan, Oliver. "The Political Thought of the *City of God* 19." *Dionysius* 11 (1987): 89–110.

———. "The Political Thought of the *City of God* 19." In *Bonds of Imperfection: Christian Politics Past and Present,* edited by Oliver O'Donovan and Joan Lockwood O'Donovan, 48–72. Grand Rapids, MI: Eerdmans, 2004.

Oort, J. van. *Jerusalem and Babylon: A Study into Augustine's City of God and the Sources of His Doctrine of the Two Cities.* Leiden: Brill, 1991.

Owen, Dorothy. *Piers Plowman: A Comparison with Some Earlier and Contemporary French Allegories.* 1912. Reprint, Folcroft, PA: Folcroft Library, 1971.

Pantin, W. A. *The English Church in the Fourteenth Century.* Cambridge: Cambridge University Press, 1955.

Pearsall, Derek. "Poverty and Poor People in *Piers Plowman.*" In *Medieval English Studies,* edited by E. D. Kennedy, R. Waldron, and J. S. Wittig, 167–85. Cambridge: Brewer, 1981.

Pelikan, Jaroslav. *Reformation of Church and Dogma (1300–1700).* Chicago: University of Chicago Press, 1984.

Pelzer, Augustus. "Les 51 articles de Guillaume Occam." *Revue d'histoire ecclésiastique* 18 (1922): 240–70.

Penny, D. Andrew. *Free Will and Predestination: The Battle over Saving Grace in Mid-Tudor England.* Woodbridge: Boydell, 1990.

Pickstock, Catherine. *After Writing: On the Liturgical Consummation of Philosophy.* Oxford: Blackwell, 1998.

Pinckaers, Servais. *The Sources of Christian Ethics.* Translated by Mary Noble. Washington, DC: Catholic University of America Press, 1995.

Radner, Ephraim, and Philip Turner. *The Fate of Communion: The Agony and the Future of a Global Church.* Grand Rapids, MI: Eerdmans, 2006.

Randi, Eugenio. "Ockham, John XXII and the Absolute Power of God." *Franciscan Studies* 46 (1986): 205–16.

———. "A Scotist Way of Distinguishing between God's Absolute and Ordained Powers." In *From Ockham to Wyclif,* edited by Anne Hudson and Michael Wilks, 43–50. Oxford: Blackwell, 1987.

Raw, Barbara. "Piers and the Image of God in Man." In *Piers Plowman: Critical Approaches,* edited by S. S. Hussey, 143–79. London: Methuen, 1969.

Rist, John M. *Augustine: Ancient Thought Baptized.* Cambridge: Cambridge University Press, 1994.

Rivière, Jean. *Le dogme de la Rédemption au début du moyen âge.* Paris: Vrin, 1934.

Robertson, D. W., and B. F. Huppé. *Piers Plowman and Scriptural Tradition.* Princeton: Princeton University Press, 1951.

Rosemann, Philipp W. *Peter Lombard.* Oxford: Oxford University Press, 2004.

Ruokanen, Miika. *Theology of Social Life in Augustine's De Civitate Dei.* Göttingen: Vandenhoeck and Ruprecht, 1993.

Russell, F. H. "Persuading the Donatists: Augustine's Coercion by Words." In *The Limits of Ancient Christianity,* edited by E. Klingshire and Mark Vessey, 115–30. Ann Arbor: University of Michigan Press, 1999.

Russell, G. H. "The Salvation of the Heathen: The Exploration of a Theme in *Piers Plowman.*" *Journal of the Warburg and Courtauld Institute* 29 (1966): 101–16.

Saak, Eric L. *High Way to Heaven: The Augustinian Platform between Reform and Reformation, 1292–1524.* Leiden: Brill, 2002.

Saarinen, Risto. *Weakness of the Will in Medieval Thought from Augustine to Buridan.* Leiden: Brill, 1994.

Salter, Elizabeth. "*Piers Plowman*: An Introduction." In *English and International: Studies in the Literature, Art, and Patronage of Medieval England,* edited by Derek Pearsall and Nicolette Zeeman, ch. 5. Cambridge: Cambridge University Press, 1988.

———. "*Piers Plowman* and the Pilgrimage to Truth." *Essays and Studies* 11 (1958): 1–16.

Sanchis, D. "*Samaritanus ille*: L'exégèse augustinienne de la parabole du bon Samaritain." *Recherches de science religieuse* 40 (1961): 406–27.

Schindler, David C. "Freedom beyond Our Choosing: Augustine on the Will and Its Objects." In *Augustine and Politics,* ed. John Doody, Kevin L. Hughes, and Kim Paffenroth, ch. 4. Lanham, MD: Lexington Books, 2005.

Schulze, Manfred. "'Via Gregorii' in Forschung und Quellen." In *Gregor von Rimini: Werk und Wirkung bis zur Reformation,* 1–126. Berlin: de Gruyter, 1981.

Shepherd, Geoffrey. "Poverty in *Piers Plowman*." In *Social Relations and Ideas,* edited by T. H. Aston, P. R. Coss, and C. Dyer, 169–89. Cambridge: Cambridge University Press, 1983.

Shogimen, Takashi. *Ockham and Political Discourse in the Late Middle Ages.* Cambridge: Cambridge University Press, 2007.

Simpson, James. *The Oxford English Literary History.* Vol. 2. *1350–1547: Reform and Cultural Revolution.* Oxford: Oxford University Press, 2002.

———. *Piers Plowman: An Introduction to the B-Text.* London: Longman, 1990.

Smalley, Beryl. *English Friars and Antiquity in the Early Fourteenth Century.* Oxford: Blackwell, 1965.

Smith, Ben. *Traditional Imagery of Charity in Piers Plowman.* The Hague: Mouton, 1966.

Smith, D. Vance. *The Book of the Incipit: Beginnings in the Fourteenth Century.* Minneapolis: University of Minnesota Press, 2001.

Spade, Paul V. *The Cambridge Companion to Ockham.* Cambridge: Cambridge University Press, 1999.

Steiner, Emily. *Documentary Culture and the Making of Medieval English Literature.* Cambridge: Cambridge University Press, 2003.

St.-Jacques, Raymond. "Langland's Bells of the Resurrection and the Easter Liturgy." *English Studies in Canada* 3 (1977): 129–35.

———. "Langland's Christ-Knight and the Liturgy." *Revue de l'Université d'Ottawa* 37 (1967): 144–58.

———. "The Liturgical Associations of Langland's Samaritan." *Traditio* 25 (1969): 217–30.

Stump, Eleonore. *Aquinas*. London: Routledge, 2003.

Taylor, Charles. *A Secular Age*. Cambridge, MA: Harvard University Press, 2007.

———. *Sources of the Self: The Making of the Modern Identity*. Cambridge: Cambridge University Press, 1989.

TeSelle, Eugene. *Augustine the Theologian*. New York: Herder and Herder, 1970.

Teske, Roland J. "The Good Samaritan (Lk 10:29–37) in Augustine's Exegesis." In *Augustine: Biblical Exegete*, edited by F. Van Fleteren and J. C. Schnaubelt, 347–67. New York: Lang, 2001.

Torre, Bartholomew de la. *Thomas Bradwardine and the Contingency of Futures: The Possibility of Human Freedom*. Notre Dame: University of Notre Dame Press, 1987.

Torrell, Jean-Pierre. *Saint Thomas Aquinas*. Vol. 1. *The Person and His Work*. Washington, DC: Catholic University of America Press, 1996.

———. *Saint Thomas Aquinas*. Vol. 2. *Spiritual Master*. Washington, DC: Catholic University of America Press, 2003.

Vanneste, Alfred. *The Dogma of Original Sin*. Translated by Edward P. Collins. Brussels: Vander Callens, 1975. Originally published as *Het dogma van de erfzonde* (Tielt: Lannoo, 1969).

Vasta, Edward. *Piers Plowman: The Spiritual Basis of Piers Plowman*. The Hague: Mouton, 1965.

Vaughan, M. F. "The Liturgical Perspectives of *Piers Plowman* B, XVI–XIX." *Studies in Medieval and Renaissance History* 3 (1980): 87–155.

———. "'Til I gan Awake': The Conversion of the Dreamer into Narrator in *Piers Plowman* B." *Yearbook of Langland Studies* 5 (1991): 175–92.

Vignaux, Paul. *Justification et prédestination au XIVe siècle*. Paris: Leroux, 1934.

Vitto, Cindy L. *The Virtuous Pagan in Middle English Literature*. Philadelphia: American Philosophical Society, 1989.

Wailes, Stephen L. *Medieval Allegories of Jesus' Parables*. Berkeley: University of California Press, 1987.

Waldron, R. A. "Langland's Originality: The Christ-Knight and the Harrowing of Hell." In *Middle English Religious and Ethical Literature*, edited by G. Kratzmann and J. Simpson, 68–81. Cambridge: Brewer, 1986.

Watson, Nicholas. "Visions of Inclusion: Universal Salvation and Vernacular Theology in Post-Reformation England." *Journal of Medieval and Early Modern Studies* 27 (1997): 145–88.

Wawrykow, Joseph P. *God's Grace and Human Action: "Merit" in the Theology of Thomas Aquinas*. Notre Dame: University of Notre Dame Press, 1995.

Wenzel, Siegfried. *The Sin of Sloth: "Acedia" in Medieval Thought and Literature*. Chapel Hill: University of North Carolina Press, 1960.

Werner, Karl. *Der Augustinismus in der Scholastik des spätern Mittelalters.* Vol. 3 of *Die Scholastik des späteren Mittelalters.* 1883. Reprint, New York: B. Franklin, 1960.

Wetzel, James. *Augustine and the Limits of Virtue.* Cambridge: Cambridge University Press, 1992.

Whatley, Gordon. "*Piers Plowman* B 12.277–94: Notes on Language, Text, and Theology." *Modern Philology* 82 (1984): 1–12.

———. "The Uses of Hagiography: The Legend of Pope Gregory and the Emperor Trajan in the Middle Ages." *Viator* 15 (1984): 25–63.

White, Hugh. *Nature and Salvation in Piers Plowman.* Cambridge: Brewer, 1988.

Williams, Rowan. "Politics and the Soul: A Reading of the *City of God.*" *Milltown Studies* 19/20 (1987): 55–72.

———. *Why Study the Past? The Quest for the Historical Church.* Grand Rapids, MI: Eerdmans, 2005.

———. *The Wound of Knowledge.* 2nd ed. London: Darton, Longman and Todd, 2002.

Wittgenstein, Ludwig. *Philosophical Investigations.* Translated by G. E. M. Anscombe. Oxford: Blackwell, 1963.

Wittig, J. S. "*Piers Plowman* B IX–XII: Elements in the Design of the Inward Journey." *Traditio* 28 (1972): 211–80.

Wood, Rega. "Ockham's Repudiation of Pelagianism." In *The Cambridge Companion to Ockham,* edited by Paul V. Spade. Cambridge: Cambridge University Press, 1999.

Woolf, Rosemary. *The English Religious Lyric in the Middle Ages.* Oxford: Oxford University Press, 1968.

———. "The Tearing of the Pardon." In *Piers Plowman: Critical Approaches,* edited by S. S. Hussey, 50–75. London: Methuen, 1969.

———. "The Theme of Christ the Lover-Knight in Middle English Literature." *Review of English Studies* 13 (1962): 1–16.

Zeeman, Nicolette. *Piers Plowman and the Medieval Discourse of Desire.* Cambridge: Cambridge University Press, 2006.

DAVID AERS

is the James B. Duke Professor of English

and Religious Studies at Duke University.

Among his books is *Sanctifying Signs: Making Christian Tradition in Late Medieval England* (University of Notre Dame Press, 2004).